Shots in the Sand

A Diary of the Desert War
1941 – 1942

J.M.G. HALSTED OBE
(One-time The Queen's Bays)

This inspired logo of the 1st Century A.D.
was used in the 20th Century on the cover
of *Per Christum Vinces*, Prayers in Time of
War, published by Longman, Green and Co.
in October 1939, price 6d.
   My Mother gave me a copy which I have
by me still.

First Published in 1990 by Gooday Publishers
P.O. Box 60, East Wittering, West Sussex PO20 8RA

British Library Cataloguing in Publication Data

Halsted, J.M.G.
   Shots in the sand: a diary of the desert war.
   1. World War 2. North African campaign. Army
operations during North African Campaign of World War 2.
   I. Title
   940.5423092

ISBN 1−870568−19−2

Typeset in Times by Woodfield Publishing Services, Fontwell, Sussex.
Printed in Great Britain by Hollen Street Press, Slough, Berks.

*I dedicate this book to the memory
of all those officers and men of the Queen's Bays
who did not return.*

Acknowledgements

The author wishes gratefully to acknowledge assistance and permission to use items from the following: *The Times* (26 November 1941 and 10 June 1943); *Anatomy of a Tank* (Macdonald & Co.); *Bayonets in Radcliffe Square* (Farrand Press); The Queen's Bays Regimental History (Warren & Sons); *Operation Victory* (Hodder & Stoughton); *Tanks in Battle* (Sphere Books); Lord Cobbold on John Knebworth; *A Full Life* (Collins); *Rommel* (Collins); *Long Range Desert Group* (originally published by Collins in 1945 and recently reissued, with a new foreword by General David Lloyd-Owen by Greenhill Books); *High Flight* (Magee family and This England, who have published the complete works of John Magee, the Pilot Poet); The B.B.C. 'A Tank Officer Speaks'.

Contents

Foreword

BY GENERAL SIR JACK HARMAN, GCB, OBE, MC.

As a former member of the Queen's Bays with whom I served throughout the North African and Italian campaigns, I am proud that Michael Halsted, a wartime officer, wishes to publish this account of his involvement some forty-eight years after the events occurred.

Many books have been written about the Desert War in Libya. Few have described the reminiscences of a young Troop Leader of a British Cavalry Regiment. His recollections of the lifestyle in England, of the move to the Middle East and of the early part of the campaign are worthy of preservation.

Michael Halsted first describes his early life. He came from the conventional background of young British cavalry officers of the early war years. He had been to a public school and, like some, his university studies had been disrupted by the war. His father was a serving officer of distinction.

But Michael himself was in no way conventional. For one of his age he appears to have been much given to introspection. His diary is frank and revealing. Sometimes he displays perception and sensitivity. On other occasions he is almost naive. He was sustained by his strong Christian principles and beliefs. He was a prolific writer of letters—not always to young ladies!

His desert diary, due no doubt to 'security' inhibitions, does not give a very coherent picture of events as they occurred. Not that this matters; Regimental Histories and War Diaries exist for the chronicling of events. What the diary does portray are the social mores of a cavalry squadron at the time. It reveals the relationship and the interdependence of the tank crew, of the Troop and the Squadron. It also records the relationship between officers, non-commissioned officers and troopers.

It shows the life within the squadron when not in contact with the enemy—the arrival of rations and occasionally extra 'goodies' when they could be provided. But the arrival of mail was the single most important occasion of all. Essential training in the use of new equipment and weapons is covered. Navigation, always a trial to the beginner, receives much attention; and navigational triumph and disaster is faithfully recorded. As I recall, a brother officer was sent in the early days on a short errand. We waited many hours for his reappearance. When asked how long his trip had been, he replied: "8 miles there and 154 miles back."

I think the author's strictures on many of our military leaders in early 1942 are fair, and were generally felt at the time. I also agree with him that we were operating with unreliable equipment and that our tank guns were frequently out-ranged.

Michael was very badly wounded on the first day of the Battle of Gazala. His courage and fortitude at the time was an example to us all. He was greatly missed. He had been an excellent comrade of originality and determination. We much admired his strength of will to regain health and fitness. We were delighted when he was able to enjoy for a year the glamour and glitter of a wartime United States. It was tragic for him, his regiment and the Army that his state of health precluded further military service. He left to become a schoolmaster at his old school.

He had given so much.

J.W.H.

QUOTES FROM OLD CAVALRY JOURNALS (1923)

'At the present moment there is a school of thought, unthoughtful in the main, which considers that the Cavalry 'IDEA' is part of an obsolete doctrine.'

'The tank will not drive the Cavalry from the battlefield; it will in the future increase its radius of action.'

'No amount of mechanical or scientific ingenuity will save the Nation which is content to rely entirely on SUCH AIDS.'

'There is every possibility of a bullet being invented which would make the tank (with its innate clumsiness as compared with a horseman) as vulnerable, if not more so, than a Cavalryman.'

Introduction

The campaign in North Africa has been described as 'one of the most interesting in the history of war' by Colonel H.C.B. Rogers in his accurate and succinct book *Tanks in Battle* (Seeley Service, 1965). He goes on: 'from O'Connor's lightning victories until the capitulation of the German armies in Tunisia, it was coloured by such dash of cavalry on the battlefield as had not been seen since the Napoleonic wars.'

Not only was I in a splendid cavalry regiment, The Queen's Bays, but I really enjoyed our modern arm, the tank. My war had three compensations: the regiment, our tanks and the desert. It was a unique life and I am compelled to describe it.

On Salisbury Plain on 8th August 1941, Averill Harriman, accompanied by Sir Winston Churchill, Field Marshal Alanbrooke* and other General Officers including my father, presented the First Armoured Division, on behalf of President Roosevelt, with American Stuart light tanks (known as 'Honeys'). We now learned that we were destined for North Africa, and we were a bit puzzled as to why we were going to such a God-forsaken part of the world. Just before we left I had the privilege of supper with General Alexander, GOC Southern Command, and my father who was his Major-General of Administration. General Alexander, whom we both greatly admired, explained the strategic importance of North Africa at the time, and I was cheered by his parting words: 'Never mind. The desert is a grand place to fight in.' How right he was; the terrain and climate were ideal for tank warfare, as I was to find out.

Many books have been written about the desert campaigns, the horrors and the heroism: but little about daily life in tanks. In 1943, while I was having my wounds patched up in hospital in England, I tried to describe the special camaraderie of a tank crew in a broadcast talk, *A Tank Officer Speaks*:

* As he became.

1

I have a passion for tanks. It's no use arguing with a fighter pilot or a submariner or a gunner. Each one will tell you firmly that his job is the best and that he would not be in any other for the world. That is just as it should be. A man fights best if he loves his weapon. It is no use arguing with me. I would never be in anything else but tanks. I will tell you why. In tanks the individual counts for much, but he cannot fight alone.

A tank and its crew must be taken together. Their lives centre round it. It is their home on tracks. They depend on it for their lives and their toll of the enemy. Its efficiency depends on their care of its engine, guns and wireless. They grow very fond of their tank and treat it like a good friend. It has its name painted on the side of the turret. Any other exterior decoration, including camouflage, is done by them too. It is excellent having a fine machine to centre one's life around. It is even better to fight in a tank with a first-class crew of real friends.

I will tell you about my men and my tank, Sunloch. (All our squadron tanks are named after Grand National winners.) Pullyblank, my driver, drove a lorry in civvy street. There is nothing he doesn't know about the inside of Sunloch. He's driven it anywhere it will go. Up and down wadis, through rocks, mud and sand, according to the country. Through rivers, streets and houses, Pullyblank can take it and I know he and it will get us there and go on again afterwards to the next objective. Driving imposes great strain, but the driver's task has not ended when the tank has come to a standstill. He cannot rest until maintenance and repairs have been done and Sunloch has been refilled with petrol, oil and water.

My gunner was a cotton operative working in a big northern factory. I have the utmost confidence in him. He's an expert shot with a 2-pounder or Besa gun. His gun always works. He always finds and hits the target. He doesn't say much, but when he does he speaks with an air of authority and that's how the friendly arguments start. We don't argue with him about guns. His name is Lenny Swire.

My wireless operator is a young hairdresser from Yorkshire: strong, cheerful and quite a bit of a lad. He never fails to get the squadron leader on the air for my orders to come through or my reports to get back. He juggles with codes and maps on his knee and fiddles deftly with inaccessible knobs. He loads the guns at the same time and keeps them working, and passes me up anything I may want, such as maps, food or tommy gun. His name is Tom Bradley and he's pretty good with a mouth-organ as well as with scissors and comb. Sometimes he plays his instrument down the intercom loudspeaker for the benefit of other tanks if they are halted close by.

These three men depend on me for their lives, yet I was only an undergraduate when the war started; but I was keen on arms and armour from boyhood. From my viewpoint in the turret I've got to spot the enemy first, and order Pullyblank into position so that Swire can shoot and we can still keep station with other tanks. I have to understand my wireless orders and act on them immediately. The two other tanks in my troop conform to me but they hear the orders too. I must be able to navigate correctly and know where I am all the time. Pullyblank with his visor closed can rarely see anything of what's going on. He relies on my orders and obeys them with instinctive action. If they are good orders, he doesn't waste time or get so worn out, and we go to the right place.

All of us like reading. We've got our actions instinctive now. We can often sit quietly reading with our earphones on, waiting for the orders to move. We've found that a tin of sweets is a good thing to keep handy. Lewis Carroll is a good prelude to a battle. Bradley prefers Thorne Smith or the latest French novel, but he is quite surprised that he likes some of the books that I lend him. Books and sweets are soon put away when the phones begin to crackle.

Sunloch is very like a caravan, but there is much more to it. It is a model of interior planning and contains everything to hand that a machine of destruction might require. It is rather fun stowing it with all the requirements of war and our personal belongings as well. Most of ours are strung on the outside, together with all the useful things we can pick up on the way. We have learned to pack and unpack very quickly. We have learned to live, eat and sleep at one minute's notice.

The maxim is: never get out more than you are actually using. When you have used it, put it back. The same with shaving as with eating. Washing and shaving becomes a fine art in the desert. My record is for shaving my face and washing my hands, feet and neck in one enamel mug of water. I used it for porridge afterwards when I had swilled it out. Swire's the best at cooking, so he is sort of cook without portfolio. We all help him, the same as we all work on the tank. We are all capable of doing a bit of each other's jobs. Swire and Pullyblank help with the maintenance if they have finished the guns and wireless, or Bradley may help them clean the guns. I go and get orders and information from the squadron leader with the other troop leaders, but help and inspect my other tanks when I get back.

I've got tanks in my blood somehow. The very roar of the engine as it swings into life thrills me. I love the surge of power and speed as we rush across the flat plains of the desert. I am excited by the recoil and the roar of the gun and the whipping of the belt through the Besa, like cloth through a sewing-machine. I like to look round at everything in its place inside, especially the racks of shining shells, which I delight in stacking.

I huddle comfortably in my seat and press my forehead on the periscope pad, feeling confident at the thickness of the armour; and never more so than when stuff thuds on the outside and bullets make a futile rattling.

It's very pleasant in leaguer, especially if the rest is not hurried. We set to and stretch our tank sheet along the windward side, pegged out and propped with spare lengths of wireless mast or a crowbar. The wind goes over the top and we can make our beds snug inside and eat and sleep and talk when the work is done. It seems funny sleeping with a wall of bogie wheels. They look as if they might stay still always and never move; but we feel happy knowing that those same bogies will be rattling and rumbling underneath us next day.

3

Pullyblank, Bradley and Swire choose to sleep in a row at the closed end of the tank sheet. I sleep across their feet at the open end. When we can take anything off we have it ready to put on again at once. I always hang my collar on a bogie hub and put my studs in my hat. I never lost them in six months. Living and working together we know each other very well, and the result is ideal teamwork. Inside the bivvy and out, we are friends. Our actions become instinctive. The minimum of orders are needed. We understand each other, and know quite a lot about each other's lives. We share the same food, fun and danger and boredom, and think about the same thing—home—all the time. We examine each other's photographs with interest and approval and bring them out many times. It is my job to censor their letters home; sometimes I can help with the spelling.

When we have had some food and char and it is dark, we sit and talk or write letters or play cards by the light of an inspection lamp. Then we can sleep and take our turns at guard, perched on the top of the turret perhaps, and straining our ears more than our eyes. If on the move but leaguered at night, the supply column may arrive and we all turn out as the lorries drive down the lines of the tanks dealing out water, petrol, food and ammunition, and sometimes mail as well.

It feels quite strange suddenly getting a letter from home in those circumstances. I got a parcel one night containing, among other things, glucose tablets. Owing to a sudden move they furnished my next breakfast. One night I was so tired that I couldn't read my letters till next morning. It's seldom that I leave them unopened for a second.

Sometimes there is not time to stop and have a brew up and then Bradley will fish about in the ration box and feed Swire, Pullyblank and myself with his own creations of biscuit sandwiches. Not that he has a very great choice. It's not much fun fighting before breakfast, but it's often a good time to attack, with the sun in the enemy's eyes. During a sandstorm, when we had no tank sheet left, we had our evening meal inside the tank. It was a specially good meal. It started with bully and biscuits, admittedly, but it ended up with bottles of Chianti and cigars: 'spoils of war'. Such are the pleasant moments of tank fighting and there are many more of them. The unpleasant ones are made so much easier because we are sharing them together.

I was only in the Western Desert with the regiment from November 1941 to May 1942. I was wounded on 27th May, on the first day of the Battle of Gazala. My tank was penetrated by an anti-tank shell. Driver Wilson was wounded (Pullyblank being away), and loader Mounsey was killed. My war at the sharp end was thus far too short. But who can tell? I may have been lucky to have been wounded when I was; certainly I was lucky to survive; but I have always wished I could have done more. I am sorry that this action forced me to leave my crew and many other good friends, both officers and men. They were indeed compensations of war. I shall never forget them. In fact it is they who have inspired this book: together with many other men and women who all through my life have contributed so much to my happiness. In John Milton's words: 'With a gladsome mind I praise the Lord for he is kind.' Shakespeare's Polonius in *Hamlet* gives the best advice a father can give his son, and I often repeat it: 'The friends thou hast, and their adoption tried, grapple them to thy soul with hoops of steel'. More especially I remember my friends in the regiment. When the day came to join, I found myself among friends of the highest calibre. In the starkness and dangers of the Western Desert 'we happy few, we band of brothers' faced in harmony the most stringent tests of friendship. In C Squadron, for instance, we troop leaders were undergraduates sent to war. The more sensitive of us, as I now understand, hated the game, but were none the less brave or effective. Luckily my life had in a way prepared me for all this because, as a fellow officer remarked I was more military-minded than some.

Part One
Prelude 1920 – 1941

1
Army Family

My early life and attitudes were influenced by my army father and his career, and by a number of his interests, constantly concerned with guns and gunpowder! An army career meant, for us, small pay and postings anywhere at any time. Mama had to move house twenty-four times in my first eighteen years, while battling with ill-health. She had poise and charm and the sweetest and most caring nature. She said she never once left me alone as a baby or small child and she saw to it that I learned to write as early as possible, so that when I was away I could always tell her if I was unhappy.

In 1926 Papa expected to go out to command the Legation Guard in Peking: and exceptionally Mama did part with me at the age of six. I was sent to a pre-preparatory boarding school, Eastacre in Winchester, run by the admirable Mr and Mrs Marsham. The motto was: 'Be clean, straight and keen.' Although my first day on my own was a bit traumatic I soon grew to love the boarding school life: making friends, learning how to work, how to read and what to read; and among other accomplishments how to shoot with a target air-rifle. Mama made many friends and wrote excellent letters herself. I was very close to her. From her I realised the importance of seeking friends—and keeping them.

One friend, which he undoubtedly is, who has seen it all almost from the beginning and is still around, is Edward Bear. When I was four, at Seaford in Sussex, Mama took me down town one day to the toy shop. There I saw, suspended above the counter, a teddy bear I just had to have. I have him still: Edward, a most reliable bear, a great character, and closest friend. Mama's court dressmaker fitted him out with a striped shirt, a blue and a brown suit, a 'British warm' and a rather daring red smock. He was a great favourite of Papa's; and he wears a major-general's insignia on his smock. I loved to hear Papa talking to him about this and that: sometimes about my lassitude or

9

failings! Edward Bear is two years older than Winnie-the-Pooh, and 'very well preserved'.

My paternal grandfather came from an old Sussex family but emigrated to Australia where Papa, one of eight boys and girls, was born in 1890. Life was hard for the large family in New South Wales, so when an aunt and her husband in England offered to help, Papa, at the age of eight, was the one chosen to be sent back to the Old Country to their care. Uncle and Aunt gave Papa a good education and home in well-off town and country surroundings, but he received very little money and no love. His was a sad life and a shut-in one. He found it very hard to show any emotion or affection towards his own family. He never saw his parents again. But he made good and I grew to be proud of him, though I once called him 'Old Mildew' (from some fictional character) which amused him at the age of forty-five! He was wounded twice in the First World War, and served in Palestine and India for short periods between the wars. In 1940 as BGS I Corps (Brigadier General Staff) Papa ran a beach organisation at Dunkirk. He ended up in 1944–45 as Vice-Quartermaster-General.

I admired his qualities, particularly his concern for his fellow men and his judgement of them. He set standards of behaviour and achievement which I could not measure up to. The same went for his practical good sense and his uncompromising honesty. His attempts to teach me useful skills or sports had some effect, but as an only child I could not fulfil all his hopes for a son: as a cricketer or a game shot, for instance. I was also very different in outlook and interests. I remember two valuable bits of his advice: 'When you have decided on a job, stick to it.' And: 'Face up to a crisis or impending one at once, whatever the disagreeable consequences. If you do not, you will prolong your misery and store up even worse consequences.'

Unfortunately I never felt close to him. We were never able to have a heart-to-heart over anything: certainly not over girls. But Mama and I could, and did! 'Safety in numbers,' she said, and watched with interest and concern from the sidelines. Papa and I did better by post. I wrote to him everything I could and received fine letters back. But it wasn't until 1942, when I was pretty badly wounded and in hospital in Cairo—the story which my diary tells—that a wonderful letter from Papa was read to me. Then I realised how much he cared for me. How much he could care. He helped to save my life, I know it.

Papa and I both tried to join the Navy, but he couldn't because they lowered the age limit the year he was to go to Osborne; and I couldn't because when I volunteered, at the time of the Munich crisis, I did not live near enough to a drill hall. We were both thrilled by the idea of naval warfare and great guns in traversing turrets. However the Army did us both very well. For me a tank made a very good substitute for a destroyer. I saw my first tank, a derelict First World War Mark IV or V, when I was with Papa on Salisbury Plain, aged six. I was fascinated, and never forgot that moment.

Most of the time we lived in the Aldershot-Camberley area, where it was grand being an army child with so many children from similar backgrounds to play with. At a great fancy dress party, aged five, I wore my first uniform, a replica of a Guards officer's dress uniform, complete with bearskin and sword. I clearly remember being pushed around for the group photograph so that I should pose properly at attention.

I fired my first shot at the age of six. Papa supported his single-barrel hammer ·410 for me to aim at a poor sparrow. It fell dead. The pathetic bundle of feathers was solemnly threaded on to a wood and leather 'game' carrier which Papa had made for me. Papa then produced a cartoon which he had kept from a boys' paper of his youth. It shows an urchin with a dead blackbird dangling from a stick over his shoulder, with the caption: 'I shot him twice, grappled with him and finished him off with my trusty knife.'

Real life began for me when I was ten, when I was given my own first gun, a beautiful little hammerless Army and Navy Stores ·410. After lots of practice at flying starlings or rabbits at corn-cutting, I shot my first pheasant two years later. The adults were quite surprised at what that little gun could do. I came to enjoy using Papa's ·22 magazine rifle, and also, under supervision and in very safe areas, his ·22 Savage Hi-power rifle. But I really loved hand guns. I progressed through pea pistol, potato pistol, water pistol to a 'Dollar (five-shilling) Air Pistol', and on to more powerful ones. At sixteen I was given Papa's ·32 Webley and Scott automatic pistol which he had been issued with in Ireland in the twenties. I slept with his lovely Wilkinson-Webley ·450 revolver under my pillow; it had a beautiful fitted leather case. And I had the great red volume of the Army and Navy Stores catalogue by my bed, always open at the gun department pages.

My delight in explosives began to manifest itself about now. At prep school (Southdown, at Seaford in Sussex, run by a Mr and Mrs Perfect!) we were allowed to order fireworks to be set off for us on Guy Fawkes night, and I always ordered loud bangers. I had come to enjoy the bangs created when Papa was using black powder charges to blow up tree stumps or split great logs. I loved joining him on such occasions. Curtis and Harvey's black gunpowder, in its green cartons, cost 3/6d (35p) a 1lb in those days, and could be bought over the counter at any good ironmonger's along with lengths of safety fuse.

One most popular diversion, exclusive to Papa in the early days, was the firing of 'Mons Meg'. This was a lovely little 8-inch barrel model field gun which Papa had acquired in the Great War. Such occasions had to be meticulously planned for safety. Mons Meg fired lead balls of approximately 16-bore diameter propelled by the same black powder, using a charge measure determined earlier by Papa by trial—luckily no error. We would 'help' Papa mould the projectiles, using a pincer mould for the lead melted on the kitchen stove. We fired Mons Meg in an 'embrasure' in a 'fort' in an old gravel pit. She wasn't very accurate. In fact we had to aim half-way towards the target and a little to the left. Each gunner in the crew from my friends had his allotted task. How we loved the whole drill of setting her up, measuring out the charge, pouring it down the barrel, ramming it well, rolling down the ball and tamping it lightly. Then came the priming of the touch-hole, laying her, cutting and inserting a short length of safety fuse, and lighting it on the command 'Fire!' Then we took cover and rejoiced at the fuse's sizzle and the woosh and wallop as Mons Meg went off. As the smoke cleared we would dash down to examine the target, or more usually try to find where the ball had struck in the ground round about.

When Papa moved from the Staff College to the War Office, Mama took a cottage at Eversley; and as I grew older in my early teens I found many congenial friends round about, mostly army children but many other young people. My greatest friend of all was Bob Langton, who lived nearby with an invalid father, a wonderful mother and two very social older brothers. Bob was at Marlborough, as several of my best friends have been. Bob was a year older than I. He had money and lived in some style. But he was humble, keen, bright, inventive, enthusiastic and ready for anything. Thanks to him and Papa my holidays were filled with fun, laughter and nonsense.

Our activities are best described in a section of Papa's obituary in the *Lancashire Lad*:

> General Halsted was an extremely modest and retiring man but to those who knew him well he was full of humour, kindness and interest. A facet of his character not known to many was his kindness, care for, and infinite patience with young people. Whilst at the Staff College and

living at Eversley he organised many boys' cricket matches, camps and shoots, and other often imaginative and inspired diversions, all of which he planned as meticulously as any military operation, and which gave infinite pleasure to his son and other young people. (See Note p. 16)

They certainly did. One lasting satisfying spin-off was that Papa opened my eyes to the natural world through books such as *Peter Penniless Gamekeeper and Gentleman*, *Woodcraft* or *Insect Life of Pond and Stream*; and by going with me quietly by day and night learning to stalk and observing creatures and birds and to recognise their traces and their sounds or cries. One of the most thrilling sounds in nature is that of snipe drumming in the springtime. Another is the hoot of the tawny owl; and another the call of the eider duck.

Papa was not a social bird, but he realised that we young people had adolescent stirrings and he was very good at chauffeuring me to and from parties or dances. Then Bob got his own car, and he was soon able to teach me to drive: an easier process, I felt, than with Papa. Bob and I and other friends were fortunate in having the Aldershot Club as our social and sports centre. Here I once saw Papa play cricket for the Command against a brilliant West Indies team under Leary Constantine. I have never seen such magical fielding since. Bob and I were a year or two in age below John Betjeman's Joan Hunter Dunn set and her attendant subalterns, but we learned quite fast as we joined in rather warily. Most warily, I remember, during an Aldershot Club dance when a large rat ran round the inner edge of the ballroom balcony. I can imagine what the girls would have felt, adding to their shrieks and yells, if the rat had fallen to the floor. I know what I felt; and I remembered the axiom, 'Whenever about to deal with rats, tuck your trousers into your socks first.'

Bob Langton was a bit more wary of girls than I was, so there was never any competition between us. The great joy I had in his company was exploring the Cotswolds and Exmoor, for instance, and reading Henry Williamson; or shooting vermin, or going to point-to-points, or playing tennis. Or doing anything harmless but slightly mad when obeying the rules of the 'What Next? Club' we founded. The one rule said: 'If fifty per cent of the members (there were two) ever says, "Let's do... something or other, such as drive all night," the club had to do it'. Bob joined the army when war came, but when tired of the phoney war transferred to the RAF. To my everlasting sadness he was shot down and killed while bombing the Ploesti oilfields in Rumania on the night of the 9th/10th August 1943.

I was now (1934 – 38) at my public school, Bradfield College, in beautiful peaceful Berkshire countryside. Here I had an idyllic time after my own fashion. In school I decided to work only in the five subjects needed for School Certificate, which left me plenty of spare time for out-of-school activities. I modelled certain of these on Rudyard Kipling's *Stalky and Co*. I found that there were others around me who also dreamed of catapults and such offensive weapons; and that I had the ability to lead like-minded irregulars. The histories of irregular forces have always captivated me. We, following *Stalky and Co.*, soon possessed saloon pistols, firing BB bulleted caps. They had 9-inch smooth barrels, and would go nicely down the trouser leg and hook on to the braces. The barrel length increased the accuracy and allowed the pistol to be rested on the left forearm to give a steadier shot.

While other bona fide young sportsmen quietly fly-fished the Pang below the playing fields, we shot rabbits and grey squirrels on school property, out of earshot. We were doing our country a service, weren't we? We didn't have the deadly gang rivalry which runs throughout *Stalky and Co*, but we did have catapult battles in Great House Woods, or friendly duels with air pistols, aiming at one's opponent's presentation of a tight-trousered bottom at the appointed distance. A hit would not half sting, but never penetrate. The money for ammunition, as well as for Mars Bars from the tuck shop, used to come from my 'fairy godmother's regular supply of ten-shilling notes. She was a great lady who lived in a lovely house beyond the little cottage at Banstead where we lived for a time. She and Mama got on famously. Her son Harry was in The Queen's Bays. So it all began.

I enjoyed the regular OTC very much, and learned all I could as quickly as I could of weapons and tactics. Weapons included the wonderful Vickers machine gun, thanks to Val Liddell the art master who still felt affection for the weapon he had used in World War I. He taught us the Vickers inside and out. For tactics, I got myself into the position of the one and only staff bugler, even though I could never blow more than a few notes. It was my idea, so as to give the CO greater control on Field Days, and myself an insight into what was meant to be happening.

On the sporting side of weaponry I mastered the ·303 Lee-Enfield service rifle and got into the school shooting eight. We came second in the inter-schools Ashburton Shield at Bisley in 1938. I loved the atmosphere on the wide open ranges: all the coaching camaraderie; the social side of the club house in which we were accommodated; the smell of Young's ·303 oil; the snick of bolts; judging the minutest shifts of wind, the hair's-breadth precision and physical control required; the ripple of rifle shots along the firing-point; and the muted buzz of spectators' excitement behind the firers as vital shots were signalled and values recorded on blackboards. When off duty I could go and bang away happily on the pistol ranges. Revolvers were provided.

Mama, with our maid Dora, moved back to Seaford (my birthplace), and I was able to make many new friends. Here there was, one might say, a more cultural inter-family social life than at Camberley. The kindness and generosity which Mama and I received, although we lived once more in a humble semi-detached were priceless and unforgettable. The sort of contribution I could make was to organise skirmishes or battles on the Downs, such as the Great Sham Battle between the Bashi Bazooks (Turkish Irregulars) and the Gurkhas, pukka regulars. The curate came as haven for the wounded, and heaven perhaps for the 'dead'. The girls came as nurses; and the casualty rate was thereby high. One combatant was Ronald Boyle, whom I was happy to meet again in hospital in the war. Mrs Boyle helped Mama with the commissariat. I was armed with an 1870 Mauser rifle converted to a 12-bore and firing blanks loaded for me by the gun shop in Lewes.

A special friend from Seaford days was Brian Foster (at Felsted): a rather silent, retiring chap, who nevertheless tackled everything which came his way quietly and competently: rabbiting, exploring, firing Mons Meg (now in my charge); or target practice with the smooth-bore double-barrelled break-open No. 4 (bulleted caps) hammer pistols we had acquired. We felt we had graduated to the real thing almost, though they lacked velocity and accuracy. Brian had a very attractive sister, Roslyn*, who was equally sporting. She was of course made welcome at all our manly activities. Brian joined the RAF in the war, and to the surprise of all of us became an admired and decorated squadron leader and Pathfinder: DSO, DFC and Bar. I was very proud of him. It so happened that one week in the summer of 1941, my regiment was down on the coast in its anti-invasion role. We were doing some field-firing behind Seaford Head just where Brian and I used to fire Mons Meg. Brian was on leave and I took him in my turret on one run: 'Driver slow, gunner traverse left, 1600 yards, hornets (enemy tanks) stationary

*One of Roslyn's sons is Andrew Bridge, the internationally acclaimed theatre lighting engineer, with *Phantom of the Opera* in the USA and Lloyds Building at home among his awards!

near bushes.' 'On.' 'FIRE!' Woosh, thump, jangle-jangle (shell case ejected). 'No thank you,' said Brian, relieved to dismount. So he proved my point in my later broadcast, that one needs to choose one's arm in order to fight best. Brian survived the war, but he was killed in 1952 flying the prototype of the Vickers Valiant.

Brian's death was a terrible blow to me and I believe a loss to the nation. The rest of his crew escaped but he was the last to eject and did not make it. The A.O.C. at his funeral said: 'I told Vickers I was sending them the finest pilot under my command.'

Back at school, very satisfying memories of Bradfield were the productions of classical plays in the original Greek in the replica Greek theatre created in the 1900s from a chalk pit. I was understudy to the shepherd and a make-up man in *Oedipus Tyrannus* in 1937. A Greek government representative was impressed enough to recommend that we should perform in Athens the following year. We were to go out on a Greek warship, but the Munich crisis intervened. Since the war performances have been given at Salamis and Athens. Lucky chaps. In my last year I took the part of Oberon in *A Midsummer Night's Dream*. The theatre is ideal for such plays. This is my happiest memory. The saddest memory alas is that over eighty of my contemporaries were killed in World War II: a high proportion out of a total of some 350 boys. Puck was played by J.P. Hopewell. He survived the war, and you will meet him later. On Puck's 'so good night unto you all' my time as a boy at Bradfield came to an end. I now hoped to go up to Oxford, but Papa hadn't the means, and we didn't know what to do.

The means came by post.

Note: Papa's Obituary appeared in the *Lancashire Lad* of Spring 1981. It was by a great Loyal we both admired: Brigadier Geoffrey Rimbault, CBE, DSO, MC, DL, who is happily still with us.

2

Bayonets in Radcliffe Square

One day in the spring of 1938 Papa received the Free Foresters' Cricket Club fixture list by post and discarded an accompanying pink sheet. But Mama retrieved this. It was an offer of a scholarship to Oxford for sons of members! I bless whoever chose St Edmund (Teddy) Hall for me. Like Bradfield it was small and friendly, and we all knew each other. I throve on the Hall's family atmosphere and total unpretentiousness. I was supremely happy among many congenial friends: chief among them was Charles Robathan, also from Marlborough. We began by sharing a room in the annexe and remained close friends for fifty years. Early in September Mama got me to drive her and our maid Dora over to Oxford so that they could clean and soft-furnish and decorate our room. Charles arrived before me on 6th October and asked our splendid scout Charlie, 'Has Mr Halsted arrived yet?' 'Lor', sir, he's been arriving for the last month'. My actual arrival was by train and on foot with hand luggage. As I walked down Queen's Lane I felt that the shades of centuries were accompanying me, and I rejoiced.

Many friends, such as Dennis Salt or Eric Sudale, Scott Leathart, Michael Powell and Roy McIsaac remain friends today: but I still feel the loss of the lively, cheerful John Merifield who became a flying hero like Brian Foster. Professor R.V. Jones mentions him in his fascinating book *Most Secret War*[1]: 'I was taken up by John Merifield whom the other pilots described as the best Mossie[2] pilot in the Air Force'.

But the greatest friend to us all was the Principal, A.B. Emden, 'the Abe'. He was a genius for taking pains over his college and his undergraduates. I would rather have risked upsetting my father than have incurred the Abe's displeasure. It was through him, I am sure,

[1] R.V. Jones, *Most Secret War*, Hamish Hamilton 1978.
[2] Mosquitoes of the PRU (Photographic Reconnaissance Unit): precursors of the U2.

that the SCR were so human and understanding of us all. We happily chanted their names to the tune of Frère Jacques:

> A.B. Emden, A.B. Emden, Kelly too, Kelly too:
> Ramsay, Fletcher, Irvine: Ramsay, Fletcher, Irvine:
> And the Old Brew, and the Old Brew.

The Old Brew was our elderly senior tutor, G.R. Brewis (1871 – 1955). We loved him for his manners and charm, his humour and his lively lectures on Logic, Latin and History. 'Boadicea,' he would tell us, 'was a woman with the maximum of courage, and the minimum of clothing.' When lecturing on John Stuart Mill, our gallant First World War soldier could never resist demonstrating how to throw a Mills bomb over the 'parapet' of the High Table. It was not long before I was doing the demonstrating for another war.

My room-mate Charles found me a right twit to start with, and I was a bit upset by his levity. I was very serious about this marvellous opportunity and the need to do well for my parents' sake. I tried to take Pass Mods in one go in my first term, but that was beyond my capability however hard I worked. 'Mon. 7th Nov. Eleven hours work.' 'Mon. 14th Nov. Work, work, sleep, work.' Well, I got all four subjects, French, Logic, Latin and History, by 28th March 1939. Then I could settle down to work and enjoy life at a reasonable time distance from my degree exams.

My diaries are hardly illuminating, but they do contain facts. 'Mon. 24th April. Can I work at 9 a.m.? No.' 'Wed. 26th. Beloff lecture at Corpus, above my head, but nice girl.' April: 'Now I must learn to work, but so many nights out.' May: 'Time passes quick when you work.' And it passed very slowly and painfully when I didn't, as a poem I wrote at the time, illustrates:

Working Late*

Grope from dinner,
Grope to waste more precious minutes
Lingering in the JCR
Propped against the piano,
Fumbling with the *Oxford Mail*:
Soaking tit-bits
Only meant for Cowley workers.
Tear away from rag-time:

*This appeared in *Oxford*, the Journal of the Oxford Society, December 1988.

Shiver through the Quad
And quickly light the gas
In cheerless room.
Stare pathetically at open books,
Sharpen pencil,
Fumble with a pad,
And hope that someone comes
To waste more time.
Numbed brain, numbed body,
Huddled, comatose.
The hourly stupor grows,
And midnight sees
The conscience-stricken student
Empty bellied, empty brained.

Ten days after coming up in October 1938 I joined the OUOTC. I was a pretty well qualified cadet—extra qualified considering Val Liddell and the Vickers gun. Luckily I could join the newly formed Light Tank Unit; so I became pretty familiar with the Vickers Mark IV or V light tanks, as driver or gunner or tank commander. I became very proud of our little force, as we drove through the town to charge about on Port Meadow. My one embarrassment was breaking down outside the Randolph Hotel in a cloud of smoke. Captain Chamberlayne was our co-operative adjutant, Mr McLagan our officer; and Sergeant Aris from the Royal Tank Corps our solid Establishment. We admired him and he became a useful friend. From my diary: 'A very nice chap. He lives at Cley and reads Henry Williamson.'

On March 19th 1939, my diary reads: 'Another European crisis brewing. Oh dear!' On the 20th I was driven to Tidworth for a short vacation attachment to The Queen's Bays, and I recalled how highly my fairy godmother, Mrs Misa, had spoken of the regiment. I soon agreed with her, but I never dreamed what my visit would lead to.

The Queen's Bays was one of the first of the cavalry regiments to realise that tanks and not horses were to be their lot, and that war was a probability. My initiation and training with them was very valuable, and it moulded my outlook on life in the immediate future; centred more on the army than on the academic, and certainly on cavalry tanks. When I returned to Oxford for the summer term, I see that in early May I took my tank on a recruiting drive through the town, and parked it near the circus entrance to Botley Road. 'Great fun answering questions.'

For conventional sport I had my fencing, and also tennis. For shooting I joined, and soon ran, the Oxford University Revolver

Association, or OU Republican Army as we became known; but we were loyal to the crown. I had now appropriated Papa's ·450 Wilkinson-Webley; which could easily be fitted with Parker-Hale's ingenious and accurate ·22 adaptor; and as easily disassembled. This revolver and Papa's sword are now in the Wilkinson Museum. This is because we have documentation that Papa's Uncle Harry went with the new subaltern of the Loyals in May 1910 to Wilkinson's in Pall Mall, to buy these items for his nephew. Papa was taken down to the basement range for a trial shot and scored a bullseye.

In due course we took on the Oxford City CID and beat them. I have the cutting from the *Oxford Mail* to prove that we won by 43 points, and that (forgive me) I made top score—easily top on the Dummy Man. I find target shooting a bit artificial, so I organised an unofficial outdoor range of our own on Hinksey Hill, thanks to a kind farmer. Here we would shoot balloons on strings or other forms of static breakable targets, sometimes while on the move oneself. It paid off.

After the revolver match our opponents invited us to have a drink at the Mitre Hotel bar, out-of-bounds to us, but how could we refuse? I was sitting on a bar stool with my felt hat on my knee. Detective Inspector Guyt, their team captain, was sitting next to me. Very quietly he said: 'Put your hat on.' I looked perplexed and he said it again more firmly, so I complied. 'Just stay as you are,' he said. 'Keep on drinking but don't turn round.' I did so until he said; 'Relax now.' I took my hat off, turned and saw the proctors going out of the door!

I became mechanised myself in my second year when I bought a second-hand BSA motor-bike for twenty-eight guineas, and fitted it as required by the proctors with a little square green identification light. One of my only pillion passengers was my sporting history tutor George Ramsey, who braved trips into the Cotswolds where he would search for particular small antique items, such as a brass trivet I remember—very suitable for Oxford teas. I couldn't afford a car, but I did admire the lovely little open Sunbeam-Talbots which more affluent undergraduates possessed, and I enjoyed seeing charming girl passengers with their hair streaming in the wind.

When I reached the stage of wanting to transport a young lady myself, I did not, like Everlasting Percy, 'put her on the carrier', but like Percy it did occur to me that 'someday I'd hope to marry 'er', as I shall recount. But first of all I had to learn the knack of handling the combination of bike and side-car, which I bought for her greater comfort. Straight away I tootled off on it to collect her, via Blue Boar Lane, intending to turn down St Aldates. At the bend round the Blue Boar itself I leaned nonchalantly left in the manner of riding a single machine. Nothing happened, except that I went straight on into the bar of the Blue Boar, through the double swing doors, which let me in gently and lessened my bump against the counter. The general tone of the landlord and his regulars indicated that I was not particularly welcome. Besides, I was now out-of-bounds. But they pushed me out good-humouredly enough. At St Aldates I firmly turned the handlebars left and my journey continued safely.

Other activities of mine were joining the Oxford Union, and becoming a Teller through regular speaking. I recall the prophetic debate on May 11th 1939, 'Chamberlain must go', with Ellen Wilkinson and Christopher Hollis as visiting main speakers. The motion was carried by thirty votes. I became treasurer of the OU Play-reading Society. This is one enjoyment which I have been able to follow all through my post-war British Council career. I can't have lasted long in my earlier post because money is not my strong point. My diary says: 'Nice girls and it ought to be fun.' I must have felt on firmer ground.

I have a very special reason to recall joining Toc H. I did this as part of my Christian belief, and because I believed in the endeavours of the Oxford branch to bring town and gown closer together. On my first day I was met by the hostess on duty, Mrs Lonsdale-Cooper. She was a naval widow with a son (who fought at Narvik) and two daughters. She had a very large heart, but a pretty small income; yet she was prepared to take me and several other lucky young men into her family circle. She was a brave, determined, no-nonsense, highly capable lady. Her family were just like her. She kept us all in order and smoothed off rough edges firmly and kindly. 'Nora L.-C.' had a lovely cottage, Lane End, on Boar's Hill, and a very useful little Morris 8 saloon, FWE 955 (I can't forget), known as the Green Fiend. The GF always seemed to have petrol. As an only child myself, I was very happy in such company and surroundings which enabled me to escape from university life, and to join the circle of the L.-C.s' Oxford family friends. In fact I became very close to Leslie, the younger daughter. Her image and character and correspondence were to become strong elements in my ability to survive the desert life.

The Long Vac of summer 1939 came, and I worked as waiter, handyman and entertainer at a family-run holiday hotel in Broadstairs. Soon after I had returned home to Hartley Wintney in Hants, war was declared. On the same morning, 3rd September, I drove to Oxford and reported to Colonel Wood, the Officer Commanding the OUOTC. He told me to report at 3 p.m. I quote: 'Tremendous activity there. Got my medical papers from Dr Hobson at the Radcliffe. Rested in Teddy Hall until 3 p.m., when I was enlisted. Had my medical in Holywell Manor. Grade II. Took till 5.30 p.m.. I was the first recruit.'

A week later I was told that I had not been passed fit for active service, so I should return to Oxford in October. This I did and as an OTC instructor I was made a reserved occupation. '*Wed. 18th October*. We drilled on New College ground and did preliminary bayonet practice.' We often marched through the town from Manor Road, stopping to drill where there was space, and an audience. Radcliffe Square was a good open space for bayonet practice. Sometimes we would drill without arms on Broad Walk. Once we were inspected there by the famous and romantic-looking one-eyed and one-armed General Carton de Wiart, and that was a thrill. I enjoyed all this much more than my History studies. I can't speak for the rank and file, but the war obviously gave them motivation.

One day Major-General Swinton gave a lecture to us staff only, on the 'History of the Tank.' *Diary*: 'Most interesting and secret.' If I had known how far Britain was behind Germany in tank development I might have opted for the Royal Artillery Unit of the OUOTC. The Gunners have always had a tremendous reputation. I was soon to find out in the Western Desert how far behind we were in tank design, arms and armour, and how often 'the Guns' saved us.

Life at Oxford went on. We had come to terms with girls, it seems. Charles and I, public school innocents in single sex colleges, had at first found the ubiquity, not even propinquity, of girls unfamiliar and disturbing. By 1940 my diary is laconic but full of girls' names, and the titles of history books to read; and also popular tunes: *If Only I Had Wings*, *Save a Little Sunshine*, *Fools Rush In*, *Six Lessons from Madame Le Zonga* (in what?).

Of course I joined the LDV (Local Defence Volunteers) and was required for regular guard duty—at the science labs, for reasons not divulged to me. Churchill brilliantly changed our name to Home Guard. I had an armband as uniform, my own rifle and revolver. My rifle was a windfall. I found a lovely little ·303 Lee-Enfield Mounted Infantry carbine in the garage in Eversley of a sporting widow, Mrs Johnson, and she gave it to me. Spruced up, it was very serviceable and handy. I took it to war with me. Otherwise I don't know where my arms would have come from. I was so keen that I had my side-car camouflage painted. I stayed at Oxford through June and July, rejoicing at having had Papa safely back from Dunkirk. He had managed to climb up a landing net into a destroyer. Then I went to Lyme Regis, a favourite haunt of Mama's, to do some serious reading. The Battle of Britain was above us. A German fighter pilot was brought ashore and the ladies of Lyme shook their fists at him. I felt frustrated and helpless.

However, Mama had been working on the specialists who had treated me in the past, declaring that I was now obviously super-fit. So we appealed, and armed with a dossier testifying to this effect I appeared before another Oxford board. Somewhere off St Giles an elderly medico in a white coat sat behind a table. He was wearing an old Bradfieldian tie, and so was I. 'An old Bradfieldian, I see. What can I do for you?' 'Pass me A1, sir.' He signed without a word. I had sat no degree, but I did not care. I was off to the war.

3
Off to the War

My diary for Friday 4th October 1940 reads: 'Term starts. Yeah!' This brief entry was because I was already in the 101st Officer Cadet Training Unit, Blackdown. We were rather sad not to be at the other OCTU at Sandhurst, because Blackdown was bleak, not on the edge of congenial Camberley, and very much out in the sticks on the blasted heath of Bagshot Sands.

We were a mixed lot of tweed-jacketed, grey-flannelled undergraduates with a few older men. There was one worldly-wise amateur jockey; also a great character from Oxfordshire, an artist and humorist, 'Buzz' Burrows with a fund of 'simple countryman' stories in perfect dialect.

Under the redoubtable Colonel Munt we were bashed into shape by very reasonable NCOs, but they meant business. I enjoyed most of it, having trained seriously as a cadet for so long. But it wasn't quite so agreeable when in the first week they found the barrack floor poorly polished, and we had to take off all the top layer with garden hoes and try again. We were all keen to pass out well so as to be able to join the regiment of our choice, so no grumbles. My chosen regiment was of course The Queen's Bays. It had been a help going to them on attachment from Oxford. But after all my experience and getting top marks in Military Law, for instance (No, I wasn't a barrack-room lawyer!), I only passed Grade C. My attitude must have lost me marks one day. But I learned a lesson. We were out all over the heath on a cross-country motorcycling exercise, fast and furious. I roared up a steep little sandy pimple, got to the top all right but did not shut off in time, so the bike and I flew up in the air into the resilient heather beyond. The sergeant reached me as I was picking myself up. 'I'm all right, sergeant,' I said brightly. 'Never mind you,' was the immediate reply. 'How's your effing motorbike?'

I did better on the parade ground as I really enjoyed drill, and had a pretty good voice: 'For inspection—port pistols!' Tank crews were not armed with rifles.

Not all our training was at Blackdown. For driving and maintenance we went to Bovington camp in Dorset. For gunnery we went to Lulworth, where the mess had very fine port which we were generously allowed to drink. We didn't have much gunnery practice, only three 2-pounder rounds per man, but they gave one the feel of the business at last. I'm glad I didn't know then how puny this little gun was.

Back at Blackdown I was finally paraded by myself outside the adjutant's office on the verandah, and up walked Lieutenant-Colonel G.W.C. (Tom) Draffen, a short, neat figure with a gentle manner and friendly, encouraging face, often with a great grin. I sprang smartly to attention, saluted, and in response to a greeting and a question, with my hands firmly by my sides, I said: 'Colonel, I haven't any money and I don't ride a horse, but I want to join The Queen's Bays.' He accepted me. Now I was off to the war, and, as I soon discovered, in the best possible company. At heart I knew this; but in reality it was better than I could have imagined. There was something about the officers and men of The Queen's Bays which I had already felt from the earlier Tidworth days but could not define. I soon understood that the very name and special tradition of this cavalry regiment connoted unconcern in the face of problems or misfortunes, overcome by a cheerful self-assurance in all circumstances, and possessing a kindness and gentleness of spirit which permeated relationships in all facets of army life. And how they could fight!

The following appeared in The Queen's Bays Families Association Newsletter of May 1944, written by an old Bay who preferred to remain anonymous.

Salute to the Bays

Would you know anything of pride—that's gained in mighty ways?
For if you don't you cannot know the glory of the Bays.
Such history as they have made will outlive any life,
With tales of battles, heroic deeds and glory in the strife!

They fought at Lucknow, Mons and Marne, Messines and Ypres too,
And can you e'er forget these names and all they mean to you?
When England stood in danger from the fierce and bloody foe,
While in the thick of battles' strife The Bays fought to and fro.

Can you but wonder that our Queen is their proud C-in-C?
Or that, with fighters such as these, our England shall be free?
Or that to wear just such a badge is one great source of pride –
Which represents a record that is known the nation wide?

When first they formed, just visualise those sleek and stately mounts
That carried in their saddles men who had the thing that counts;
The pride of England's cavalry, a brilliant cavalcade;
Presenting an imposing sight both on and off parade.

It was a blow, to say the least, when they were mechanized.
To say good-bye to faithful friends that by the Bays were prized.
But still their name in glory stood, as once more into war
Went forth The Bays on 'armoured mounts' to pay another score.

'For King and Country'—these the words, the motto of The Bays.
Simple it is, but means so much, a real expressive phrase.
It shows devotion to a cause that ne'er in life shall die—
A cause so soundly handed down these years for you and I.

Uphold that cause, then, England's sons! Let not your footsteps lag!
Remember all those fighting men that fell beneath our flag.
Remember, too, that gallant throng, worthy of every praise—
The second Regiment of Horse, the bonny, bonny Bays.

For though their polished finery is lost in lumbering tanks,
Their record stands, and always will, amongst its many ranks;
And when we emerge victorious, the last great battle won,
They'll need a standard larger still to inscribe their Honours on.

One day I would be proud to have been present at such a Battle
Honour: Gazala it was to be.

The next week or two were nerve-racking as I tried to make sure
that I had absolutely the correct uniform, badges, shirts, ties, hats,
Sam Browne, black shoes, etc., as required by the adjutant. I must
admit that I greatly enjoyed the visits to Huntsman, the regimental
tailor in Savile Row, and seeing my special Queen's Bays uniform and
accessories materialise. I was very proud that I would be distinctively
accoutred. I still have my beautiful pale heavyweight service dress
trousers for tough weather conditions. My jacket and pigskin Sam
Browne were handed on to the next generation.

So here we go. *Diary: 'Sunday 2nd February 1941. I join the QBs.*
One minute to 4 p.m. by Ma's watch and I'm sitting in the ante-room in a
house on the Pride of the Valley—Tilford Road. Mrs Langton sent me

out in a taxi to Elstead and I have come over with four other officers in a three-ton lorry with all my odds and ends of kit. I felt rather glum at first, but I met the colonel and the adjutant and had a chat. I feel better now the journey is over with these cheerful young officers wearing all sorts of odd clothing, SD and no belt, etc. I am wearing Pa's old British warm and hope it will do. The Lieutenant who met me here is nice, and I am by a fire reading the papers and waiting developments. It is no longer snowing. I can hardly believe I am an officer, but it feels good.'

It didn't take long to have me integrated, nor for me to feel at home thanks to the kindness and understanding of 'Margo' Asquith our C Squadron leader, and Michael Erleigh, 'Spud' Patchett, 'Bing' Crosbie-Dawson of the seniors: and through the marvellous get-together spirit among the other subalterns: Jimmy Cumming, Stephen Christie-Miller, Ben Hough, Joe Radice and others. Margo endeared himself to me right away. Next morning was raining and unpleasant. He came down to breakfast, looked out of the window, placed the tips of his fingers together and said: 'Not a very nice day for the officers.' Later on he introduced me to the marvellous music of Ernesto Lecuona and his Cuban Boys. *'Escalvo soy'* *'Cancion'*, etc. Superb stuff! I had all the best titles written down on April 26th. Can recordings be found today? It wasn't so easy to meet chaps from A and B Squadrons, or RHQ, because the regiment was spread out in the towns of Milford and Elstead as well as Tilford. The whole must have been a job to administer.

The first thing that happened to me was my introduction to the NCOs and troopers of No. 4 Troop, my troop. A fateful occasion for both sides. I am at this moment referring to the notes I made on Friday 7th February 1941, about each one as he was described to me beforehand! Luckily I added the fact that my driver, Lance/Cpl Pullyblank—'Good driver', it says: (very, very true). 'Had been a footman at Cowdray Park'. We got separated in the desert, but I have been able to make contact with him after forty-six years just through that tiny clue. We have had great natters, and he has written interesting letters to me, historical letters, covering the whole of the rest of his war in North Africa and Italy, which thank God he survived intact. His first letter is included on p. 117 of this book.

It was an unreal life at Tilford. We trained as hard as we could in the wooded area around us, Hankley and Tilford Commons and their environs. We had Cruiser tanks to begin with, fast and smooth no doubt, but not what we crews hoped would be really fine 'Armoured Fighting

Vehicles'. Here is a specimen squadron leader's instructions, as taken down in my diary:

> Keep 100x between tanks, halted or moving. Do not bunch in cover. Don't rush for isolated cover. When rallying, tanks in troops must still keep distances. Cross open ground quickly. Harbouring: Switch off as soon as possible. Give petrol, oil, ammo and food requirements in writing to SQMs. Get tanks ready again immediately.

Some of the time we were deployed towards the South Downs as an anti-invasion force. We would have done our best but we were not a powerful deterrent, few in number and rather poorly armed.

Winston Churchill came down on 14th February with General Sikorski and General de Gaulle. No doubt the PM had ordered what to my mind was a ludicrous attempt to impress these heroes. Some tank troops were hidden in a wood, and at a signal they charged in a body across a meadow past the little group. Quite impressive *in vacuo*—but against opposition? Pullyblank was borrowed to drive a Cruiser tank fast across the little river Wey on Tilford Common. This entailed having to career straight off the steep bank. His tank didn't jump the gap. He plonked into the river with a great whoosh and nearly drowned, but got across by keeping going. Other tanks and crews went off elsewhere and were bidden to charge through old houses, guns in reverse, of course. I believe it was for a Ministry of Information 'heartening of the populace' film!

When we were free, in this shake-down period, we used to dash up to London and have a great time. My education was just beginning. The usual meeting place was the Berkeley Buttery. The Berkeley was an elegant and friendly, unstuffy, hotel. I don't know how I afforded to join in with the gayer sparks who were obviously continuing their normal 'playboy' activities: but I was able to take my part in such night haunts as the Coconut Grove, the Orchid Room, or the Ladder Club. The money didn't worry me. This is reflected in my diary when I met my father in September. Eat, drink and be merry was the order of the day, and alas some did die 'on the morrow'. I was very lucky in having a handy inexpensive London base at Rosa Lewis' 'Cavendish Hotel' in Jermyn Street (where she had been set up by King Edward VII, I understand). This was thanks to my being introduced to Rosa by my uncle Hubert Howard-Tripp, who had been one of the Cavendish clientele since the First World War. He had now rejoined the army with the rank of captain. In due course he became Papa's staff captain in South Wales District. At the end of the war he put in some pretty good service in Belgium as a Civil Affairs Officer, and a street in Willebroek was renamed Captain Tripp Straat in 1947.

Rosa and her niece Edith Jeffery kindly accepted me. Charles was an inscrutable but most helpful butler, barman, gentleman's gentleman and everything else, and Sissy was the no-nonsense sporting waitress. I was able to stay at the Cavendish now and again for the odd dance, as my diary reminds me, and some of my happiest memories of life off duty, in war and peace, were centred on the Cavendish Hotel, with Kippy, Rosa's West Highland (near)-White always alert on the front doorstep. No questions were asked at the Cavendish. There were some unusual goings-on I used to notice, but I supposed they were within the category 'gentlemanly'.

Back on the job, life was never dull if one kept alert. For one brief but highly diverting period I was off to Gatwick, attached to an Army Co-operation Squadron flying Lysanders. I thoroughly enjoyed myself and greatly approved of the co-operation given to this representative of the Royal Armoured Corps. The only niggle was that I was warned to watch out for Polish fighter pilots, who were apt to shoot first if they couldn't identify a plane; and a Lysander was a rather unusual aircraft around the English countryside. A pilot one day agreed to fly me over the Royal Naval School for Officers' Daughters, evacuated to the country. There I dropped a message for Leslie on what appeared to be the headmistress's lawn. Lysanders were lovely, comfortable, slow low-flying aircraft so I could see the pouch and streamer collected by the gardener and borne indoors. I heard later that the headmistress was pretty sporting. She gave Leslie the letter enclosed, but warned her: 'If you will have boy-friends, you must keep them under control.'

In April I was given some leave and was able to go to Exmoor with Bob Langton: he who had first introduced me to this beautiful region, and to the Cotswolds, giving me a greater awareness and appreciation of the English countryside. I wrote this in my pocket diary:

The world, the human world, doesn't seem to matter. Even such a small portion of so small an island seems remote from the complications of a human war. Even our human ties seem to fade and become insignificant parts of our life on earth. I feel as if I am apart, as if it would not matter if I never returned to Tilford and no one would be any the wiser. God is the only Being here it seems, and he is sufficient company for the birds and the animals and we who seek the solitude and beauty of Exmoor. But we do belong down below (for the human world is down below here) among our fellow men. . .

Now I must return to earth, to home, to billets, to the war, because if I do not there will be no home, no loved ones, no friends for company. . . Some of us will not be here, but seeing through the eyes of Heaven, will be rejoicing with us. . . God who watches over us, please keep us safe if it be thy will, when once the battle is won, that we may enjoy not the fruits of victory but the beauty that is timeless. Give us the chance to help others in the way, that they may enjoy the beauties of life too, and live in Peace in the shadow of the hills, and listen to the music of the waters, that is Nature's own organ music, while the birds sing in praise.

The month of May contained much sadness. Mama died of cancer in Brandon Lodge Nursing Home, Leamington Spa on the 15th. Papa sent a Motor Contact Officer that morning to tell me the news. I had this to say:

4.30 p.m. Am sitting in the Gaiety Tea Shop, Leamington Spa. have just met Pa outside Brandon Lodge. He got out of CXB 508 and said, 'I didn't want you to come really. Ma passed away at four o'clock this morning.' This is that hand of death that so many brave ones feel. This is the birth of life that makes us thankful, so deeply thankful for the life of our Lord Jesus Christ. How melancholy we feel if we think with regret about all the joys of the past, and how glad we can feel that we are nearer now to one another, being with God alone and no earthly barrier between. What could I not write, and what will I not write, of the devotion and companionship of Mother. Every memory comes flooding back, tumbling over themselves in my head, with their pictures clear before my eyes. I will tell of it all—but now I will not cry. I will not be sad. I will rather stand alone, trusting always in God. Oh God, hear me, forgive me, and help me to stand as thy witness even as my mother was.

Mama is buried at Hartley Wintney, and lies not far from one of the very great men who saved Britain in the war, Field Marshal Lord Alanbrooke. She has a neat and most original brick grave and headstone, as she had wanted. Luckily both Papa and I could be there. I read the lesson. Poor man, what a grievous loss at the age of fifty-one. I felt most inadequate.

The regiment moved to Marlborough on 2nd June 1941. I travelled on my Triumph Tiger 80, a lovely bike. I thoroughly enjoyed that form of transport, and the machines of those days: the Royal Enfield Bullet, the Matchless, Velocette, Scott Squirrel, Brough Superior, etc. Now a great life began. The officers' mess was the Ailesbury Arms Hotel, the sergeants' in the Town Hall. I had comic little rooms round the corner above Figgins the greengrocer, but very private. Regimental Headquarters' and one squadron's tanks were all parked down the centre of the great wide High Street. The Polly Tea Rooms were going strong, and the young officers would take their morning coffees there, to the fury of the regimental sergeant-major whose office was opposite, just too far for us to hear what he thought of us. We in C Squadron were out at Ogbourne Maizey, and the other squadron was at Ogbourne St George; delightful surroundings. The Marlborough Downs were ideal for deploying armoured units; but there was one snag. We were ordered on no account to churn up Joe Lawson's gallops*. When we had been down in Sussex on anti-invasion alert a farmer had shouted up at Joe Radice in his tank: 'You do more damage than the bloody bombs.' On a more serious note, we were very thin on the ground. Stephen Christie-Miller's comment was: '"Troop Training" One tank up: two imaginary ones behind!' England is really too small for tank training. We were amateurs compared to the Afrika Korps. Rommel knew all about us, as Bays prisoners who later escaped, reported. But we won.

Two diversions came my lucky way. I was sent off to Birmingham for a few days to the factory of Mechanisation and Aero, who were making the Crusader tanks we were now getting. It was useful to become acquainted with every part of this tank and where it fitted in and what it did; but not being a mechanic I wasn't a chap who could in the long run make full use of the information. But the other aspect of my visit may have been useful! I was urged to cheer on the workers. I did my best, day and night; well, not all that late. Saturday 14th June, I quote: 'Another most amazing interlude. Am in the gallery of Grand Casino, Birmingham, having done a good deal of dancing with quite a range of girls. It is really very funny just not dancing, when many girls are quite curious as to what I am doing. I spotted a girl in the gallery or royal circle, but at close quarters (I am at the next table) I am not quite so sure—Dear! Dear! I am told that Birmingham girls are not as good as Liverpool, and not half as good as those of Chesterfield.' I never got to Chesterfield.

Another day, back at Marlborough, I was sent down near the coast with my troop to give a demonstration to the RAF. Though

---

* *The Times* of September 16, 1910 reprinting army manoeuvres (which included the Queen's Bays) mentions the same problem: '. . . coming from the East Coast, where the cult of the gamebird has absolutely forbidden military manoeuvres, the Colchester Brigade has literally lost the habit of taking advantage of free woodland.'

I have absolutely no recollection of the event I mention it because I am rather proud of this letter from RAF Headquarters in Southampton which reached my colonel:

Dear Tom,

The tank demonstration went off with great success this morning. Everybody was extremely interested and pleased, with the exception of the farmer, and it looks as though I shall probably have about £200 bill to face.

Young Halsted in command was most helpful and intelligent. He gave an extremely good exposition of the duties and characteristics of armoured regiments, and in every way conducted a first-class show.

I am extremely indebted to him and to you for doing it.

Yours truly

(signed) H.W. Hall

I think that was damn decent. By God, we needed the RAF. Without air cover we would have been quickly reduced to wrecks of tanks and men.

About this time I got hold of a copy of *Army Training Manual No. 49* written by Montgomery. In it the game of cross-country rugger was recommended. So I said, 'OK chaps, get changed: we're off to the ground.' The ground I chose was a meadow reached by a five-barred gate at the roadside. This gate was one goal. The other goal was the entrance to a cart tunnel through a railway embankment beyond a stream. It was a great game: no rules such as off-side or knock-on, of course, and no scrum as such. Rules for self-preservation only. The game required tactics, deception, co-ordination, back-up, exploitation and goals. The men enjoyed it. They certainly needed lots of even more vigorous and tough training, as Montgomery found out and instituted when he arrived in Egypt. During our game they soon latched on to an added bonus, tackling me in the stream and getting me as wet as possible. I think this was in revenge for taking them through an electric fence one day without warning them.—'Come on lads!'

I am afraid I don't know what the chaps got up to in the evenings, but I should have found out if they were content. I was lucky in being very near, by motor bike, to my admirable cousins Geoff and Edith Peters who lived at Hungerford. I could go down to them at their lovely Mill House, any time, and enjoy the peace and charm. One or two of us young officers, I may say, sometimes found an agreeable source of companionship in several of the girls employed by Billy Rootes' organisation evacuated just down the Bath Road at Ramsbury. Theirs was a strenuous war effort.

Happily for us all, HM the Queen, our Colonel-in-Chief, paid us a visit on 18th September. We had a group photograph taken with her in the garden of the Ailesbury Arms. I wrote: 'It was a very exciting day being so near to Her Majesty. I marvelled at her simplicity.' Forty-seven years later I was proud to be beside HM the Queen Mother on the fiftieth anniversary of her becoming Colonel-in-Chief. I looked at that photograph with her, and she remarked: 'It takes you back, doesn't it?' In that photograph I am clean shaven. I thought it was time I grew a military moustache. I tended what appeared on my upper lip, but it was so scruffy in early September that I was told to shave it off, and not to try again until after the Queen had been to luncheon. My moustache had taken a long time to grow, so one day I asked the RSM what the secret of his was, and what he recommended for me. 'Goose turd, sir, spread on thickly at noights.' Another lesson learned.

Somewhere at sea on the voyage to Egypt, later in the year, the senior officers decided to have a 'horse race' based on the subalterns' moustaches. We were given halters of life jackets and led into 'the ring' round which the seniors sat, making bets on the form they saw paraded before them, each having 'drawn a horse'. The Padre drew me, poor chap, and his horse came in last.

But let me tell the next part of the story in the exact words which I began to write in my diary just five days after the Queen's visit. The original volumes are in the Regimental Museum in Cardiff Castle.

Part Two

Diary of a Tank Troop Leader
September 1941 – June 1942

4

Convoy to Egypt

THE DIARY VERBATIM

September 23rd 1941

The start of my great adventure. We 'proceed overseas' from Marlborough, Wiltshire. I don't think I have every enjoyed myself more than these last four months at Marlborough and Ogbourne Maizey. Gosh! What a send off. Almost a month's warning, and ample time, if time is ever ample, to get everything in order and see everyone. I cannot write it all here, nor name all my many friends to whom I owe an everlasting debt for all the fun and hospitality. Cousin Geoff and Edith Peters, Miss Sandys, the Findlay family, and all at the College.

Spud Patchett as temporary squadron leader made life heaven at Ogbourne, for when there was nothing to do, he would let us 'slide' and Bob lent me Abraham in which I could nip around and to Oxford. Winston secured us an extra week's leave at the end of August and then for me life began.

I was blessed with the society of Leslie Lonsdale-Cooper, and all her family, my kindest and most generous friends. I cannot write enough about Lane End, and all it means to me. I have only room to mention the few wonderful days which made my life a dream.

Firstly the Plum Day, when we went to Broadway in the Green Fiend and met Olly on his motor bike, and Leslie and I climbed the tower on Fish Hill, and a vision of my ruling love, the countryside, was revealed to me in the presence of my heart's love, Leslie. All day I had my regimental brooch in my pocket to give her. . . wondering when I should. In the end I gave it as I left to walk back at night to Mrs Taylor's, and what an agony that weekend was, as I never heard till four days later.

Then there were the two grand dances at the Ailesbury Arms, but who wants to hear about it, and I don't think I want to tell of those happy days or of the days near Chedworth; but I cannot help mentioning that Friday when we went to London, or the last time I saw her in the middle of Marlborough, waving goodbye at the wheel of the GF after the visit of Her Majesty the Queen. I could not have left after a happier time, and the difference having Leslie made. If it had not been for her, my departure would have been a much more matter-of-fact affair to me. Father and I never say very much about things; and Mother sees us in a different Light and no longer lives in pain or worry, for which I do thank God.

Major Sykes lent me his car on the last evening and I had the great privilege of dinner at HQ Southern Command, Wilton House, with Lieutenant-General Alexander and Pa. I got the usual ticking off after dinner up in Pa's room over my chaotic accounts, but Pa gave me £35 to cover my kit, which was very kind as I had spent a lot of money over it all. In fact while in England with the regiment I never saved anything, and I do want to save so that one day I may be able to set up house—with Leslie? Who knows. Such things are in God's hands. . .

Then, out to the big Humber car, backed her round to the yard, guided by Pa. A handshake, a word of good luck from him. 'Heaven knows when we shall meet again,' I think he said. 'You have got to be QMG anyhow,' I replied. He laughed, and I let in the clutch, sliding off into the dark and the fog, over Salisbury Plain.

So I completed twenty-one years and a few months in England before leaving it for the first time. On the morrow, final hectic packing, lunch at the Ailesbury Arms, and all the wives there looking so very glum. No transport, so I shoulder my pack and set off on foot to the station with someone, but Stephen Christie-Miller turns up in his minute little car, and we pile on, four up, all over it, and are tipped off at the station. Miraculously we sort out all the baggage, Swire gathers up all my belongings, and we pull out on time.

A journey from 2.30 p.m. till 10.20 a.m. Two pangs on the journey—we stopped in Oxford station, and I saw Hinksey Hill receding as if for ever. That little bit of road I have so often paced with my bicycle, eager for the reward at the top where Lane End lies. We had also stopped at Hungerford for Brigade to come aboard.

Six in a carriage with not much food, but we managed all right, and I was able to shave in a little water from my water bottle, and save some tea in my thermos at Leicester for an early morning cup on waking.

Embarkation. September 24th

A port which no one had actually mentioned before. All went off very smoothly, and James was on board to greet us. In a cabin with him and Ben Hough. The *Empire Pride* is a very small but brand new motor ship of the Ministry of Supply and run by Bibby Line. Everything very slap-up for the officers, and all bright and untouched. What a surprise to find sheets, towels and bedclothes, and native servants who produce hot water when you ring a bell.

Meals are sumptuous, of many courses, and very well served by Indians in a smart kit. We shall eat and eat. Joyful discovery that it is all free. The big gesture of the Government for her homesick forces! The first chance to save money comes at once, and furthermore drinks and smokes seem ridiculously cheap— Whisky 3d, fifty Players 1/8d. Cigarettes and cigarettes, what a paradise for some.

September 25th – 30th

An unpleasant period of sitting in the Clyde off Gourock, waiting and waiting to sail. Very trying for the chaps who are cramped down below, and find hammocks odd things to sleep in at first. They have very little room to put anything, and lounge around miserably, leaning over the rail, thinking of home and writing letters.

I am lucky. I have found a job. I am training crews from various squadrons to man the 12-pounder gun on the poop with the aid of 'Guns'. Mr Davies, the Third Officer, is training a crew under Sgt McLean and such stalwarts as Cpl Waterhouse and Smith, for the 4-inch gun. I have always fancied naval gunnery and here is my chance. Everyone else is very keen too. I already feel an ache to be with the Navy and out on one of the destroyers or corvettes that slip in and out so businesslike. Neil Bruce is out in a corvette somewhere, and I think of Billy Normand and how Leslie loves the sea. What if I was a Sub. now? Well! Perhaps I should not be where I am now, and should not have been able to have all the fun I did either. It would have been different, but what's the use of thinking of that?

I think of Leslie all the time. Everyone thinks of home, and puts up photos in their cabins, and I am so happy to be able to do so too.

Gunnery goes on every day and we practise on Catalinas and Sunderlands and mainly on seagulls. It gives us something to do for

39

we are far too near home in time and space. All my spare time I write letter after letter, in a frantic effort to catch up on all the people I have neglected in the past months. Up to the last few minutes of posting (for mail to go ashore before we leave) I wrote madly. I asked the Padre for an envelope, and took sixteen! Each letter became shorter than the last, but perhaps they will be just received as a gesture. I still have more to write, but they must wait until the mood takes me on the voyage. I hope it will!

September 30th

A fine evening, and I am up on the gun. We are off! Glimmers of light show us the vague forms of other ships in the convoy. We try with the aid of glasses to distinguish how many there are. The moon lights up the estuary, and we pass the winking light buoys and form single file to pass through the bar. As we glide by the guard ship, we raise a cheer which is answered by the crew, and so we enter the open sea, under the protection of the Silent Service, and manning our own little guns. I don't think very much, as I think I have thought it all during the past week.

October 1st – 5th

Shambles—hundreds seasick. I staggered to the poop but was very ill, and couldn't eat, and had to retire to bed. I am in a second class cabin now with Peter Willett, James Cumming and Ben. There is no room, no air, horrible smells, and a closed porthole.

Three miserable days in bed. Eating a little lying down, thinking of Leslie, gazing at her portrait, appalled by the thought of joining the Navy! I couldn't stand it down on the mess decks where there was utter chaos, smell and sprawling troopers crammed together. Thank goodness I have a bed to lie on, but I wish I could do something for my chaps—Swire hasn't appeared for days.

Gradually the sea calms and I find my feet and my stomach again. Training was supposed to have started but came to a standstill. Stalwart chaps on the poop keep a watch, but we have to take anyone on his feet. I am no use as gunnery officer, but luckily Ronny Dallas was hale and hearty. James was too, and he used to come in and laugh at me, but I didn't see the joke for a long time, and could only groan.

In the end we all recover, more or less, but a queasy feeling remains in the stomach for some days.

October 6th – 13th

Now we settle in the first straight stretch of the voyage. Training begins in earnest and we manage quite well with the usual individual stuff, compass, gunnery etc., with lectures in the afternoon. It is not easy to keep the chaps amused all the time but we manage to vary it a bit, with a great inter-troop general knowledge tournament and other talks. Tony lectures on music and Nick Carter on South Africa. I am preparing one on Libya and reading as much as I can find on the subject. The days get warmer and we change into drill and wear topees. It is difficult to walk about at night without treading on recumbent forms.

I get Swire to pitch my camp bed in a certain spot and creep into it about 10 p.m. I love that, and generally fall asleep listening to the wind and the lapping and breaking waves curling away from the bows, watching the vague forms of the other ships and the stars overhead, peering through the upper structure of the ship as it rises and falls.

It is then and in the early morning when I pick up my bed out of the way of the deck scrubbers and retire to my bunk for an hour or so, that I lie and think of Leslie. I like to imagine all sorts of delicious fancies. What it will be like the moment I return and can dash to Lane End. What it would be like getting engaged to Leslie and being married at St Aldate's. What I should do and where I should find a home. Suddenly I come to my senses and fall asleep with a prayer to God.

I went to a second class cabin to remain with James and Co., and get on marvellously, but I don't enjoy the second class dining room even though there is Chris, Stephen, Robin and Tony and the Padre.

We are lucky over not contacting the Germans. We have only had two or three alarms; on which of course I dashed to my gun with Tony and all the chaps, who were as keen as anything. One morning we saw a Fokke-Wulf Condor and the cruiser fired. It disappeared and we heard no more. Perhaps it didn't like the look of our escort, which is pretty heavy: a cruiser, an aircraft carrier and about eight destroyers. These Fairey Swordfish are interesting to watch taking off and landing, and also the Walrus off the cruiser. The aircraft carrier left us opposite Gib and some of the destroyers too.

The evenings I find are the most difficult times. Everyone seems to settle down to cards, but I don't like them and will not play. I hate losing money for one thing, and think it rather a waste of time for another. I much prefer to settle down with a book, but I won't deny that even that tires occasionally and I long to sit on deck and chat about home and things. The Padre comes occasionally, and I like him, but he is rather a fool at times. Not very deep somehow and his manner grates a bit sometimes, but he's a 'good fellow'!

I loved Ernest Hemingway's *For Whom the Bell Tolls*, though others do not seem so enthusiastic. I like its intimacy, its clarity and minuteness. Then I spent some days with *David Copperfield* and that was a real job, though heavy to read every spare moment. I could sit and discuss all those lovable, curious and horrible characters. *Libyan Sands* by R. Bagnold is a book that intrigues me. I have a real desire to see this great desert for myself, and discover whether I could go off into its desolate places for fun. No doubt I shall have to go in somewhat different circumstances into some parts of it. I think I shall be able to appreciate it as I am a country lover, or is that love confined to England? We shall see.

Major Jarvis on Egypt is most entertaining but he does not touch on the Romance! He is too old a hand to be deluded by that idea I suppose, but I am fired with a real desire to see something of the great dead civilisation now unveiled.

I used to talk to many people about Egypt while at home and I remember turning over the pages of the *Cambridge Ancient History* with delight. Baedeker's bald guide gives me a foretaste, rather dry-cooked, but H.V. Morton fires me with a thrilling sense of the great past. Egyptian life centred round death and the tomb and we can see something of the living death that they tried so hard to make into a continuance of life. All the time I wish I knew more history. I get very excited when I read about St Paul or about ancient Greece. I want to put myself into the sandals of a man of the past and see all the glory and feel as he felt. I have longed to travel in this vein as well as to see countries as they are. It was in the past that I used to drive with Bob, or with Father. A castle, a monastery, a villa site, a house with ancient associations, fills me with a sense of awe and a longing to know and feel more. Perhaps on this enforced travel I shall be lucky enough to see something that I have long wanted to see. Perhaps then I shall feel my curiosity sated and take no further interest, for in the past I never bothered to learn anything wholly, but dabbled in many things, and made the army and guns my real hobby, and these do not lead very far in themselves. I have guns enough now, and some of the travel too!

The sea shows us something of its denizens. Flying fish, which are queer little things much smaller than I expected, for I imagined a sort of herring affair, would flop on deck any time with foot-long wings. Some have seen dolphins and sharks too.

We near land now, and all settle down to letter writing. I write to Leslie, Father and Cousin Geoff and Edith. I have to censor my chaps' letters, which is an interesting job. Normally I do not come across their private lives and it is comforting to feel that they think the same as I do, and write about home and those they love. I wonder what they would think of my letters? My operator Bradley has a girl friend like I have, and I think he hopes to marry her on his return. I hope he can, as I hope I can marry my darling.

The little map case is rather an odd frame for her photos but it is serviceable enough. How I wonder what she thinks of me. Does she know that I love her as I do. . . ? I long for a letter, but we cannot expect mail till the end of the journey.

October 14th

Lunch time, and land is in sight! A new continent. African hills can be seen rising steeply to the clouds and I feel quite a thrill. I spent all the afternoon in the boiling sun on the gun platform where I have a good view of the procedure of a convoy entering Freetown, Sierra Leone. Destroyers and sloops and MTBs and launches all dashing about as we form single file and pass slowly through the boom. We cheer the little boom ship with its few whites, and crew of grinning Africans.

We pass our escort cruisers, *Dorsetshire* and *Devonshire* which has Chris's cousin on board. The *Dorsetshire*, or one of them, sank the *Bismarck*. Then we see the mass of other craft. Three or four miles of ships in the huge mouth of the river. On our starboard, the little town with its motley collection of curious-shaped and soft-coloured houses and buildings.

Great thrill, another ship has nurses on board who wave to us. What a time they must have!

On the same side, the first little bits of projecting land with palm trees and coast defences and little lagoons looked in the burning sun just like an exhibition model in a glass case, floodlit. Above the town tower tiers of hills rising to a main peak like the top of Cleopatra's Needle. The whole is covered in a mass of thick vegetation, and dark clouds float round the summits, the only clouds in the sky. The water reflects the green of the hills which is so different from Scotland, but we can see that the earth is red like Devon.

We anchor opposite an RAF Sunderland station and near some oil tanks, camouflaged, by a small jetty. On the far side of the smooth green water there is a long low line of trees, which we are told contains mangrove swamps and certainly looks very sinister stretching the whole way round. From the town across the bay ply little native sailing boats with curious inverted triangular sails. We see one or two little canoes with natives ready to come alongside. It is very, very hot, and as darkness falls it still remains hot. The oil tanker comes alongside and couples up and works with a floodlight later. Our accommodation ladder is lowered and that is also floodlit. In fact lights twinkle all round and portholes are only partially shaded. This partial blackout has quite a stimulating effect and we feel much freer. We cease to carry our life jackets everywhere, too.

October 15th – 18th

Horribly hot. We sweat and sweat, and nothing can get rid of the sweat as the air is too moist for it to evaporate. Iced drinks are all the coolth we have, and that is inadequate. PT in the morning and boxing sparring are very hard work and men drip on the deck. My shirt only lasts comfortably till lunch time, or tea at the most. It is dreadful in the cabin and a blessing to be able to sleep on deck, but it never seems to grow cool at night.

Nearly every night there is a wonderful sight to be seen. The sky is lit up by electric storms, and often vivid flashes light up the bay and the ships. There is no rain, but occasional vivid streaks of fork lightning show where a storm is in progress. One night we were hit by a storm and it was heralded by a clap of thunder like a ship blowing up or a bomb bursting, so sharp was it. Lightning and other stage effects were terrifying. I can now see that not all Dorothy Lamour's dilemmas are unreal. The rain came down like a million hoses, and the wind howled and whipped the calm water into curling waves. Then suddenly it passed and I could creep into my bed on deck with the air a bit cooler.

I could write a lot about the natives who came alongside diving for pennies, or more when they could get it. They made the chaps laugh and part up with a good grace. One chap who styled himself Charlie, and spoke good English but with comic prattle, wore a bowler, an old school tie and a moth-eaten bathing dress. He was good value indeed and must rank as a real stout heart. Their canoes were beautifully fashioned, and they baled with wooden scoops when the bottom filled from their climbing in and out. They were tireless and would carry on for hours on end, diving and diving. What marvellous bodies they had, and how puny most of us look beside them. I believe that the port natives are very spoiled, though.

We longed to go ashore just for a bit to explore, or go for a sail in such an inviting setting, but it was obvious that we could not do so or the convoy would have swamped the town, nor were there boats enough to take us off.

One night the matron of the RN *Oxfordshire* hospital ship came aboard for dinner with some other MM officers. That caused a great stir, and the band who play in the first class dining room did very well, so did Jojo Baker and others on the microphone afterwards. The band work very hard under Major Barclay and practise every day, playing sometimes at dinner and sometimes a quartet afterwards by the grand piano in the smoking room.

We never tire of watching the great Sunderland flying boats taking off and landing. One day we saw a great launch full of RAF go by with a very Empire-building and bronzed officer posed by the cabin. Tony Dean noticed this and remarked to me. I thought he might.

I am afraid I do not often go on to the mess decks as the smell and heat are awful. The chaps keep out as much as possible and the hatches are off and the wind chutes up, which help. The decks have awnings over them which give some shade. The blower system in the cabins and saloon is excellent. The officers always seem to be better off than the men, somehow.

We are soon tired of gazing at Freetown and look forward to cool breezes again, even though we go nearer the Equator yet. We loll about feeling very limp and sweaty.

Sunday October 19th

Went to the 8 a.m. service as usual. We hold it in the first class saloon now as it is so well attended. I love that service for it brings me nearest to God and to those whom God watches over at home. The 10.30 service is now on the Boat Deck, with the band on a hatch in the middle of the congregation, which is very large and quite voluntary. The Padre's sermons are shorter and much better now, and I think appreciated. It is the best way I think to make a sermon simple with one idea which will stick when driven home. An elaborately constructed sermon, however well balanced and delivered, fails to go over more often than not. There is no need to go by time when making up a sermon, except of course to limit it! I liked the idea of the watch with movable pointer screwed on to the pulpit of Marlborough College chapel.

At last we are off, and sail quietly away in the afternoon and soon see nothing but sea all round. The convoy has changed a bit, too.

October 20th – 29th

We aim for Cape Town now, and hope to get there in about ten days. No one ever knows anything on this ship till it actually happens. We never knew when we were starting originally or where we were going. We still don't know our final destination, or whether we change ships, or even if we are going to Cape Town at all. We may go to Durban, but Cape Town is favoured.

Had one very interesting evening talking to Nick Carter who was a South African business man. He joined the RAC when war broke out just when he should have returned to the Cape. He went to Blackdown and is in the 8th Hussars. Married in South Africa, his wife died in childbirth and he has a daughter of seven years. I remember him coming to join us at Ogbourne with his new young wife who he said was rather a nuisance as they were only married in June and she wanted to be with him as much as possible. We were rather shocked at this outburst, but I have since discovered that he is only as outspoken as all South Africans are. He is quite a good chap and gets asked many questions nowadays.

He told me how he came to get married, and how he went for a quiet honeymoon to Zeals in Wiltshire to a little cottage lent by an aunt-in-law. I was very interested to hear all about it as that is what I long for. I wonder whether I shall be able to marry or not, when and if I return. Will Leslie wait for me? Will I feel the same towards her, or what will happen? I do so hope everything will be all right. Many chaps are married and have happy homes and children. I am too young yet, I know, but I think of these things so much more now I have met Leslie. Gosh! She is a marvel. A wonderful brain, and so versatile. She can do anything in the house, and anything out of the house. Gardening, carpentry, walking, games, everything. She is my ideal and I love her so. Pray God that she likes me and that we may marry one day.

What shall I do when I return? I do not know. If and when are the big questions, which are too vague and problematical even to be speculated. Shall I feel like continuing with my original design, Holy Orders? I hope so, and yet I am not quite sure. I am very weak and think I want everything my own way.

My idea of happiness is a cottage in the country with Leslie. Father will have a cottage, I hope, and I shall have lots of furniture and things if they escape the bombs. With luck I shall have a little money, too. Father will put something by for me, and I may be lucky somewhere else. I hope I can save on this campaign. I am not spending very much on the voyage and have my remaining cash sewn up in my belt where it is not easy to get out. I do not bet with it, but do drink a little. Luckily an iced orange drink was only 3d in the heat. I must not spend in Cairo either, but save it all for Leslie and the future.

What a thought. What an incentive to work and fight for. Leslie my saint and angel. She is at Carr Sanders Secretarial College now*, training for a job. I am sure she will do wonderfully, but I wonder if she will wait for me. Could she possibly like me enough? Nothing can tell me that, and I can only long for letters and write my best ones back. Can I tell her exactly what I feel, or would that be premature? I think I had better hold on for a bit and leave the big guns till last.

Mother watches over me I am sure, and she will watch over Leslie and know what is best. I am sorry she only saw her once, but I am glad she did manage that. Alas! She and I were never fated to stay in Oxford together.

October 30th – November 3rd

I have just spent four of the most amazing days of my life. Amazing in that they were unique and a most novel experience. It will be a long, long time before the vivid memory dies.

It began on the evening of Thursday, October 29th. Land sighted! Table Mountain in view. The Cape, of which we had heard so much from Carter and about which we had all been thinking for so long. Somewhere where we could go ashore once again—for five weeks seemed so long to us who had been accustomed to so much freedom and licence.

Gradually the sea calmed, for it had been unpleasantly choppy from the evening before when we had the concert, and the mountain line became clearer and Nick Carter pointed out Devil's Peak, Lion's Head, the Twelve Apostles. Everyone came to ask him questions about hotels and things to do. I thought of what I should do, and built up a

* Evacuated to Stanway House, Gloucestershire.

picture in my mind of what Cape Town was like. A faint memory of an old picture post card kept coming into my mind. I began to feel excited and an air of expectancy crept over everyone. We drew nearer and nearer, then darkness fell.

During dinner I eagerly chatted to Colonel B and Colonel W and then hurried over my dessert and up on deck to see what was doing. During periods of excitement or even minor interest everyone crowds on deck. A passing ship, a bird, an aeroplane stirs a hum of excitement, but now. . . The sight that greeted me on the boat deck sent me scurrying down to tell Colonel Williams to come up as soon as he could so as not to miss it.

The ship was moving slowly in under the lee of Signal Hill and Table Mountain. All rolling had ceased, but the wind blew and it was cold enough to wear an overcoat. I carried my field glasses, too.

The lights! At the foot of the mountain shadows a semi-circular band of lights blazed out over the bay. Sea Point lay on our right, Cape Town just hidden round the corner, but the lights of the lowlands north of the town curved round and trailed into nothing on our left, where low hills continued the circle of the bay. I was thrilled to see those lights twinkling away, winking at war, inviting us to share what lay behind. We could see lines of streets, promenades, large houses, neon signs, all winking through the cold air. In the darker shadows car lights flashed fanwise for a moment to be lost in the blaze of the town proper.

Then the lights of the harbour control began to flash and the lighthouse beam swept again and again across the bay. Navigation lights appeared at the convoy mastheads, and we crowded the rail to watch the pilot boat come alongside. Instructions were roared to us through a megaphone and the troops below raised a cheer as the string of figures ended, the boat sheered off and we moved to our anchorage for the night. As the anchor rumbled down, the officers collected their bets in the smoke room. I remember that I walked round the deck very cheerfully with Chris Parker and then retired to bed as I could not go on gazing at those lights, for all that they meant.

October 31st

I awoke to find the ship moving into harbour and rushed in PT kit to the poop until we were in the dock. Our first sight of Table Mountain in light. Its sheer rise is remarkable, but it is so close to the town and rises without any foothills. The town shines bright with a maze of small white houses with red roofs, and a few tall modern buildings with writing on them. It is a joy to see cars and buses and people again. I can see also the other ships berthed, with every rail filled with waiting men.

When shall we get off? What shall we do? Stephen gets a copy of the *Cape Times*, which is a novelty and shows a foretaste of what we may expect. Good news for the racers, too, as the Met is being run tomorrow. We hang about for about an hour while officials come aboard and various cars drive up to the gangway.

Our 'first woman' is a striking dark sergeant of the South African Women's Auxiliary Force who drives a huge blue American car. She is cheered as she drives by and smiles in return. The men throw pennies and tanners to the ragged, dirty crowd of coloured dock workers and roar with laughter as they scramble in the quayside dirt and fight for the sixpences. I have never seen a more horrible-looking lot of men, but they seem cheerful and turn willingly enough to man the big dock cranes. Our hatches are opened and the derricks manned. Someone has seen Allin going off for the money with a suitcase and a tommy gun, and G.G. Smith goes off in a car. There is hope we shall get off when they return. Suddenly I see George and John T.-W. with some coloured slips on deck. The passes have come. We rush to claim them for ourselves and to sign our men's.

What a scramble there is on the mess decks. Everyone wants to go ashore, but someone has to be an orderly. The sergeant-major does his best while I rush off and get money for my chaps and five pounds for myself.

Officers can go off at 11 a.m. The Padre, the Doc, Michael Pollock and I step off together. I do not notice my first step on shore, the thought comes to me later on, down the dock. The old *Empire Pride* looks quite impressive from the shore, but nothing compared to the *Dominion Monarch* or *Strathaird*. We walk the whole way out of the docks wondering what is in store for us.

A great institution the Information Bureau, which is staffed by hard-working ladies with maps of the town. These and their instructions are most welcome, and when the Padre has telephoned the Archbishop we march off up into the town, clutching our papers and leaving a host of men and officers, asking and being informed on every point and many car rides being arranged.

By now we are hot and hungry, and in the main street a lady makes us buy charitable greetings cards with a poem on, to send home. She tells us to lunch at Markham's, and we go in there. Everyone looks at us, or so we think. It is odd to feel a stranger, but grand to order a nice meal, and we like the brown bread and butter with the soup. Half way through, the manageress comes up and says 'You gentlemen have been the guests of the gentlemen sitting at the next table. He is a well-known business man and he has just lost his son.' We are amazed and quite taken aback. Such a thing has never happened to me before and our host has left anyhow. So we thank him on one of our greeting cards and sign our names and leave it till he comes again. Raspberries and cream are marvellous—a dream come true. We find the whole town a dream.

The shops are full of everything to eat and smoke and wear. Piles of chocolates and sweets and food lie on the shop counters. Nothing is rationed. The streets are full of petrol-eating American cars, and garages serve a non-stop flow of that precious liquid. I feel as if I want to buy everything I see, and with difficulty stop myself from rushing everywhere just to look at all the inviting things in the shops. I have an urge to buy something, so we go off and send parcels home from a big store which specialises in this job and everything is cut-and-dried easy. I send Leslie silk stockings, perhaps rather rashly, and the family sweets and dried fruit, and Mrs L.-C. tea and sugar.

Then we try the Post Office for cabling home but it is too crowded and we step into the street wondering what next.

A small lady with a Hillman Minx was inviting Major Wilkinson and Pat McCloud to go out, but they could not, so she asked us. She said she was going to Stellenbosch, about 30 miles, and we accepted with alacrity although we thought we would spend the first day feeling our way quietly and perhaps go to a cinema in the evening. I even refused an offer to go dancing at the Kelvin Grove—7.15 at the War Memorial for transport.

The lady was Scotch, very talkative, a rather dangerous driver, and wearing an RAMC brooch. She was an evacuee herself, living with her three children in a flat in Rondebosch, a suburb, having come out a year ago, her husband being a DMS GHQ Cairo. With five of us in the little car we were not comfortable, so she let me drive when we reached the big national road on the edge of the town. I was thankful in a double way! Mrs Lees talked and talked about everything but mainly Edinburgh medicine of 1923 or 24! What a change indeed from the last five weeks, to be at the wheel of a car speeding out into the country in South Africa.

After about an hour we reached Stellenbosch. A quiet, shady, peaceful little university town with many old Dutch houses still remaining. It seemed with its wide streets like a town in the Middle West such as the films portray, and the others thought it like France.

I was informed that I was to meet a very charming girl. We drew up at an office, and Cynthia came out, and a cheerful man named Gerald Lunt too. Cynthia was all I wanted to see. Duminy was her name and she was of French Huguenot descent. She spoke cheerfully and frankly with a delightful accent which never failed to charm me all the time we were together. I will not only remember her for that. She was beautiful and charming to us all. (Because I had been five weeks away from female society? No!) She would have been striking anywhere, and when she got into Mr Lunt's car to go for a drive, I got in too, with Mrs Lees, Mike and the Doc in the other.

What a drive we had. In a big American car on cambered roads built for speed we sped to Jonker's Hoek in the mountains and then to Hells Hockte. It was breathtaking. The mountain passes, the mountains, the fruit and vineyards, the strange birds and trees, the natives and their little dwellings in the valleys, the speed, the sunshine and Cynthia.

All too quickly we returned to Stellenbosch. Thoughts of Cynthia have put out of my mind the interlude before the drive, when we all went to the local hotel to 'wash and brush up', and the Hebrew hostess invited us all to drinks. At 3.30 in the afternoon choice was difficult so we had orange gin as she did, and liked it very much. We also met a Nazi agent, as we were told by Mrs Lees. We were to learn a lot more about the German influence in South Africa. Stellenbosch itself is a very strong centre of Afrikaans and Nazi sentiment. Over the last twenty years, the Germans have been very clever with their propaganda. The Boer War is excellent ground on which to build hatred in the hearts of men who never forget even though they may forgive, in obedience to the command of their all-embracing Bible.

We had dinner together in the café of the cinema, and again cream with strawberries this time, lots more brown bread and butter, passion fruit juice and a salad grill. Simple fare in simple surroundings with charming people, *and* a delightful girl. How lucky I was. Then we bade goodbye to Cynthia and returned to Cape Town in the dark.

No blackout, no fumbling, stumbling, and cursing. It was lovely and I revelled in every minute of it. Late at night the shops seemed to be open, laden with fruit and other things to eat. Neon lights blazed, car lights glared and I marvelled at it all. No worry on reaching Mrs Lees flat about curtains. We flicked on the lights and gazed at the town through open windows in childish delight at being restored to the light that had been extinguished in Europe for two years. The Doc took a bath, and we listened to music once again on the wireless. I think the Padre had a bath too, for I never got one as the water was cold, but by then it was latish and we all climbed into the car again, but did not drive straight back to the docks. We went to the university first and had a marvellous view of the town. I met a very nice medical student taking the air. He told me his name was Bailey and invited me to call again.

We drove down by a roundabout way to see more, and at the docks declared we would stick to Mrs Lees for the next day at least. I wanted to see Cynthia again as soon as possible, but I had competition from the Padre I knew, and we had to march next morning. We walked to the boat astonished at our luck, and marvelling at the wonder of it all. I felt like dancing down the quay. I was too happy to feel tired, and eventually fell asleep thinking eagerly of the morrow having thanked God for that chance meeting.

For the first day we had done very well indeed and many people envied our luck as we told them all about it next morning. Paper and ink in my hand cannot tell of the infinite variety of things I saw or of the many complex feelings I had. I loved it all, and I seemed to feel a new life and vigour, at the same time wondering at it all, and occasionally thinking that it was perhaps a dream.

November 1st

A dash for papers being sold at the gangway which we could read at breakfast! Then parade in khaki drill and a scurry to borrow topees and bits of clothing which had been packed in the hold ready to move ships. We did not envisage a march through the town, but by 9 a.m. we were all drawn up on the quay with the Rifle Brigade and the 9th Lancers.

At about 10 a.m. we marched out of the docks with a South African band in front. It was very, very hard to march as the band was scarcely audible to us who were some way back. A few people cheered at intervals, and clapped too. Hundreds stared and smiled. I felt very proud and whispered to the chaps not to look at the beautiful girls but to march their best. We marched a long way, and certainly saw the town all right. Back to the ship after a brief halt. A hurried change, a scramble for passes, and a convenient taxi rushed me to the shops with half an hour to spare before they closed. I found a fine bookshop and had a brief but happy browse. So much to see, such a desire to buy.

After lunch at Del Monico's, very posh and very much *the* place, Doc and I took a train to Rondebosch and the Padre went to deal with a confirmation candidate and the Archbishop of Cape Town. Mrs Lees and her children piled into her car and off we went for another remarkable drive. Everywhere we went we met officers and men from the convoy. Every car seemed full of sightseeing soldiers. I am in Africa now! On we drive round the winding road to Constantia where we can see the Indian Ocean, False Bay and Muisenburg with Simonstown hidden on the right. The Indian Ocean is warm at once compared to the Atlantic round the corner and the bathing is calm and safe compared with Hout Bay on the Atlantic which we visited next.

The mountains were very impressive and the sea very powerful, or so I felt, but I thought the whole area rather false and rather showy and not the real Africa. The Marine Drive back to Sea Point, though, was very impressive and I felt myself driving extra carefully so as to avoid the 1,000-foot plunge over the precipice into the sea.

We got back to the flat very late but there was a welcome tea waiting for us. The domestic problem is easy if you can get a good coloured servant, and Mrs Lees has been very lucky. The idea is to go dancing later on, and an Anne Petrie is coming as a partner for the Padre. I am hoping for Cynthia to come but there is no word from her when Anne arrives. Anne is dark and pretty and I like her at once, but Cynthia has taken the wind out of my sails. Padre finds Anne all he wants and Doc seems unmindful of anyone in particular—we presume Mrs Lees will be his partner.

Leslie, I thought of you at the dance at the Rotunda down on the seafront where we had booked a table for five. No Cynthia, and so we had to share our partners and I hate that. I wrote my immediate impressions in my pocket book, and Leslie was much in my thoughts. We drank orange gin and Van der Hum, and ate sandwiches and fruit salad at steel-framed tables and chairs. The band were not very ambitious but the acoustics were good in the big circular domed dance hall. It was all rather tinselly and shallow though, so unlike the Mayfair and its soft carpets and lights. I don't expect to find the Mayfair on Sea Point, but I like soft lights and carpeted stairs! We had quite good fun and I was pleased when Anne said I danced all right. Dancing with Jean Lees I schemed to meet Cynthia again, and she promised she would find out about it tomorrow. I hoped we might go out to Stellenbosch again.

It was interesting to watch all the people there: university students, a few South African forces, and many people speaking Afrikaans. I like the sound of Afrikaans, but the bilingual business is an awful nuisance in the country. All signs, notices, books, speeches, etc., have to be duplicated, and it is a waste and many people realise it.

The dance finished sharp at 12 p.m. We heard the South African national anthem and then sang 'God Save the King'. Everyone seemed to become cheerfully noisy then, and rushed about as they finished up their drinks, and the management turned out the lights hintingly. We did not meet many people or feel any active opposition, but Jean told us that there were some scoffers watching the march that morning. She was standing in the crowd with the children, but I failed to see her though she saw me.

Sunday November 2nd

Doc and I got off at 10.30 and Jean was waiting at the dock gates to drive us to the Scotch Presbyterian church. I had never been before and I liked it. I liked the people and the minister and I thought the public baptism he conducted was a splendid way for a baby to enter God's church. I missed the familiar service though, and the absence of the altar worried me a bit at first! After the service we went round to the vestry and met the minister and one or two others including the British Astronomer at Cape Town, a delightful and typically vague man with two watches in his pocket, both different but I couldn't make out what they were for. I liked the minister who was intense, and drew himself up stiffly to attention when he shook hands. He was most sincere and appeared well-liked, and certainly his week's programme that he read from his dais seemed very full.

The afternoon saw our big adventure! Doc, Jean, the children and I set off for the Sir Lowrie Pass, leaving Padre and Anne together somewhere in the town! I drove, and though I had to concentrate on the road ahead, I thoroughly enjoyed it afterwards! Quite frankly I was overawed by the mountains and the big roads seemingly miles from anywhere; and apprehensive lest the car should break down.

The view across the flats to the coast mountains was impressive. On either side grew queer trees, shrubs and flowers like one finds in greenhouses. Occasionally on the lower slopes we came across native boys holding out bunches of beautiful coloured flowers, and from what I saw, they sold them all right.

At the top of Sir Lowrie, Jean enquired from a native at a cottage if we could do the Viljoen Pass to Paarl, and he said that the road was in good order. Jean had never dared to venture alone but she felt quite confident now, but I didn't feel so good! However, off we went, and up and up a very pretty red sand and gravel road through trees and small plantations. Away below us, below the rocks and crags, and mountain streams, stretched the very fertile valley in every shade of green. It looked like a picture postcard with the sun and clouds. My eyes were glued to the wheel, as a slip and we should have come to a very sticky end.

From the top of the pass, which seemed endless and full of tricky bends, I could see a new country below. It looked rather like England with rolling green fields, and other patches of dark and light on a rolling countryside. Trees appeared in small woods and near there was the usual little white farm. The red road wound down at fantastic length, twisting and doubling on itself, and all of it visible. Down at the bottom we seemed in a new country, and all round us behind and on the left, and again in front, in the far distance the mountains shut us off from the sea and apparently civilisation!

How minute this little corner of South Africa appears on the map. How huge and unfriendly it appeared to me, a stranger, on an unknown road, driving a rather precious cargo. Going on and on farther away from home, I felt slightly uneasy. I asked where we were, and got vague replies from Jean who knew we had to turn left somewhere. I began to believe that in South Africa a mile is equal to a league. However, there didn't seem much point in retracing our steps. At last after passing many little farms with apparently no life at all, I saw at the very end of the valley, a bridge beyond which a sharp rock rose which meant we could only turn left or right. A signpost told us we were all right, and I branched left for Paarl, still an unknown distance away. Jean thought it was about six miles but I had my doubts. We headed along a gravel road across the bottom of a wild valley between mountains rising on either side—heading for the mountains in front, for a pass which appeared to rise into the clouds.

I realised we must break through the barrier to reach Paarl. I didn't like the idea much, which was silly of me, but the mountains began to hedge me in somehow and I was unused to hills I could not run up on foot. I felt miles from anywhere and it was about 5 p.m. One car we asked said Paarl was 35–40 miles which shook me but did not surprise me very much, though it did Jean!

Fransch Hoek proved to be a real pass. On and on and up and up with a steep precipice below us all the time. A gravel road and small stone blocks to mark the edge. I should have hated the clouds to descend from the peaks, or darkness. But we had no horrors! We crawled up, more often in second gear with the others nosing impatiently up in top! Soon I let them pass, and we chugged on quite happily, marvelling at the view all round us, and feeling the cold air. But this was nothing to the sight that greeted us at the top of the pass just as we began to descend. The sun away on our left shone with slanting gold beams through the shadows and clouds of grey black mountains rising sheer from the ground, leaving their grim sides in dark outline. To our right the sun shone upon more mountains, flooding the crags and slopes with yellow light which made the natural colours even more picturesque.

Away in front of us were white clouds out in the light of the plain, forming a background which reflected white and reddening shafts of light on the narrow valley below. I had never seen such a lovely sight as that beautiful green, fertile Fransch Hoek valley presented in the evening light. Its fruit is renowned all over England, its beauty was the greatest view I have yet seen. I thought of my friends who have travelled in Austria and other parts of Europe. What would they think of this? Was this quite ordinary to them? Never mind, it was new and wonderful to me, and I drove slowly down, exulting in it all, and feeling so happy now that we were safely over.

At the bottom we stopped and ate oranges, and then sped away north-west through the little town of Fransch Hoek, which from the top of the pass had looked fairy-like and unreal. A very beautifully constructed model of charming little white houses with red roofs, hiding among the abundant green. Habitations well placed and roads wide and straight, just as the Boers had built them for their wagons. A signpost showed us the way to Stellenbosch and I hoped we should be able to see Cynthia. I should have loved the drive with Cynthia, but never mind! It began to grow dark and the children grew sleepy as we hummed through the well lit suburbs. I cheered as we parked by the flat, and in we went to prepare food, which we all needed!

November 3rd

PT on the docks from 9.15 − 10.00 and great apprehension lest we should not be allowed ashore, as rumour had it. But hurray, the passes arrived with a proviso. We had to be back by 12 p.m., and that meant we were on our last day. I had visions of dancing with Cynthia, and Jean went over to Stellenbosch to see her in the morning.

In the meanwhile we all spent the morning shopping, and I hunted the bookshops but without much satisfaction. I had the urge to buy but couldn't make up my mind. In the end I bought: a star map, two other maps, *Far from the Madding Crowd* by Hardy, and what do you think?—Bell's *Standard Elocutionist*, the modern edition. It may be useful one day! Then lunch at Markham's where I gorged on strawberries and cream and chocolate.

We decided to do Table Mountain as there was little cloud and the sun really shining. Catching the first bus after lunch, we climbed and climbed, and eventually a special bus took us to the lower cable station.

I was quite keyed up as we waited our turn. We stood overlooking the town below us from quite a height, and as we watched we saw the *Dominion Monarch* move out to anchor in the bay. Poor chaps! Confined on board away from all the fun. How we should hate that. I hoped we should sail right away when once we embarked. Then, 'This way please!' and into the little swaying car we climbed when it came to rest on a downward run. We began to climb. I felt quite weak in the legs as I watched the vertical face of the mountain sliding slowly beneath us. The cable grew steeper and our rise slower. The other car slid down past us at a great speed, but could we make it? At last we crept into a tower balanced on the very edge of the rock. Rather shakily I made my way through the crowd in the curio and visitors' book room to the misty platform on the far side. At the end of this the mountain top stretched away for its three miles or whatever it is. Westwards the Atlantic ocean breakers appeared as they rolled over the rocks of the curving coastline which we had never seen before. The mountain chain stretched away southward and at the end on the left there was the Indian Ocean shining through the clouds and the sun. The cloud formation was peculiar. A cold breeze blew strongly from the Atlantic and curling over the top of Table Mountain, a continuous cloud formed making the air chilly and obscuring the view. Luckily no more than this developed and our view of Cape Town and Table Bay was uninterrupted.

It was a remarkable view, exactly like being in an aeroplane. We could see our 'hell ship' in the dock, and rejoiced to be free of it for a time. The Bay looked wonderful and the still blue sea, so very unlike England. The Hottentot mountains were away in the dim distance, vague outlines merging in the cloud which always seems to gather on mountain tops.

The descent was easy and enjoyable but the sheer face sliding by at our rear was still grim, and it was more fun to watch the pine trees grow bigger and bigger until finally they closed in upon us and towered above as we came to rest in the white-walled 'station'.

I had another disappointment after tea. Anne and Padre came into the bookshop as I was mooning round and said that Cynthia could not come as she could not get back in the morning early enough. Anne's friend would come instead. That meant I should not see Cynthia again, and I was sad.

When Doc and I reached Rondebosch only the children were in, so I slid off in a taxi to the university to see Bailey. Luckily, he was in, but unluckily many of the buildings were closed. However, I enjoyed walking round and asking questions, and telling him about my life and Oxford. I heard quite a bit about the Afrikaaner question, and I sympathise a little with them. We passed many very pretty undergraduates who were very well dressed and as a selection far superior to a casual selection at Oxford. M.B. asked me to stay to dinner which I should have enjoyed very much but I rang the flat and found that they expected me, so he ran me back in his car. He will become an army doctor, and we may meet again. At least I have found one male friend here which will be a solid connection if we ever meet up again.

Jean had brought some wine samples from Constantia, so we settled down to a hearty but unfortunately hasty meal. Then Anne's office friend turned up, Lynette Ryall. I could not quite make her out—but we were hurrying to get our booked seats at the cinema. At any rate she was very, very pretty, or at least so to my mind. She was slim and blonde and cheerful and desirable.

The car arrangement was splendid and I wish we had been going dancing. Anne sat on Padre's knees and Lynette on mine, as we hurtled along to the cinema, with Jean driving at suicidal speed, but we arrived in time. Cynthia was rather forgotten, and I loved having Lynette to cuddle! I only wish we could have danced and gone romancing perhaps! She had an odd voice, and in England I think I would have classed her as a 'pretty secretary', but here she was Anne's friend and obviously on the same level. Unluckily I did not have very long to worry my head about her.

I couldn't do much in the cinema but prattle away and enjoy it with her, and eat chocolates. She was a good cinema companion for we both very much appreciated this film, Leslie Howard in *Pimpernel Smith*. A very clever bit of direction, slick acting, witty dialogue and mild propaganda. I wanted to see it when Leslie said she was going to it in Oxford, but I never thought or imagined the actual circumstances in which I should actually do so.

I suppose all the girls who meet convoys know what most chaps are after, but I felt that to start anything with Lynette would have been cold-blooded and unfair to Cynthia, let alone my darling Leslie. I thought of her a lot, and Padre told me he thought of his wife, and somehow didn't quite believe what he was doing; for such an idea that less than two months after leaving his wife, he would be rather 'gone' on a pretty and sweet girl at Cape Town, would never have occurred to him earlier on. Was I being unloyal to Leslie? What would she expect of me? What was the limit to which I might go, and was the Padre's limit to be any stricter? However, there was luckily (or unluckily!) no occasion or opportunity for either of us to get worried. Still with our girls on our knees—what an amazing change from our dull and celibate life on board!—we drove for some last eats to the Doll's House, an interesting little road house affair. Here you park your car and flick your lights up and down, indicating to native waiters that you wish to order food. You order, and the food and drink is brought on a small tray and attached to the side of your car. Decadent? Lazy? One doesn't worry at that time of night, but at least it was indigestible and uncomfortable with six people in and out of a small car. Never mind. It was all fun, and the society exciting.

The parting came too soon. Down at the docks there were crowds of cars decanting sorrowing officers and men, regretfully disentangling themselves from their guides and hostesses. Some staggered up on foot rather the worse for wear, and some turned up in style but packed like sardines in a one-horse buggy, which rather detracted from the dignity of their poses! We wended our way down to the quayside rather sadly and regretfully, keeping well away from the menace of speeding cars.

Climbing aboard on the stroke of midnight we gathered to reminisce and chatter for a while, examining parcels in the smoking room.

Then bed, and many memories.

November 4th

I awoke to find the ship moving and hurried on deck to find us sliding out into the bay where all the ships were gathering, anchors up. We were spared the agony of hours gazing at that pleasant shore, for when the last ship came out, we steamed away in silence, no one apparently noticing as they went to work on just another morning.

I am sure we all felt alike. Worse than leaving Gourock somehow, for then we were miles from home and irrevocably parted, and leaving a not very cheerful place with which we were bored to death. Now our interest and feelings had been roused very swiftly. We had found new friends and new experiences, which were all the more delightful after our dull and rather depressing time. So soon, we had to leave it all, just as we were really getting going, and yet we were not leaving home, only a port of call. How much we have to thank Cape Town for, and how well they did it as if we were the first and last troops to come in.

But it was no good moaning. We were on our weary way again to unknown destinies. Dates with Death perhaps? At any rate we had had some marvellous dates with Life. There were no parades, everyone was exhausted and many slept. Minds were too full to speak. That night, no laughter or cards after dinner. We all crept away to bed.

Sunday November 9th

Back into tropical kit and scorching sun, but a tempering cool breeze keeps us energetic. There is too much time to contemplate. I keep dreaming and thinking of what war will be like. Reading of horrors means nothing. Pictures of horrors raise no lasting emotion. Somehow I cannot picture Ben, Stephen and Tony and the like being treated with brute violence as fierce tank leaders, spreading death with crushing force, and having death flung back at them. I cannot think of myself as the target of bullet, bomb or knife. Somehow I don't see myself as an enemy to be destroyed. But it doesn't do to think very far. Who is going to get home, and when, and in what condition? What pretty wife or sweetheart will become a sorrowing widow of one of our men? What hopeful, cheerful family will become fatherless? I am so glad I cannot know. It is in the hands of fate, and God will watch over our lives and see how we come through it all. Who could tell what fun we would have at Cape Town? Who can tell what luck we may yet have?

November 11th – 13th

(Armistice Day) The bugles blew and we rose from sitting discussing Browning gun stoppages. I always think of Uncle Donald when I think of the last war. He must have been a wonderful man, and so like his sister. He and his brother Cyril were killed. Their names are on the war memorial at St. John's, Hampstead.

I think we stood and thought somewhat of ourselves too, at that moment. We cannot help thinking of the future as we know so little of it at all, not even our destination. What a waste death is, but we all know it is, so what's the use of talking platitudes? I don't mind the thought of being killed at all. Mother has passed on before me, and only Father would be left rather lonely perhaps.

What would Leslie care! A passing regret and then I hope no more than a memory of our friendship and a wonder at what might have been. But I want to live as I want as many as possible to survive. Is it all luck, I wonder, or what? I want to live because I have not yet seen life to the full, and I am sure I have not justified my existence, if I ever can.

There is so much that I want to see and do. I long to travel the world and see the natural and man-made beauties both of the past and the present. I have been reading H.V. Morton's *Through Lands of the Bible*, and his words thrill me. How much more enjoyment he must get from knowing so much history. What a poor historian I am, who groped his way along the Honours syllabus at Teddy Hall.

My yearning for more knowledge never seems to get me very far. I never do much about it. I did buy a history of the ancient world at Cape Town, though. I have been reading, too, of great men, Smuts and Allenby. I used to long to be famous and get to the top of everything at school. My ambition to be a bishop? I don't know now. I think I should be content to live unnoticed by the world at large. I want to survive this war to return to England and earn to be able to live in the country, among all that I love of England.

Above all I want to be worthy of Leslie, and if granted that privilege by God, to marry her. Life is not complete without marriage, and I think I have found the most perfect companion. I do love her so, and love to talk about her to Ben or Peter or James when they will listen. I wonder what she thinks about it, though? Would it be fair or wise to write all in a letter to her? Somehow I do not think the time is ripe, but I will write such a letter and send it home to be sent on to her if I am killed. Shall I be lucky like Father, or shall I be like Uncle Donald? Our Father. . . thy will be done, on earth as it is in Heaven.

Perhaps someone will be good enough to send her my diaries, too.

November 14th

A great sight and heartening for us all. HMS [*Repulse* omitted], our ocean escort, steamed slowly up and down the lanes of ships so that we could all get a good look at her. Sailors were in lines on deck, and the marine band was playing, and the captain stood high up above the bridge, a tall white-clad figure, field glasses in hand, very strong and silent. We cheered like mad, and they cheered too, but I only longed to go aboard as a visitor. I don't quite know whether the sea is my real life or not.

I am very content with my lot really, but I don't know at all what action in the desert is going to be like. I am now preparing a lecture on Libya and learning all I can about it. I am sure it will not be unpleasant all the time, but I expect I shall fear the desert, or is it only mountains that fill me with that strange feeling? Morton feels the Libyan monotony very overpowering. Jarvis rather cheerfully dislikes it at times. Bagnold respects but loves it all, with its stillness and its strange life.

General Alexander's parting words to me give me much comfort at this moment.

I hope we get time to settle down before we have to start fighting, though, as many of my troop are new to the job and have never fired a 2-pounder gun or driven a Mk VI Cruiser. We shall see.

November 15th

Training is rather deadly now, but fatigues paralyse it more than anything. I am never sure who knows what, and it is all rather difficult. I hope for the best, but I don't think we have achieved as much as we might, somehow.

Now that seven weeks have gone by, and there is the prospect of another week only on board, I feel rather panicky, and want to rush on and teach all my chaps everything this week. But I shall have to be content, as we cannot now do more.

I wonder what a German regiment would be like. Conditions are not too cheerful for the chaps, though. The smell of sweat coming up through the hatches is not very pleasant even for those above. At night it is horrible for those below who are herded together. Even those who sleep on deck lie in packed ranks and it is very hard not to tread on bodies when crossing the deck after dark. Food is on the whole good but it varies, while ours is excellent, of course.

We have a lot of fun really, and with Major Al Barclay and his band, and singing after dinner in the saloon. I find time passes pretty quickly, as I always seem to have something to do. Plenty to read for one thing, and a lecture on Libya which keeps me very busy. I have been reading Armstrong's *Grey Steel*, on Smuts. I am afraid I am not very taken with the person he portrays. I cannot tolerate carelessness or recklessness where men's lives are concerned.

What a difference with Allenby. I have been reading Wavell's early chapters on the South African war. I think I can picture it all so much better now that I have had a glimpse of the country. Allenby never risked lives unnecessarily and he must have been brilliant in his fieldcraft.

What a wonderful chance we now have with our Cruiser tanks. A troop leader's job should prove a most interesting one, given a bit of luck. C Squadron is a grand one. George Streeter is a real dear and very human. Quite one of us and not a bit stuck up. I like Netty Streeter very much too, a sweet girl, and they are a charming pair. Spud Patchett is an ace. I think he is a man we all love, rather like a good-natured spaniel. His wife Doodie is one whom I am very taken by, and his little daughter looks a bundle of fun. I am sure that it is because they are so happily married that they are what they are. Margo wasn't married and he was odd at times, very much in a rut. Bing Crosbie-Dawson is the other one of the family trio, who is equally charming and friendly. He can only be described as being exactly like his Golden Labrador 'Amber'—but then you don't know Amber, I'm afraid.

Peter Frankau is senior subaltern. The Ram! Large moustache, very capable, rather a pose of arrogance, 'bloody fellow!' attitude, which is not really true. Unfortunately his family life is far from happy, I am sure. I don't think his men quite appreciate him and he appears ruthless but I think he is an excellent tank officer.

Joe Radice, BNC, rather a butt of everyone else. He is an excellent fellow, but his rather nervous manner and his habit of missing things, make him appear a fool which he very definitely is not. A very knowledgeable chap if he gets his chance, but I'm not sure what he will do if he finds himself going spare in Libya! Who am I to say anything about anyone, when I am as likely to make a balls as anyone? What we want is a couple of months training at least in the desert, when we land. We may get a week if we are lucky.

Stephen Christie-Miller, Trinity and a very sound fellow whom I admire very much. He is a bit of a child in the company of Robin and Tony, though I like all three very much. Robin is married and has a baby son. How nice to be able to marry young. James Cumming is very much admired by his naval friend Billy Normand, but I can't see it.

Tony Dean is a very good sort of level-headed chap. King's School Canterbury, but missed Cambridge owing to the war. What a shame for him. He loves Canterbury and music, and plays the trumpet. James was at Cambridge, as were Ben Hough and Peter Willett. I wonder how different James would be if he had come to Oxford. There is a wide difference between the two places beside outward appearance. Oh for Oxford! What doesn't that name mean to me now? Everything I have valued and all I love.

What a grand lot of chaps to set out with, from Colonel Tom Draffen downwards. I have no real friend somehow, but I like them all. I do wish Charles Robathan or Bob Langton or Stuart Cooke were with me, but they are far away. I must write to them soon.

November 17th

Went over the ship's engines with my friend the electrician, by kind permission of the chief. It was most interesting, especially the 'tunnel' with the silent revolving prop shafts, at the end of which you can hear the propellers threshing the water. I am glad I am not doomed to be in the heat and roar, shut away from the light and all that's going on. I like to see how things work and a ship is a new one on me.

November 18th

Land again! Rather grim-looking cliffs and rocks of Cape Guardafui, or some such name, I'm afraid I haven't looked it up. A Vichy submarine reported, so we zig-zag and so cannot make Aden tomorrow, I believe.

Delivered my lecture on Libya which had taken a long time to prepare, but I enjoyed it. I don't quite know who enjoyed the result, but Padre said it was good but pretty gloomy. I gave my impression of the desert which was perhaps fairly grim, but I am not depressed by it or the thought of living in it. I am rather excited at the thought of all the new sights and experiences that await us.

November 19th

A wonderful sunset which is on our port bow, as we are going westward. Above it hung the evening star, Venus. Never have I seen it looking so lovely. No jewel could ever compare with that sight, which I feel quite inadequate to describe. I can only remember it in its beauty.

I thought I should enjoy reading *Trekking On* by Colonel Denis Reitz, the author of *Commando* which I loved. I found the chapters on the Great War very depressing. Trench life graphically described doesn't fit in very well at the moment. I am afraid I am rather given to introspection. I find myself dreaming about things that may or might happen. I am afraid these are not only confined to rosy hopes. Peter Willett and Co, say they imagine I am rather efficient and warlike. I like guns and things which somehow I cannot reconcile to war. I like firing guns but I hate the thought of men dying. I loathe it. It appals me when I think of what every nation lost in the flower of its manhood in the last war. Father survived and I am the result. Uncle Donald did not, and so he has no son to bear the stamp of his marvellous character. What a calamity indeed, let alone the loss of a great man. It is odd that I should think of him so much. He and Mother were very, very alike, and I shall never forget his portrait on Colonel Greenhill's Chinese sideboard at the Green Cottage (which he had lent to us). When taking 'light' at Toc H at Oxford, I always used to think of him: 'With proud thanksgiving let us remember our elder brethren.' Toc H was responsible for my meeting Leslie.

A wave swept over me as I sat on deck. I was reading Denis Reitz's early struggles in Madagascar and I admired that man. I do not know what it is to have no money at all. I have never been without money, thanks to generous friends and the self-sacrifice of Father and Mother. Anyhow, I thought that perhaps I might go to Australia at the end of the war to 'seek my fortune'. Supposing I could persuade Leslie to come with me? Should we be old enough, would she come, would I be able to support her? Anyhow I have many relations out there, but I am afraid I have neglected them very much. I must try and write now before it is too late and I have to fight instead of living a life of ease.

November 20th (Aden)

Land again, and our last port of call. I was roused at 6.30 a.m. to find a brilliant sun and blue sky. Peering through the porthole I could see high, barren tawny rocks picked out in fierce relief by the sun behind the ship. I hurried on deck to peer through glasses at white dots of sails which I instantly recognised as feluccas or dhows, by their shape. I have seen so many in pictures.

We took a pilot on board as we came to rest in the bay, leading the convoy in. The other ships, strung out into the sun right to the horizon, were a fine sight. Our bearded pilot came from one of the many little launches that fussed around us, and soon we were into the harbour itself. Copper tried to get PT started, but there were far too many interesting things to see as we leaned on one rail or hurried to the other. HMS — was a grand sight and I only wish I could go over her now that I am old enough to appreciate technicalities! The liner — on the other side was quite impressive at close quarters, but our eyes, I think, were mainly for the sights of the port. Gosh! The rocks look grim and bare and dirty, and the little cluster of houses with the curious looking Crescent Hotel in the foreground.

A comic series of important personages came aboard from an equally curious fleet of little motor boats with their black crews, in uniform or not as the case may be. Policemen alone we could recognise. We were quite close to the shore and could see cars and lorries and sometimes army trucks buzzing along the front. All the cars seemed to be little Fords, unlike our last port where no car seemed to be under 20 hp!

We saw our first camels too, dragging small carts at a very unhurried pace, though I was most surprised to see one trotting once! The people we could see all wore coloured clothes of voluminous proportions, and turbans, and at one moment we had the privilege of watching through glasses the complicated procedure of a 'gentleman' putting his on.

The main business of the day was oiling and watering. An unfortunate but entirely unavoidable air lock in the oil tanks (as we afterwards discovered) caused fountains of oil to spew upon the deck for a considerable period. What a waste of oil, but luckily it did not catch fire, or do any damage in its course over the decks and down the ship's side. Portholes were closed in time, but recumbent figures had to shift rapidly from their resting places.

George Rich and Peter Glyn got out their fishing lines, but I don't think they had any luck, although we could see a few cigar-shaped fish. When I heaved George's weight and paternoster over the side for him, there was a most sad accident as the line would not hold it, and all his tackle sank to the bottom!

The colonel, Jimmy Dance, the brigadier, Jerry Horton and Alex Barclay went visiting and were luckily invited on to HMS —. I was most interested to hear all about it from Jimmy. I am not so sure again that I wouldn't like to be on board her. A dull life at times? I don't know—I am not finding this trip dull now. I am sure our life won't be dull anyhow as—flash!—the news has come that the Libyan campaign has begun already without us! We thought we would be in at the start, but no, the General Staff have thrown a surprise and even the 22nd Armoured Brigade are not there yet. They had three weeks' leave at Durban, and went on farms, etc. The lucky dogs—I could have done with a few more days at Cape Town!

Having done our jobs we draw out into the bay for the night where we see a most wonderful sunset behind mountains that look like the moon. The peaks have the appearance of sound waves on paper! Curving round from them to the right is a thin white circular strip with mountains faintly visible in the far distant haze. That is the desert of Arabia. Our first acquaintance.

November 21st – 23rd

Steaming fast by ourselves up the Red Sea. The last lap to what? To battle, murder, and sudden death. To the Pyramids and the Sphinx and the desert beyond. Soon we shall hear the familiar rumble of our good old steeds. News keeps coming in of the campaign and we wonder what our role will be, and think of the chaps in it now.

I served again at Holy Communion. George and Bing were there too. The 10.30 a.m. service was very impressive and the hymns well chosen and the sermon well received. Padre spoke on the Twenty-third Psalm, 'The Lord is my shepherd, therefore can I lack nothing'. Mother wrote that out while I was undergoing my operation. I think of Mother more now, and yet remembrance of her seems curiously dulled somehow. Perhaps just as well for me.

November 24th

Our last day on board, I think. I feel curiously depressed. My imagination is running away with me. I keep thinking of the battles in Libya and all my visions of the future seem to take on another light. I cannot shake off this depression and I wander about in an odd manner which I cannot control. What a fool I am.

Reading *Far from the Madding Crowd* cheers me a bit, or rather takes my mind away from it all, but I finish this after lunch and creep away to sleep till I have to conduct a kit inspection, and after tea I creep away again and watch the sunset, which is a fine one tonight. The dark clouds of last night gave me a feeling of grimness.

I must not think of what may follow. I must recover quickly and put my nose down to the job. It will be all right once there is something to do. At the moment we sit talking, wondering, surmising, reminiscing.

My darling Leslie is much in my thoughts now. I think of her every moment, through all the band and the shouting and jollification. I think of all the Leslies and all the wives and I wonder who will be the lucky ones. I must go up now and join all the fun and games of our last night's celebrations. You would not wish me to be mooning around. That will not get me anywhere. Well, I think of you always and find great comfort.

Now we step into the future and action! The battle roars on a few hundred miles away. The First Armoured Division is coming to fly the flag and give the news some pep. Yes! That's it! I won't be cowed by it all. Here I am, and I will make the best of it, and put myself in God's hands.

Thy will be done. . .

5

Western Desert

November 25th (Port Said)

In port, and at the end of our sea voyage. The morning spent in steaming up the Gulf with bare rocks on either side shining dull yellow and gold in the sun. Felt very queer, pondering on our future as we eagerly scan the news sheet, and then as the officials come aboard we hear more of the action, and fear we may go up very soon without much training. Never mind, we shall have to do our best. I believe most of the casualties have been in vehicles, but the thought of casualties makes one feel rather odd. Quickly Ben, James, Peter and I pack up Cabin 44 and tip the old native boys. Then I wander round and round the ship, finding it difficult to settle down to anything. Finally I decide to write my final letter to Leslie in case I get pipped off. I do so want her to know how much I love her. Perhaps she will not receive it favourably; I mean, I wonder how she would receive it. I hope she will never have to, because I do so want to return to her if I am lucky enough.

John Lyon, I am sorry to say, shot himself this morning, and died shortly afterwards in the ship's hospital. A depressing start for us, and very, very sad as he leaves a young wife and child, and Evvie Hambro his brother-in-law was on the dock to meet him.

It took a long time for us to get ashore with all our valises and packs, and then it grew dark on the quayside as we waited to march to camp. Lorries were few and the baggage was slowly got rid of as the trucks and their black drivers honked through the crowds of rather bewildered men and officers. At last we started off, all laden with kit, and as we passed through the dock gates, two Arabs issued us with hot tea and a bun. I shall not forget that march in a hurry. It was a long five miles on a narrow road, and lorries kept roaring up behind with blazing lights, crowding us into the side. We passed right through the town, through the smells, the lights, the gaping populace, past dirty houses, tall houses, poky little shops, crowded tawdry cafés filled with Arabs. Over crossroads, past better houses, along the edge of the railway, still chased by lorries. Peter and I brought up the rear and we were followed by two black-gowned figures carrying rifles, presumably protecting us from the crowd who pattered along behind. They were a cheerful lot, and seemed to shout encouraging remarks, though perhaps there were many evil faces leering at us through the little tiny lattice windows with pale blue lights emanating through! Right through the town and out along the main road beyond. My feet in shoes filled with sand began to feel it, my shoulders weighed down with full equipment began to ache. However, we got in in good style, though it was a bit of a strain on top of no exercise at all. A camp on sand awaited us. Our first bit of sand. No kit had arrived, so we had to put our overcoats down for the time being and go and seek some food. This was laid on well, stew, bread, jam, butter and tea or oranges. All this we fell on and enjoyed it, though it was very different from the *Empire Pride*!

It was very cold and the men had a hard night as kit was late, but we all got it in the end, and settled in on a floor of sand.

November 26th

Up well before dawn, and a cold wash and shave, and then a quick pack up before breakfast, which consisted of bacon and jam mostly. The way we eat now is very different from our ship style, but even the most superior of officers are as adaptable as any and no one complains at all. That, I think, is a rather interesting fact when people talk of the army who live a life of luxury and ease. When it comes to hard living it is not so hard to get down to it.

Another march followed soon after the sun came up, which it did in fine fashion and in marvellous colour with the air crystal clear. It was fine to see the sun touch the mountains which seemed to change shape as the shadows changed. It was very cold, but gradually the sun asserted itself so that as we stood on the railway track by our train, the sun soon warmed us. Soon we were off on our all-day journey, given a send-off too by a prison camp full of Italians. Some waved, others gave the Fascist salute, others made curious head-chopping motions!

The journey was most interesting, which made up for it being so slow. We stopped at every station where crowds of crooked vendors came along with fruit and chocolate, hard boiled eggs, rolls, magazines and sexy stories. We all tendered large value notes and in many cases got handed back a collection of spurious coins for change, as the natives so easily played on our ignorance. We had bully beef and bread on board, so we could eat all day and sleep at intervals between jumping up and looking at new sights and views out of the windows of the carriage. Camels and donkeys being ridden by a strange assortment of Arabs and Egyptians, or loaded with huge burdens, though they looked quite well cared for. When the train went slowly, small boys and other vendors would jump on to sell things or ask for baksheesh!

We went right across the cultivated area of the Nile delta and over both mouths of the river. It was interesting to see all the irrigated fields and the old bullocks turning water wheels. Most of the fields seem to contain cotton and we saw dumps of cotton bales at some stations.

Villages were comic affairs. Some houses were of mud and some of plaster. All had flat roofs piled with brush, on which chickens scratched. It looked odd in the larger towns to see normal-looking houses at the bottom, finishing on top with a delapidated mess of brushwood. Every place looked as if it had suffered a severe blitz many years previously and had never been rebuilt. All the way along we were cheered by people and crowds seemed to gather at the stations. Everyone seemed very friendly. The sun went down in a very nice setting but not quite H.V. Morton style, though the moon came up bright and beautifully clear.

It was dark when we finally arrived at our little destination station. A hot meal was laid on for everyone and we were soon aboard lorries to our camp in the desert.

A rather bewildering moonlight drive, and very bumpy. In the bright light we found Spud waiting to show us our tents, and we were soon busy putting up the side curtains and collecting lamps ready to seize on our luggage when it should arrive. It took a long time to come but when it did we were under our blankets very soon and asleep. It was a very cold night, but we were quite snug.

November 27th – December 9th

A most pleasant time in a rest camp, so-called, where we have been preparing hard for war. The first time we have been really on the job since about April. Everyone was very, very browned off at the end of the voyage, but now that we are busy there is a very different atmosphere. For a day or two we got no equipment and we spent the time making ourselves comfortable, exploring the desert in the neighbourhood, and visiting **Amriya**, the little village which we discovered in the morning was about five miles away.

Our camp is Ikingi camp, well out of the horrible dirty, dusty traffic-sprawled camp area. It is just on the edge of the desert and we can see the Mediterranean peering through the far sand dunes. My first view of the Mediterranean. Between the sea and us is a small strip of lagoon which appears to be tidal, but there are no duck there! Away on the other side the desert stretches for miles, and miles, and miles.

We have had quite fun, first with prismatic compasses on foot and then in tanks, doing some navigating on the way to the range which is some seventeen miles away. My first experience of the desert was in a truck with Peter Sykes, Basil Nicholson and George Rich and Peter Glyn. We found the site for the range without much difficulty, on a compass bearing, and then we set off across country for seventeen miles. We arrived back at Ikingi Maryut just about a quarter-mile out, and felt very pleased with ourselves. However, the journey for the chaps in the back of this large tin-bodied lorry was very unpleasant. I know because I was in it! It was horrible bumping over the coarse grass tufts, but on the hard smooth sand we fairly bowled along. When we got back we felt very pleased with ourselves and quite confident in the knowledge that we had picked up, and also taught, on the ship.

Days have really been quite hectic. Lorries have been dashing hither and thither. Chaps have been in and out of Alexandria fetching tanks, and our days have been well occupied preparing and fitting them, and rushing around trying to get hold of more and more stores. There is a very nice officers' shop in Amriya which provides all the necessaries which we have forgotten. Especially, nice suede rubber-soled sandshoes and boots, which we all bought very soon, and now find very useful and comfortable. We get up fairly early in the morning and work from eight till twelve when we have lunch. Tea is at four and dinner at seven. It gets dark about five, which makes any activity after tea difficult.

Our tent is very cosy now. Peter, James, Tony and Stephen and I all fit in very well, and we manage a table as well. We have an oil lamp and sometimes candles, but they are rare. Torch batteries don't last very long but a torch is needed to read in bed. I like lamp light except when trying to pack!

I enjoy the evenings best of all. There is nothing much to do after dinner so we go to bed. I am reading a most delightful book, *Guy and Pauline* by Compton Mackenzie. It is all about Burford and Oxford and the Cotswolds and a boy and girl. I love the way it is written and a lot of it is very like my thoughts and dreams. I have written to Leslie about it. I wonder what she will think of it.

The nights are usually very cold, but it is lovely in a warm tent with plenty of blankets. One night was very windy but the tent held up all right. We have had only a few showers of rain all the time, which makes a lot of difference. I dislike rain more than anything except when just going for a walk in it. However, a sandstorm is almost as unpleasant, and very uncomfortable. Some days we have had a slight wind which swirls the sand about a bit, but twice we have had a pukka storm when movement became very difficult, and I put on my gas mask for a bit! Goggles are essential always, but even they cannot keep sand out of nose, ears, mouth and neck!

When there is no wind it is all right and we have now got used to the sand in the tent, which at first we found very trying. Nothing escapes it. Everything we possess is covered all the time with a thin film, but we have learned now that it does no harm and we only dust things when we want to use or wear them. Sand is clean stuff and the camp never looks dirty, but it is always dusty and far worse in this area where thousands of vehicles and troops have churned it up for so long. A tank can be seen from miles away by the huge cloud of dust it raises. A lorry is nearly as bad. If you travel with the wind, your own dust sometimes obscures your own view in front.

Atmosphere varies very much in the mess and in the tent. At first we were all agog for news, and sat around picking up titbits about the progress of the fighting and what our fate was likely to be. We all wonder when we shall be in action and long for news of others.

A lot of people have come in to tell us about their experiences, for which we are very grateful. This is a stage further from book and training which is so valuable. Our chief is Lieut. Titlestad of the 2nd Tanks. A Rhodesian copper miner, silent, rather shaken, but very interesting and helpful. I admire him very much for the marvellous way he quietly tells us the most exciting tales, in magnificent understatements. He was stuck alone with his crew for nine days in the desert and he said, 'Oh! It was a bit boring.' He is coming up to the front with us when we go the day after tomorrow.

I have been lucky with my tanks so far for they have all come out of El Wardyan RAOC quickly and we have been able to test the guns and the wireless, and pack in all the mass of kit and fit the compasses, etc., do an oil change, paint all the signs, etc. Now we are almost ready except for our own kit, and I look at them and wonder what will be their fate and ours.

I have been able to get into Alexandria a couple of times. The first time the adjutant very conveniently sent me in to take charge of a convoy to be desert-painted. I was able to spend the whole day around the town. I had my hair cut and met a friend of George Streeter's, Capt. Jim Astley-Rushton, 7th Hussars. He had been wounded and is on leave still. His car he pinched at Benghazi! He introduced me to the Union Club where I had an excellent bath—a bath in camp means either a camp bath cold or a two-mile trip to a cold shower at Ikingi! Alexandria is not very exciting, and shopping is not good. I had very little luck in getting anything for Leslie. I did see the Coptic Church and the Greek Orthodox, which were quite interesting. I wish I could have gone over one of the battleships of the Mediterranean fleet, though.

I went in the next night with Ben Hough with A Squadron and had a very enjoyable time. I managed to buy one or two things for Leslie and we had a marvellous dinner at the Union Bar—prawns, omelette, Wiener schnitzel, mousse au chocolat, Turkish coffee. Lovely! We saw our general, Herbert Lumsden, there too with a charming girl, having run across him in the Cecil earlier on. He is a very nice man and looks very like Father. Coming out of the place, who should I meet but Mr Hiscocks who is a captain in the Marines! He was my history master at school and I liked him very much. He was at Teddy Hall and used to come to Oxford quite a lot. Unfortunately I had to dash off but I hope to contact him again. Ben and I saw a marvellous film. I really did enjoy it. James Stewart and Margaret Sullivan in *The Shop around the Corner*. A charming love story, and I just love Margaret S.

I went in again with Tony Dean, Peter Willett and Freddie Barnado to see a bit of the night life. We saw very little but for our education allowed ourselves to be conducted to an 'exhibition' by a young Egyptian. We had to pay a lot of money and I will not describe what we saw. It was certainly no thrill, but our education has certainly started at the very bottom.

A most unfortunate thing happened on Sunday night. Truck loads of chaps have been going in to Alexandria nightly to give them a bit of fun. Every night, horrible scenes of drunkenness have taken place in Mohammed Ali Square in trying to embus the party again. It was quite nauseating and very sad to see. I am sure it was because the chaps have too much money to spend. Well, on this particular night Peter took two trucks in, and coming out the sergeant-major, who was tight, turned one over (as he had insisted on driving), killing two chaps in the KRRC, and injuring a lot of our valuable tank crews. Lance corporals Pullyblank and Bradley were both in the lorry, but luckily they escaped injury. It was a miserable business and George Streeter and all of us feel very cut up. Beefy Webb was a very good chap I thought, but now he has been seriously injured and of course will never return to the regiment.

Tonight we have had a little excitement as a 10th Hussar ammo store tent went up in flames and made a merry noise.

Now as Olly and Leslie would say, 'we are ready for off.' All our heavy luggage we packed up and sent back to the base and I have only a little kit left, as I shall only lose it all I should imagine.

Tomorrow is our last day here, and then we follow the trains we have seen passing for so many days now, up to Mersa Matruh. What will happen to us? No one can tell. I hope, as everyone hopes, that I may be allowed to survive, and all my chaps with me. I should be very sorry indeed to lose any of my lovely tanks either, for they are real masterpieces of ingenuity and forethought. They contain more fittings than the best hotel in the world and I know I feel happy inside mine as long as I do not get too close to a PZ KW III or anything like that. Tomorrow, if I have time, I must write as many airgraph letters as I can. This diary I will send back to Barclays Bank in Cairo and hope to collect it again later.

Now to bed and a few more minutes of *Guy and Pauline* before sleep.

I am enjoying it all and I feel quite excited at the moment— not a bit 'going back to school feeling' though no one can enjoy anything to the full in the middle of a war. I carry my two pictures of Leslie on me now in a nice camel leather carved case. Oh! If only I can return to her whole, wouldn't that be absolutely marvellous?

Oh God. I pray thee look down upon us all, and keep us always in thy protection.

December 12th

We move from El Amriya to Mersa Matruh. Everyone up before dawn getting ready, but we didn't leave the station till 1.30 p.m.. Tony took the lorries by road at 6 a.m. to be ready for our arrival. Quite a ticklish business loading tanks on to 'flats' from a ramp. There is only an inch to spare on either side of the truck and the forward tanks have to be driven down all the length of trucks, which makes for anxious moments for driver and director.

When people travel by train, there is always a feverish rush to buy food of all sorts, and we certainly stocked our carriage well. Stephen had his petrol stove. George, Spud and I all provided food, and we had our rations in with the men's stuff. It took a long time to satisfy the RTOs and Major Q (M), that all tanks were securely fastened and shackled, but most of the iron screw shackles were rusty.

While we all stood about, two hospital trains came through and the chaps looked absolutely done in, with long beards too, and staring eyes. They seemed to cheer up at the sight of our trainload of tanks, and one or two thought we wouldn't need them and that the Germans were on the run. However, we expect we shall go into Tripoli as our job. Another rather depressing sight was a train with a load of shot-up tanks. M3s, Cruisers, MK IV and VI. We wondered how many of the crews had survived, as they looked pretty battered with large holes and scars! It was a tiring journey. Until it got dark we had a view of the desert but it was uninspiring. We passed a train of Italian and German prisoners, which was a bit more cheerful, though.

We had some amusement at a little place where crowds of children and men tried to sell us food and were continually being driven away from the train by a terribly fierce-looking policeman with a long whip; but they didn't mind him at all. They merely laughed and darted under the train to the other side. Baksheesh! Baksheesh! How one gets tired of that cry.

When it grew dark we closed everything up, brewed up a good meal of bully, onions and tinned fruit, and settled down to sleep after a good strong sip of whisky. Cpl Work had brought us a grand pannikin of tea earlier on, which was much appreciated. We have got quite used to the tinned milk, and tea, tea, tea is the order of the day every day.

As we rattled along, I read a bit more of *Guy and Pauline*, which is still lasting out. I love to be reminded of the beautiful Cotswolds, especially Burford and Swinbrook. I thought too of H.V. Morton's trip to Mersa Matruh, and Cleopatra. Our best few hours sleep we discovered we had when the train was stationary somewhere, and it wasn't till 5 a.m. that we finally fetched up. My chaps had had a bad time in the guard's van, but plenty of room for cooking.

December 13th

As it gradually grew light we rushed to unload the tanks, and stack the heavy sleepers in one of the vans. Then, piling our kit on top, we followed George around the outskirts of M.M. to our concentration area. Mersa Matruh was just like H.V.M.'s picture and looked very nice and clean, with the blue but rather stormy sea beyond. It has been very badly bombed, though.

After about four miles we reached an aerodrome surrounded by mines on a huge flat expanse of sand and scrub. We found all our lorries parked and James and Bing with the M3. George put us all out on the perimeter, and as the sun rose up we pitched our lean-tos with tank sheets and settled in. There was a lot of maintenance to do, and then we brewed tea and had a hot breakfast which was most welcome. Then a wash and shave.

All day we were much cheered by news of the Russian success and the Germans' retreat in Libya; but we hadn't much time to sit around as we had to prepare our tanks for action. We saw some of the air ambulances in action and they looked very fine planes. I wonder who go in those!

We ate high tea at 5 p.m. as it grew dark, and sipped whisky afterwards while discussing the next day's training and wireless. It grew very cold and we soon retired to bed and I slept for the first time with my crew, under the tank sheet which really made a fine tent and wind shield. I had my lilo, sleeping bag and three blankets in a kitbag on the tank and I was quite warm enough. It was very cold doing a two-hour spell of guard, though. Stars were wonderfully clear and the old Plough became visible far into the night. It was not easy getting up at 5.15! I shaved in a mug of water by the mess truck when it grew light.

Sunday December 14th

After a quick breakfast we were on the wireless sets, and at 8.45 the regiment moved off to 'Charing Cross' where the road to Siwa (199 miles) branches off the road to Sidi Barrani. Sgt McGuinness broke down there and we had to leave him to be picked up. All day we did squadron manoeuvres in the desert, landing up at Aba el Kanayis at 3 p.m., where the regiment went into open leaguer. We were right on top of a plateau and it was very, very cold. No food since breakfast at 6.30 so glad of tea at 5 p.m. I took the only opportunity and had a quick bath standing over my canvas bucket on two petrol tins. It was an icy business but worth it, as I managed to get some hot water off a sand-stove. This consists of a half of a petrol tin with sand in it. Pour petrol on and light it and things boil up very quickly. I found my tea cold, but I had had a bath! We ate as it grew dark and found some welcome whisky too, and then retired to bed at the early hour of 6.45.

Swire had an even more comfortable tent up and we had no guard as we were four men short. It hadn't been a bad day, though. I stopped some rockets over the wireless breaking down, but these were teething troubles. I have no 2-pounder cocking link and Sgt McGuinness has been recovered to LRS and will be away till spares are found. George's tank lost a bogie! Ground very stony and going gave tanks a bashing, and I fear for the tracks. No time to read, but thinking of Leslie. Sudden flashes of fun at home come back often. Desert not frightening so far. Our navigation has been good.

December 15th

Horribly cold and heavy rain at 6 a.m.. Dressing, shaving and breakfast a misery. Hope I don't get a cold in the tummy. Twelve hours sleep OK though. No sun, but biting wind. On the ridge all the morning doing maintenance.

Found a Matilda crew who have been by their broken tank six weeks! They are very much desert islanders, but cheerful. They ask for ammo and pills and Elastoplast! They hope to catch their regiment at Sidi Omar, but must be transported with their heavy tank. Most amusing to find them. Very nice lot, five men. Wind still most unpleasant and sand rising a bit. Sgt-maj. Littlejohn went over a mine yesterday, but all crew safe. Bloody fool. Not even an enemy one, and field obviously marked! Tank out of action. Wonder when I shall see McGuinness again. They are no use here without their tank anyhow. Old Bagnold and Co. who enthuse about the desert are not so far wrong. Up to now I have nothing against it at all. I have not been lost so far, and not a bit frightened of it. I have had great success with my navigation! The desert is not a bit alike. We moved through a sand and rain storm to a lovely depression where we all brassed off with our Besas. The Ram came under fire at one moment but otherwise we had a bit of fun, running down to a squadron open leaguer at 4 p.m. Stephen and Co. were lost, but were discovered about half a mile away over a hill. We had a grand brew up before moving off for the night.

Not pleasant driving at night, and worse if leading tank because of sudden drops and rises which even in daylight are troublesome and one has to go carefully. We flew into the air down a steep unseen drop, but I just had time to shout to the chaps to hold on, and we came to no harm!

December 16th

Gosh. It was a filthy night. We had two spells of guard, and it poured with rain some of the time, together with an icy wind which made my first sleep very spasmodic. Doing our second period of guard Bradley and I never spoke! We shifted our tank sheet round afterwards. We daren't rig it up, so we folded it right over ourselves. I got right into my sleeping bag, boots and all, and slept well till dawn. Tony and lorries never found us till morning though they were in camp half a mile away and heard us start up just before light.

A hard and good morning's training. Warm sun but still cold wind. My cold better, but crew still coughing and sniffing.

1 p.m. in old leaguer again, and a hot lunch ready. Tea came up almost immediately after, so it seemed. Much warmer now, but rain. We save it for washing. My gunner, Swire, wrote 'Dear Mother. We have one mug of water. We have had it for three weeks!' That rather typified our water-securing efforts. We find it very difficult already. However our strainers with ammo packing felt work well enough. A good dinner and early bed tonight. Sgt-Maj. Littlejohn appeared, and we questioned him about going over his mine! He's a bit shaken and didn't like the sensations!

The Matilda chaps at last rescued by a Scammel. I don't suppose they want to go a bit.

Got the News while brewing brekker at 7.30 a.m. on the Mersa Matruh – Siwa track. A surprise to get it on a No. 9 wireless set. Found it was 2.9 and BBC service to America. Rommel and Co. seem to be turning and fighting. No more news. An airgraph from Mrs Parsons. Nothing from home or Leslie yet.

We have a squadron mascot now. A dear little dog which would not leave the lorries at Amriya. Much nicer here than near Alex. Less dusty and overrun like Laffans plain. Spud got good canteen supplies from Mersa, so we are well stocked with sweets, etc., and our air letter cards are here. Hope for time to write as dark very quick and no lights allowed. Must carry this on my tank. We are too busy for reading and amusements while in leaguer.

December 17th

Marvellous sun. A day for short sleeves and sun goggles. What a contrast to the 15th. We had a splendid morning out at Bir Idris dashing about the desert. Coming back to lunch we had a peaceful afternoon and evening. Everything got a good airing and most people found it warm enough to have a complete bath. I managed a couple of pints but the sun chose to go in just at the wrong moment. Bed at 6 p.m. and no guard for us. Sgt McGuinness arrived at 7 p.m. and I had to guide him in my pyjamas!

December 18th

Very cold morning. Spud at work again with a false 'news' that a new German armoured division landed in Tripoli. He is a real card. As snaky and light-fingered a chap as ever lived, but charmingly Irish about it, and you can't get annoyed. I nearly did when I saw him taking my map from my case the other morning and I'm sure he pinched a bar of chocolate the other day. He was tech. adjt. for two years so he certainly knows his stuff and all the ins and outs. Wish we had a wireless. Using No. 9 is illegal and not worth the strain on the batteries. We shall have to send Tony back to Alex!

Regimental scheme today. He is coming out as my operator. 10.00 hours at one hour's notice to move to the battle area. Am in tank waiting for regimental scheme to start. 5 p.m. There was no scheme! Whole brigade moves 32 miles across the desert. A fine and encouraging sight. Cpl Dawson's tank only would not go.

Felt nervous of breaking down on rough stuff. It's not like going along a road. A bearing is not quite so clear! Halted now to go into harbour. A most beautiful sunset of grey and red. Very cold already. I have put my overcoat on. Look forward to char. Our twenty minutes halt at 3.40 was not quite long enough. We boiled up the water but had to pile everything back and pour the water into the tin again! Now we can brew up quickly before dark. All hands to the stove!

December 19th

A brew up again before light. Orders and petrol disturbed an otherwise good night. Off again at 6.30 a.m. on a trip of 73 miles. The Germans are supposed to be running and we shall be on the frontier wire by dark, at Bir Sherferzan. Two-hour maintenance halt at Bir Thelatah at 9.15. Thought lorries were coming up but they have not done so, and we haven't brewed in consequence, but have munched some bully and opened a tin of peaches for a drink. Very hot today now sun is high. Want my sun goggles when echelon get here or up to us. Half a gallon of water a day now. Not much for washing, and mugs and mess tins are hard to clean. My thermos is invaluable, and I am very glad I bought a little chocolate in Alex in spite of the price. Found a walking stick with two notches in it! Shall keep it, as it is rather nice to use and wave about. General Lumsden came by my troop when on the move earlier. I hope we were correctly spaced as he gave us a good peer! I like him very much. 2.30 p.m. Still on the same spot. Given two hours for maintenance we had to pack up before it was finished. I've had to sit watching the squadron leader's tank for ages.

Rations arrived and we had a fine brew of tea. Then a NZ supply column threw us eight loaves of bread. Splendid! Biscuits are dull. It is very boring. I wish we had *known* how long we were going to halt and then we could have done something about it; as it is we have been just sitting around.

Tried to read a bit of *Guy and Pauline*. Operator Bradley wrote a letter. Did not feel like it myself. Feeling quite cheerful and confident, though rather worried about maintenance and getting the tanks there. There are some dreadful oil nipples to find. Just flat and dusty here. A water point, I suppose. I wish we could get some.

Now carrying 12 gallons of petrol in tins on top. Two other lorries arrived. No sign of mess truck. If we are going to fight I want one or two things. Haven't shaved or washed yet. Only enough for tea!

Sun gone down. 5.30. Waiting to pass a minefield. Tanks disappearing into the glow of the sunset in clouds of curling dust. Hope we don't go far at night. It will be the devil of a job. Have just verified my tank compass error as 20 degrees. Wireless very bad now as we were warned before coming out. Just had the last drop of tea from my thermos. It wasn't much among four!

Soft colours and a moon over the sunset as I have never seen before. The thinnest moon you ever saw, a tiny rim at the bottom and the whole of the rest of the moon visible, blending almost imperceptibly in the pale green light which changes as I watch to blue. Oh, for the right setting with music! What music? The only music I can hear is the engines ticking over as we wait, sharp silhouettes peering ahead waiting to cross the minefield into leaguer.

We brewed up after dark and the light of the fires made the large assembly of tanks and lorries with men running about look like olden times.

December 20th

A good night. Very cold morning. Petrol and maintenance rather spoiled drivers' rest. On again now. Going good, but we halt at 9.20. Gunfire or bombing ahead. Marylands and fighters pass us. Hope we get long enough to wash today! Sun just warming things up.

11 a.m. After going very fast, we are in Libya. I had the distinction of leading the squadron over the frontier without knowing it, till I walked back to the white stone frontier post where Spud took a photo of Bing and me.

Whole area covered in last month's graves. Little mounds with a piece of wood and a note in a beer bottle signed by the Padre. A grim and flat place. How horrible those dead men smelt, they cannot be buried very deep. All my crew have left their stove to go and look. Basil in a scout car passes on his way to find the wire. I shall have a shave now.

4.30. Sandstorm and horrible dust raised by all vehicles. Am twenty yards off the frontier wire leading the squadron. Now I am actually moving in the long queue following the gunners; another good sight. Storm subsided, but ground gives off horrible dust which makes view very limited. Through the wire and all around for miles are traces of the battle of last month. Hundreds of graves which in the failing light are driven over. Horrible black stones on top of soft sand forms the going. Then we got on the wrong bearing and had to change course in the dark. I led the squadron in the dust and only Stephen and I reached the leaguer. All the rest went astray owing to the various Very and other lights. We were in very late and could not brew, so we had bread and bully and a nip from my brandy. Guard on top of all this and a freezing cold night with horrible wind. Brad had his boot caught in the track and had to wear only one!

Sunday December 21st

Move into open leaguer in better country and brew up with a fine heskanit fire too. Then good news, we are to remain all day, but slit trenches must be dug and guns ready from now on. The mess arrived so I got my corduroys and one or two other needfuls. A good go at maintenance but a new phase has occured for us. Remains! I found part of an ammo dump and we got a lot of bits of kit and tackle from a burnt out RAOC lorry. A bit sordid but socks and shirts are useful for the chaps. We got a German haversack and a nice petrol container which Pully had filled with C600 oil which is hard to get. Blankets too found, but two nasty accidents in the 10th Hussars. Hands blown off with an Italian grenade, and a water bottle booby trap, which went off when the chap pulled the cork out. The devils. I hope we get some good loot, though—very tempting to pick up stuff. I got .300, .303, grenades, 3-inch how, and all sorts from the RASC clearing the old dump. A good haul in horrible dusty sand which rose in clouds.

Then Spud sent me off five miles for petrol and water, to the big dump. Chap there offered me a BMW motor bike. Lovely job but wouldn't go far for sand! Met RSM and our SSM and Mike L. doing the same. I thought I had the bearing to return home by, but it got dark and we all got lost. It was very annoying and rather worrying and very cold indeed. I followed a Very light and got to Division, who were signalling for the General, where the G2 gave me the bearing of Brigade, but I only got there by luck as it was a wrong bearing! They would not fire a Very for the RSM who was at Division then.

Brigade gave me a bearing to RHQ but we failed to find it and returned but could not find Brigade again. All sorts of odd lights showing, which made it very confusing! Found a ration lorry which had decided to stay the night too. They gave us welcome bread and cheese, and I slept in their truck with the chaps as I had not an overcoat even. Very good lot, and cheerful. Down and Walker slept in their lorry as they always do. They had been lost every night! Cold feet and a hard bed but slept OK till light. Easily found Brigade then and got on bearing to Regiment, but went far right. Luckily I saw some lorries on the left and we made for them. Hooray, home and breakfast. Felt such a fool, especially as some of the other lorries not yet in. SSM went into a trench and had to walk. I cannot have allowed for deviation, but I tried to do so. Very hard in the dark, though. Glad of a rest this morning and wrote to Leslie and Cousin Edith. We shall be here tonight but we've got to move the tank to do distance judging this afternoon.

Two airgraphs for me! One from Kathleen Stapleton and one from Cousin Den. Nothing from home! A nice peaceful afternoon and a chat to Wilson, Smart and Slingerland from my lilo! It's a bigger upset for them than me to come out here. Said goodbye to *Guy and Pauline* this afternoon. A sad ending. They have been good companions. I have *Lorna Doone* now. Rather a contrast but I think I shall enjoy it. Leslie loves Exmoor. How lovely to go there with her. I remember sitting above Far End House and writing about such wonderful dreams.

News! Sudden wild rumours are around the camp. Rommel has packed in and resistance had ceased. I do not believe it, but hope. Busy getting my third tank off to RHQ for the Battery Commander of the RA to travel in. Very annoying indeed to lose one out of the troop, and lose Judge, Hinch and Hyman, but we've kept Cpl Minks. Have sent Cpl Smith. Not much of a chap and rather glad to get rid of him. Yes. It seems to be time. We are to be here for a week or so. That means Christmas here! We are having a very cheerful meal though it is getting very cold as the sun goes down. What shall we do for Christmas? Lots of chaps, Tony, Spud and Co., have got German stuff. Letters included. Rather interesting, but we should get some better stuff if we go on. I love the idea of loot. Hooray! Hooray! We are going to have a Christmas even though it is in the middle of nowhere.

December 25th—Christmas Day

A lovely night with my bed and sheets and pyjamas! Crew very snug too and we read in bed by the light of the inspection lamp.

Up for a service at 8 a.m., which was a very cold proceeding right out in the open, with a staff car driven up behind the altar which had a Union Jack on. Some gunners came as well, which was nice, and quite a lot of the officers. Still the cold west wind blowing. Breakfast was rather quick because of a regimental church parade when we all dressed up and formed square at RHQ with the gunners and infantry. Friend Allen of Oxford fencing I suddenly saw standing opposite me!

After church I wrote letters to Leslie and Pa and then we had our lunch of bully curry, soup, asparagus and tinned fruit, all of us squashed round the table in the little tent. After lunch a grand kip till tea when we sampled some of Smith's unleavened bread! Some chaps went off in a truck to see two German Mk III tanks, but they were very much battered. All my crew slept and I did too, being very glad of it. There was an officers and sergeants football match in the morning. Sergeants won 3-0. I did not play. Sgt Day crocked his leg, and is out of his tank for a bit. Very annoying for Stephen. The colonel came to have a whisky at 6 p.m. He hadn't much news of our advance: except that we shall be a large force and will move in the New Year. I believe supplies are the problem. Certainly our rations seem rather erratic.

What a devil of a place this is. Absolutely nothing and a horrid wind blowing all the time. I get very annoyed with it! Even tonight after dark I could not get straight back to my tank, but wandered around for a while. Only mail today was three for Spud and a cable for Stephen. I have had no news of home at all yet, and none from the all-important Leslie. I hope for some soon. One can only hope. Another very nice comfortable night in my camp bed. Read a bit of *Ghost Stories of an Antiquary*. Great need to ration my literature. I wish I had more.

December 26th

A big brigade scheme against the anti-tank gunners, the spare crews and the division protective troop. 4 Troop in the lead as usual. Devilish hard to keep direction over a 25-mile course which kept changing, and wind made sand very bad at times. We were a patrol forward of the regiment and had a great 'battle'. Anti-tank guns very hard to see. I wonder if they would have got us. Had some very nice side views of some of the division troop tanks, but thought Stephen was enemy at one time! Passed a crashed plane with Sgt Pilot buried inside it, with his helmet on top of the cross. What a place to be buried. Fifth this month, too.

6 p.m. They said our advance was good! That means nothing in the real thing. Horrible night as regimental orderly officer: slept in the open at the Command Post. Did two hours on, two hours off after a tiring day. Never mind—close leaguer went very smoothly.

December 27th

As all exercises at home end—the brigade beat it for home! Arrived 4 p.m.

December 28th

Day of rest and maintenance. Nice warm sun, so I had a complete wash. Great joy, an airgraph from Pa.

December 29th

Frost during the night! Day of preparation for move. Washed my hair and all my clothes in petrol (not my hair). Wrote quite a few letters, stocked up the tank from the canteen. Even greater joy. An airgraph from Leslie. Hooray! Hooray! It is marvellous. I feel quite at rest now I know her feelings more or less. I have been wondering and wondering, and thinking of her all the time. She says four letters on the way. Splendid if I get them OK, but they will take time. Odd coincidence that Pa and Leslie should both write on the same day—November 12th!

Cheerful conference this evening which went on till dark and we were issued maps of Tripoli in the moonlight. Good wireless news tonight except the Japs. Tony Dean has gone off as 2 i/c Scout Troop. Rather a good job.

December 30th

The great start at 07.00 hrs. Thoughts of home and Leslie and some flashes of anticipation for the future campaign whatever it may be. I quote:

> One more turn of the head in the gathering gloom,
> To watch her figure in the lighted door.
> One more wish that I never should turn again
> But watch her standing there for evermore.
> *Compton McKenzie*

09.40 hrs. Halted by a crashed Hurricane. Notice inside telling people not to touch as it will fly again. Peter has found a Cruiser, just where he is with a broken water pipe, and hopes to get one off it. We could do with a speedo. We are south of Sidi Rezegh now.

Quite a lot of stuff lying about. It is a very short time since they were fighting here. We've chased them a long way. At lunch time we passed through the battlefield of Bir El Gubi where the Germans and Italians had a defended position by a small fort. Whole area strewn with wreckage. At least twenty Italian tanks, all completely destroyed. Some still had bits of burned up crew inside in various stages of trying to get out. Like I read in Great War books, Mills picked up a tin hat complete with bullet holes and brains inside. There was a horrid grim, desolate little cemetery of some thirty Cameronians, 1 captain, 3 subs and 26 men, near where they had obviously attacked the trenches with bombs etc. Grisly blood-soaked stretchers still lay beside the graves with blood-soaked shell dressings and bandages. We passed a pile of Italians rolled up in blankets. The anti-tank gunners inspected them but they smelt so. Pleasant evening meal after a sixty-five mile drive in nice country with plenty of shrub, and even a few blades of grass here and there, and we could see by the clouds that it rains. During the night it certainly did. Poor James was subaltern of the leaguer guard and had to sleep in the open.

December 31st

A day of rest and frigging, as Peter's VIs have failed him and he becomes an M3 troop taking Cpl Minks from me for which I am very sorry. I am having young Thorne up as Sgt McG's gunner. He is such a nice cheerful little chap who writes the most affectionate letters to his mother, and lives in Devonshire, as a change from my north country chaps. There is no doubt they are quite different. Those from the northern towns seem more worldly somehow.

We all gathered by my tank as it was New Year's Eve and I passed my much-treasured whisky bottle round. We thought we were off at 7 a.m. to chase Rommel at Agedabia or near there. He seems to have quite a big force left though we are hammering him all the time. Churchill says the big battle for Libya not yet begun, and that he has a surprise for the troops in Libya. Are we, or the French in Tunis, the surprise I wonder?

January 1st 1942

A lovely lie in bed as orders to move were cancelled. I lay and watched the sun climb through a thin layer of cloud in a growing blaze of gold and shining greens and blues of the lightest shades imaginable.

Then we got up and had a good, slow, peaceful breakfast with no one to worry or hurry us. Not warm, however, at this hour.

January 2nd – 3rd

Still halted, spent the time practising new manoeuvres.

January 4th

On the move again. Seventy-seven miles west this time, in a fast run, but met very difficult going at one point and came down a precipice as well. Many deviations but Stephen leading, so all I had to do was bum along behind, admiring the change of scenery to small hills and escarpments—and an airgraph from Pa, which arrived with the rations when I was snug in bed!

January 5th

Horrible day! Very long journey and the whole brigade had to go single file through a huge minefield. One of B Squadron tanks was blown up, but only one chap was badly hurt. The real trouble was the dreadful dust which swamped everything, made visibility very short, covered men and vehicles in a thick layer, made our eyes smart, and shortened our tempers. Only half an hour for breakfast after three-quarters travelling in the dark. Only half an hour for 'lunch' at 3 p.m., still among mines. Day not finished yet. Crowds of vehicles and a narrow front and dust miserable at 5.15. Supposed to have another fifteen so miles to go!

5.30. Hooray. Orders to open leaguer in one mile! Soon in and bedded down after a quick brew before dark. High wind and rain. Horrid! Stood around, all of us, listening to the Home Service news. Not much, but our own news is a lot. General Lumsden dive bombed in his ACV, and temporarily out. The other brigade lost a lot in a clash with Rommel. We may be in action the day after tomorrow!

January 6th

Filthy rain and wind, and start advanced by three-quarters of an hour and we hardly got any breakfast—I had to navigate the regiment for the journey. Bit nervous at first, but George congratulated me as we had no queries at all from the Regimental HQ behind. Pully did it all on the tank compass though, and he had to watch out for contact bombs!

Suddenly saw a long white streak ahead on an expanse of flat and featureless desert. I had to drive up to five yards before I convinced myself that it really was a huge sheet of water! Simply amazing. Lots of bird life, a few green shrubs, and a few little flowers like crocuses. Saw some gazelle too, running between Peter's tank and mine, and I got my tommy gun out in case they should run clear of him. Duck and a few waders and two or three flocks of bustard. Water just like an estuary, and the wind and rain just like a January on any English estuary.

Spent afternoon cleaning up tank and guns from yesterday's filth and firing our machine-guns to see them OK. Miserably cold and wet with high wind. No chance of a wash or shave yet. Luckily we stay the night and manage a lovely cosy bivvy, with rain pattering outside. Feel very dirty, though. May be in action any time now. Thinking so much of home and Leslie. I do so want to get home safe to see her, but there is no one depending on me, like Len Swire's wife, or Pully and his family. It's no use thinking of it, though, but we are all rather wondering. Tony and Stephen and James and Spud and all. Who will be the lucky ones? I love life and somehow I would rather struggle along on twopence at home than go to Another World! Believe the 4th was Sunday. Far too busy to have a service, but when I lie in bed I try and pray to God, and I try and think of Him always and ask Him to take care of my darling, and if it be His will, allow me to return to see her again. We are near Jedabia* now. Just heard the sound of bombing pulsating in the night stillness. We are ready except for those tanks that have fallen by the wayside and they will be a reserve when repaired. What are we going to do, and how and when shall we do it? God knows, and in Him we must put our trust.

Goodnight Pa, and Goodnight Leslie darling. If I get pipped I want you to have this diary and your photos which are in my breast pocket safe. I hope I get yours which you say are on the way. Goodnight.

January 7th

News! Again the unexpected! We are to remain about ten days as Rommel is dug in, and we have to make a real set piece attack on him. Lovely day, with sun and little wind. Mess and A1 echelon arrive and up go all the little tents, etc. There are a few square yards of greenery in the hollow, and some poor little struggling crocuses round the area.

*Jedabia = Agedabia

Lovely wash and shave in the afternoon when the tank ready for action. Rations and water cut down again as communications are very long, but we are OK. Tony came over in the evening. It is his twenty-first birthday! We drank whisky and orangeade without any water! Got my bed and pyjamas again and a very snug bivvy. Felt very tired today, but the rest has made all the difference. Chance to write a few more letters now. Padre paid a call to our tank when I was having my 'bath' but he took no notice and brought us some stamps and airgraph; and had a pleasant chat. He is pleased with a Christmas card from Anne from Cape Town which arrived in the middle of a minefield early in the morning! Bing is going off to Benghazi tomorrow to try and get supplies. He is taking a lot of money and I hope he has luck.

January 8th

Awoke to hear AA fire and a stray shell bursting about 500 yards away. We got up fairly quickly and had our Bren gun ready with the sausages.

January 9th

Out on Squadron Exercise, we bumped a small Arab tentage with flocks of sheep, camels and goats. All training ceased as the various language exponents tried their hand at barter! We went off to the tents themselves, stopping the tanks 100 yards or so away, so as not to frighten the inhabitants too much! As it was, the women and children ran away hurriedly. Two old men came out, but tins of bully were of no avail and there were no eggs or anything to be had. So we went back to the shepherds' party and found four Arabs facing some fifteen English, complete deadlock but all smiles. Pullyblank and I advanced confidently with *Salaam Aleikum*, etc., and a tremendous argumentation and gesticulation ensued!

At last we managed to come to some sort of an agreement. One sheep for £1 or about four pounds of sugar—we are very short of sugar, so Spud produced £1, and a sheep was captured by one of the Arabs, and its throat cut with my knife, and it was solemnly borne to George's tank! Pretty cute those old Arabs, for they obviously had a very good bargain, but we didn't mind as money doesn't mean very much to us at the moment, and fresh meat means quite a lot! Sgt Hopkins, being farmer and butcher, soon had it skinned, etc., and hung up on their 3-inch how. We had liver and kidneys in the mess, and Cpl Work and Co. boiled the head and had a hellish brew inside their bivvy.

January 10th

Horrible wind and driving sand soon put an end to any training. Had another wash and shave inside the tank bivvy, and felt much better. It is far too cold to do anything like that in the early morning. Miserable rations today. About a spoonful of jam per man and enough sugar for two brews only and a 'small portion' of cheese à la Lyons for four men! Badly need some more jam, which is a great standby, also milk and sugar—cannot really expect much more, but Bing may have found some delicacies at Benghazi. Tinned fruit I hope for one thing, and whisky for another. It is great stuff, especially in the evenings here when we all get together over our evening meal and chat. It is quite a change to have our own company again, though my chaps are very good sorts and I like returning to them in the evening.

Rommel is no fool and has moved round the corner to El Agheila where he has the country in his favour—marsh and escarpments and wadis. He cleared out of Jedabia the day we arrived here in the last sandstorm. Now we wait to try and find his position before getting at him. He has quite a number of tanks left and we have learned to respect his 50mm gun.

A very pleasant, peaceful and homely evening in the mess tent. The harsh wind promptly died to nothing as it grew dark, and it is very cosy now. We ate a hearty meal of mutton, spaghetti, beans, biscuits and treacle. By the light of two candles, James, Spud and Major George play poker, Peter watches, puffing his pipe, Stephen writes a letter, and I read *The Egypt's Gold*.

7.45, and we all think what we should be doing at home. Spud said 'cleaning guns', and I thought of the Mill House, and the sherry coming in—I wonder if I shall have a real home some day; Father's cottage, for instance, in Berkshire? How I think of Leslie—of the past and of the future. Hope there will be an Early Service tomorrow morning. Anyhow the brigade scheme has been cancelled, which is something. Padre hasn't been round today, so we don't really know. I am sure I couldn't get to RHQ from here in the dark. George's tank is 150 yards from here and he had to come back to the mess having missed it once last night. I always bring my compass to dinner!

January 12th

A lovely sunny day with little wind. No tanks to move until further notice so we have a peaceful maintenance day. Now that we have found the Bir three miles away we have as much water as we want, but must boil it for drinking.

Bing arrived back from Benghazi with a good haul of stuff. Curaçao, kummel, cognac, milk, jam, beans, peas, tomatoes, sweets, sardines, spinach, which will give all the tanks a great supply of food which will help our short rations a lot. Pity we have to buy the stuff as it may well have been pinched by the Turks, Jews, etc., left in the town. However, that is the British way of doing things. I write now with an Italian pencil! Peter Glyn was not so British in his methods. He 'won' a donkey, and traded it later for four sheep. George Rich just shot two sheep and gave the chaps biscuits. The Germans would have shot the chaps, so they were actually quite pleased about it.

An airgraph from Pa and a letter (my first) from Cousin Edith were a great joy this morning. Had a real good wash and shave before lunch and Coles my servant came up from B Echelon and generally tended to my wants.

A most wonderful evening meal in the mess tent. Soup, rissoles, spaghetti, peas, bread, jam! Not to mention a bottle of cognac, orangeade and soda. It is very pleasant sitting round a table again, by candle light, and chatting. Sooner or later we shall have to attack old Rommel, but life is pleasant now and I think we are being very lucky as we had a square deal over not having to fight immediately anyhow.

I won't say anything more about the war, as a report from General Lumsden says that diaries off our chaps have been re-captured from the Germans and they contained a lot of valuable stuff.

Bing had a lot of interesting things to say about his four-day trip. I should love to have gone, but I am sure I should have got into trouble over looting!

January 13th

We are reduced to peace-time training again! We did an inter-troop compass night march on five different bearings over a distance of two-and-a-half mile. What a joke! Everyone was very keen, and I've not sweated so much since I came out here. Sgt Smith won by doing it in the shortest time, but he wasn't very much of a silent patrol.

January 14th

A lovely warm summer day with no wind. Most extraordinary, after wearing overcoats and scarves yesterday, to see people in short sleeves. I took my sweater off when walking back from rifle shooting with George Streeter. We shall have a good competition tomorrow. Spent nearly all the afternoon messing around the tank, having a complete bath and change of clothing.

January 15th

An amazing squadron rifle competition at petrol tins at 200 and 500 yards. 4 Troop won, which was a good show, and SHQ were bottom. Very funny. An irritating wind blowing from the exact opposite direction, blowing sand into every tent and bivvy, which had to be changed round.

Went back to Brigade to listen to Brigadier Hughs. He was very good and interesting. Nice to meet some of my acquaintances in other regiments again. Bed fairly early in a nice warm bivvy, so I had a good read. Got Mottram's *English Miss* off the Padre, which I am enjoying very much. The school part reminds me so much of Leslie and my visits to that school. Went to sleep very happy and did not wake up till 8 a.m.

January 16th

We had Holy Communion at 9.30. I stood by the colonel. Few officers came and no one else from C Squadron. It was very nice to have a celebration again. The first since Christmas. Then a parade service at 10.30 in which the South African Dutch Reformed padre assisted. He was excellent and his prayers were not the usual set piece à la Cranmer, but spontaneous and sincere, and I think they made quite an impression as they were so different. Again I find myself wondering what I shall do after the war. Remain in the army perhaps? I have a craving to be in the countryside. But who knows—the war is not over yet, and I am not home.

Sunday January 18th

Some amusing South African chaps came over in an armoured car and a truck for water. We helped them out and then had a shaving party, followed by a lot of shooting with pistol and tommy gun. They had many tales to tell of Jerry and loot and previous battles. Said they would come over with some .38 ammo.

January 19th

Horrid brigade scheme with rain and usual halts and total absence of information. However, no trouble and spare crews did well.

January 20th

Much heavy rain in quick storms. At lunch we had a sort of cloudburst with very high wind. Scene outside tent was like a Dorothy Lamour picture—all desolation and typhoon. Mess being on a nice sand scrub patch in a hollow, we soon learned why. We were flooded out in no time, and George's and Spud's and Peter's bivvys were floating. Lots of the men were drowned out too. Luckily the sun came out again, but it was most unpleasant. By an extraordinary stroke of luck a rum ration arrived at the very moment. It usually arrives a day late.

January 21st

Still sitting around enjoying ourselves and getting through a lot of reading of Penguin books provided by the Padre. Going to do some shooting on the range tomorrow. Bing still away at Benghazi. Very much look forward to his return.

At tea some KDG armoured cars came through, and one stopped. Who should be in the top but Maxwell from my old school. We were both very surprised indeed! He thought the Germans had made a sortie, but he was going back out of it, lucky man. He was always rather scruffy and dirty, and he looked just the same now!

6
Action

Woke up at 7.25 to hear Slingerland say, 'Anyone awake? We've got to move at 8.30, lorries and all!' My word we didn't half shift, and I just had time to pack all my remains and bed on the mess truck and rush and have breakfast on my tank. Everyone a bit shaken, and now Bing still away at Benghazi. I hope he manages to get all the stuff and keep it safe.

A wonderful day and hardly a cloud in the sky. The Germans have broken out with two columns of tanks, 30 and 40, and our support group have had to withdraw. Now we are halted at 12 o'clock south of Saunnu waiting for developments. This game is full of surprises.

6 p.m. In leaguer at last after rather a bloody day.

January 23rd

Did not sleep very well, felt rather jittery at the thought of action! Off early in a mist which made it all the more trying, especially when we broke down. Luckily Pully and Sgt McGuinness caught up all right.

11 a.m. Shelling on our right and a lot of smoke. Coming up we could see Jerry on the far ridge. Bit of shelling on the right and one very close to old Richardson's petrol lorry. He moved quickly. Can see one Mk VI blazing and another pulling out now. Hope chaps OK.

Whole Brigade HQ moves away to the right. 'Miki' (my wireless code name) leads the Brigade to Saunnu with my troop. Getting exciting. Sgt McGuinness breaks a track on a bad bit of going and we have to leave him to mend it, as we wheel left to Antelat.

Now C Squadron moves forward to ridge in front to see what is going on. Many lorries burning near us. Enemy not far. Peter and

Stephen move up carefully. Suddenly they are shelled and have to come zig-zagging out and we have to move too. George's tank won't start, so he has to get away from it as we draw off. We are not followed and then petrol comes up. Sgt Smith goes up in his tank and Cpl Work gets George's tank out OK. Then Cpl Smith's won't go, and rather under nose of Jerry we have to tow him back to close leaguer area. Just time for a quick brew of tea now. Very glad to go to sleep when petrol in OK.

11.30 p.m. Move in half an hour! Off we go, the whole force, for five miles. Horrible going at night. At last bed again and an odd biscuit. Suddenly I get a telegram from Cousin Edith, then all my mail. Hooray! Two from Leslie and all sorts. Too tired to read. Lovely clear night so OK in open. No sign of Sgt McGuinness.

January 24th

Off at 7 a.m. to hold the ridge. While in observation I open Mrs Mather's parcel. Hooray, some food and hanks. Both used on the spot. No time to read. No sign of Sgt McGuinness yet, I'm afraid. I spot a truck and some men on the far ridge. I suspect a trap so go up very carefully. Nothing else in sight and Cpl Smith overhauls them. They all tumble out with all their hands up. Rather a deadlock, but we are in a bit of a hurry so Bradley goes over with a tommy gun and Cpl Smith covers them with his MG. I shout '*Italiano*?' One replied, '*Nein, Deutsches*', OK, get 'em in the truck and follow me to Squadron HQ. George says 'First blood to you,' on wireless. We get them back OK and Basil and Tony come over. Luckily Bradley remembers loot. We each get a Parabellum automatic. He gets binoculars and a short bayonet. We had forgotten to disarm them!

Forward to the ridge again and then action—we shadow an 88mm gun and an anti-tank gun. Some ambulances going across the front were a lure, I'm sure. We fire to stop one, but cannot. See two tanks. Think them Italian but daren't go too far from ridge, which is our position. Then we see guns coming up with lorries and staff car. Hope to get a shot before they limber and I move up. Unluckily Cpl Smith breaks down and we have another horrid few moments towing him away.

Then they open up on us and we try and get up at them. Manage a burst or two and make them run, but then we get a shell just over the top of the turret and beat it, zig-zagging out. The big gun shells us all the way and then HQ gets shelled as guns move up right and left, Spud's tank hit and he had to leave. I take on rear link. Cpl Smith's tank fails again and they bale out and we pick them up on the way back! I wish they would blow it up. It is a nuisance! Shelling continues and then our guns get on to them and they retreat. Out we go again, and hold the ridge again. No further attack at this time. 4.30 p.m. Horrid lot of planes about from Antelat landing ground, but we brew up OK and get petrol. Very tiring indeed this, but interesting being used as a patrol. It is uncomfortable being two or three miles from help. Stephen is out now in the far distance, shadowing Antelat with some armoured cars as well. Don't like being without food. No meal now for three days and of course clothes on all the time. Our guns still shelling over our heads. It makes a nasty crack, but I have begun to realise which is which now! Someone fired at a Junkers passing overhead and it unloaded an alarming stick of bombs over near B Squadron. I saw the plane lift in the air, and then a row of bright orange flashes on the ground and a batch of black smoke. Big gun from Antelat fort now begins to shell RHQ. We withdraw into close leaguer as the light goes and the gun ceases. Very glad to get sleep again. More mail but none for me. More guns come in, which is comforting.

Sunday January 25th

Squadron pushed out on the left to watch in the early morning. No time for food or brew I'm afraid, but we had jam issued last night. Suddenly orders came for squadron to move over to right flank and help Pomfret Force with a small column. We moved over to the track and found RHQ. Change of orders again, squadron ordered to turn half right in line and attack over a ridge on some anti-tank guns and then swing left on some transport. An odd moment lining up. I could only clench my teeth and hope for the best.

'Advance, speed up,' said George, and over we went—to be met with all sorts of anti-tank fire from guns we could just make out on the ground. Saw George put out one gun and ride right up to the chaps, who had their hands up. No time for him to do anything as regiment ordered to pull over to the right instead, and gunners were on the retreat as they were disengaged a few minutes before. Stephen on wireless reports Peter wounded and apparently in a bad way. Hope he comes on. George said, 'Follow me,' and we made a bit right. Horrible jumble of guns and transport streaming away with us. No orders, so just keep on and on trying to shoot whatever appeared. However, a lot of shelling on us, as we zig-zagged away on and on in a sort of mad rush. Some guns went down for a few minutes and then we saw the German tanks coming on and on at us on two sides. Horrible as their shelling kept getting on to us, and our little guns just couldn't reach them at all. Suddenly saw the colonel alone on the right, with Basil on the front and John. Vehicles and tanks still being hit, but most got away by then.

The chaps who remained were the armoured car patrols. I drew up alongside a major who shouted, pointing back, 'Those are the boys.' We could see the PZs coming on, and a few guns went into action for a few rounds and then withdrew. Soon were left the colonel, Stephen and I and Douglas McCallan. We tried to get orders and directions on the wireless but lost touch. The sergeant-major and all sorts of odd tanks tagged on, including Dick and another colonel. The Hun came on very fast indeed, but seemed to bear left-handed towards Msus. In the end we shook him off, having seemingly been surrounded or partially so. James and George and Co. had all gone away, left too, and we lost touch with them.

Eventually we found part of Brigade, who ordered us to El Cherruba and not to Msus, where the enemy were already penetrating. There were still thousands of lorries streaming away with a few gunners left. A few Hun could be seen away to the south, still coming on and shelling a bit. Here, while deciding which way to go, we buried poor Cpl Minks who was still inside his tank which the SSM was towing. Some chaps dug his grave, but no one would face getting in properly and pulling him out, as he was in such a mess. I was a bit hesitant but had to do it in the end and John T.-W. read the service from his book. My first experience of sudden death, and I found I could cope all right.

Now we were running short of petrol. Luckily we met Brigade refuelling hurriedly in a horrible sandstorm. They began shelling us and we had to move on again. I still had no petrol. Lost the colonel for a bit, so stayed behind and waited for him. He came up and Brigade all went on. Luckily one petrol lorry was left and I have never shoved petrol in quicker. We had no funnel, but we made a makeshift and poured it in both tanks at once. Off we go again, stopping to blow up two tanks on the way. Finally we join up with a Grenadier Guards B Echelon and halt for an hour in the dark for a brew of tea. It was marvellous.

We had the hell of a job finding the leaguer, country very undulating and very hard to judge distance of Very lights although we were in touch with George who had got in with Jimmy, Peter and James.

Stephen and I were still with the colonel. Finally our dear old tank, Sunloch officially and Leslie unofficially, blew up the ghost and had to be abandoned. Piled on to Stephen's tank with most of my kit, but hoped to get the food and the rest the next day. Anyhow the colonel was determined to push on and find the leaguer, and we had to follow him, not knowing where the Germans would be next day.

It grew appallingly dark and our nightmare drive did not end till 4.45 in the morning, and then not without incident. In getting into Cherruba, Stephen's tank with ten chaps of us on board fell over a sharp drop on to the colonel's tank below. No one was hurt, but we had to leave his tank, too.

January 26th

When it grew light, Stephen and I found ourselves on B Echelon with Tom Toller, and all our chaps too. We moved away leaving George and James and all the remaining tanks to continue the fight if need be. Moving up the valley a bit we had time for rest and food and a slight wash. Found our mess truck OK. B Squadron had theirs blown up, unluckily. Had some whisky and, oh joy, was able to buy chocolate, sweets, tinned fruit and cigs off HQ squadron's canteen lorry. All day we waited for orders to move on, but they never came. Armoured cars all about, but no signs of real activity but plenty of rumours. Gradually chaps began to drift in, and we were able to take stock of the situation and see who remained and have some rest. Everyone very shaken and not a bit normal. Very odd indeed, and they all stood around very dumbly. Sgt Graham provided a wonderful meal and we met up with the colonel again. Peter F. had been crushed by a tank that morning and was away in an ambulance. Copper Blackett now confirmed a prisoner, as his crew were rescued by an armoured car after spending a night in a German leaguer. No news of Alex Barclay, Peter Glyn, Mark, or dear old Spud. Rumours that Freddy Bartholomew and Robin Lyle safe, also Henry Sherbrooke. Sgt McGuinness OK, with his crew and his tank later picked up. He had an exciting time on his own away at Saunnu.

January 27th

Felt more or less OK and ready for more work, if need be. James C. still with George and the other tanks. Don't like being away with them still in it, and anyhow I have done nothing yet. News! I am to command a Honey troop with Douglas and George to be 2 i/c under a squadron leader of another regiment. I hurriedly get three crews together from our remaining chaps with Sgt Blythe and Cpl Compton, and we pile on to a lorry with all our kit and rush off in another sandstorm.

At Cherruba we find thirteen rickety American tanks of the X Regiment and have to ferry them away to sort them out. Then it poured with rain and instead of a sandstorm we find a quagmire and everyone filthy wet and miserable. Piling on to tanks we somehow all move away and reach the regiment three miles away, passing them eating tea and not being able to have any as we have to get sorted out before dark. We are to join George now, but it is the hell of a job to sort out the tanks which will work and pile our kit on in the failing light. Then we scramble off in the dark to where George is in open leaguer with James, Michael and George Dodd. It is still beastly wet and cold, and our tanks all horrible and groggy, and we have no kit and no food, but in the end we get to sleep and it rains most of the night.

January 28th

Just an hour to look and see our tanks in daylight when we get the order to move. Consternation! We cannot fight in these as they stand, and no wireless working. In the end we are left behind and the composite regiment moves off under Colonel Forsythe.

Sorry to say goodbye to George and James again. Douglas and I go back a mile or so and join George Lacy of the 3rd Regiment with thirteen old crocks of tanks. New orders. Sandy Hope and either Douglas or I are to form two troops of tanks and join the regiment as soon as possible. We hope for a day to sort out as we go round seeing the mechanical defects. I volunteer to take my troop as I have crews all ready, so I rush off.

Then sudden scare. The enemy are five miles away. 'Move at once!' Never in my life have I had such a morning, trying hard to find three tanks which would work and getting all our kit on. After a dreadful hour I get two tanks and one crock. No one can help much and there is no food for us. The colonel said to me, 'You don't want food, all you want is ammunition!' I felt very uncomfortable as we all moved off in the afternoon to try and find the regiment. We thread our way through a mass of guns, men and tanks all advancing south through the dust. My wireless still very poor. Finally we find Peter Urquhart who orders me to join Graham Hill's squadron on the left and I drive over as he advances, and shout to him that I have joined him and then we tag on till we halt before dark for brew up. Then I find I am among delightful chaps. David Steel for one, Sandy from home for another. We have to beg food and parcel ourselves out on their tanks for something to eat. Feel better now and fit in OK as we prepare to leaguer. Meet David Allen and John, the other troop leaders, and find them very nice and amusing.

No leaguer. Instead we return twenty miles in the dark. George comes over to see me and at halts I see Sgt McGuinness and James Cumming. I get the Forces Programme on the wireless as we return all together in the moonlight. hear 'March of the Gladiators'. Very appropriate. Also 'Barcarolle' which is very moving. Very, very cold night, and a strange sort of tank. However we finally bed down at 1 a.m. inside the tank and sleep as best we can. In the morning we shall sort out our position in the regiment, and George Streeter has asked for me to join him, I think.

January 29th

Find George Streeter, which is good, and then hope for a few hours to sort our tanks out still. Luckily rations come and we wolf all we can and have a lovely mess of porridge. Mail too. Very surprising but very welcome. A cable from Leslie and one from Cousin Margaret from Bramley. Also a letter card from that very pretty girl at Cape Town, Lynette Ryall, who said she was rather timid about writing. I take off my boots and change my socks and wash face and feet in a mug full of water! Great feat.

When we have all fed, we drive over to George and all is well, and then orders to move again. Feel very much the new boy on this strange squadron and in strange regiment, but it is OK being with George. We do twenty miles with only one breakdown, thinking the enemy are advancing on Cherruba. Filthy sandstorm and I feel, as we all do, utterly miserable, but we just manage to get some tea brewed. Rest of journey done in dark and it rained but we all got into leaguer OK. Not quite sure what is happening, but know we have another day's advance to do. Rather a wet night, and we have no tank sheet now, as we never got our stuff off Sunloch.

January 30th

Slightly more in the picture today as we continue our advance, and as the day goes on we all become more cheerful, but it is tiring work for Pully driving. We are not happy yet as we still have no food and have to beg again at tea. No water either. However we find our way into close leaguer in a pleasant enough spot. Then we get a rum ration and rations come up too.

January 31st

I set off on a dawn patrol, but all clear and we open out for breakfast and hope to remain all day. Our wish is granted. We are in a very interesting spot, all hills. It makes something to see. Weather is nice but wind cold.

Manage to write to Pa and Leslie. We test and adjust our guns and get our tanks shipshape and wait events. Nothing happens, and we draw in for the night feeling much better and rested.

Sunday February 1st

Just a week since the 'do'. What a week, and what a speed it seems to have gone somehow. News that Alex Barclay and crew are safe, having walked thirty-six miles or so. Regular Sunday morning feeling as there is no hurry to get up, luckily.

Padre turned up at Mechili after the battle and he is here now and we have Holy Communion at 10.30 by a lorry. Well attended but wind horrible. More food comes and we have jam again, but water is salt. Ugh! Now we wait for the next development, whatever that may be. I think I have learned that it is no use having too much imagination. Fear is a curious thing. It is probably always with you, but there is no need to let it get the better of one. We shall do our best to make a show and keep the Germans back. It is curious how differently we seem to run things. They seem to be so much better organised on the whole, and yet we can and do win out in the end. Stephen and Co. are back now at Tobruk. I wonder what we shall do, and when we shall all be together again. The thought of a rest is pleasant, but leave does not mean home. One might just as well be here for now, to do a real job of work, and then get a rest if all goes well, and return if necessary really ready to sweep Jerry away. The Russian news gives us great confidence, but

Far East still bad. Never mind, there is America yet, and I think Jerry has his best stuff in the field now. He seems so much more clever than we are, and we always seem to be doing what he wants. It should be our turn soon. I hope Charles, Bob, Brian and Co. are all well. Wind is paralysing today. One cannot spread one's things out or wash or do anything in comfort at all.

February 2nd

Worse wind and thick driving sand all day, which makes any outdoor activity almost impossible. I daren't take my trousers off for a little sewing or do my main washing. We have orders to move tonight, but we have some real compensation today. Bing has followed us up with Musgrave and Atherton and his canteen lorry. Last out of Benghazi, last out of Cherruba and Mechili, he is here with Col. D and John and Tiny Blair and their recovery section. They recovered my dear old tank, but all the stuff had gone from it, and they were forced to blow it up in the end. So sad as it hadn't really *done* very much.

Anyhow we got the full benefit of the canteen lorry. Fifty piastres a man in cigarettes, milk, jam and vegetables. We got chocolate too, and Chianti and gin and tinned beer. What a show, *and* I got some reserve bully from Musgrave. Fancy wanting bully! However we are OK for food and there is porridge for tomorrow morning, and I got a ten-pound tin of jam off Musgrave. Oh boy! I hope we have learned a lesson and can save it all, but 'Leslie the 2nd' is a good little bus and should carry us a long way yet. We had the biggest meal I have had for weeks inside the tank, with wine and little cigars and all! It is horrible outside, but these little tanks are matey and comfortable! Bradley has found a book behind the wireless and it is a splendid book. I am loving it. It is called *Pantomime*, by G.B. Stern. It suits my sloppy sentimentality and makes me think all the more of Leslie, and paints a vivid picture of all the things I long for. Home, and fires and even cold winter days. My mind always runs to Oxford in all the seasons. Oxford which is so sacred to us and which is the heart of all that Mother loved best. Somehow I have felt her much nearer to me lately. Oh! There is little time to think, but perhaps that is a good thing. Thanks be to God for our present condition, but what of the war in Libya? Brigadier made a speech and said that the C-in-C. had everything in hand and knew exactly what he was doing, and that we were not to be pessimistic, and that we had done well, but I am sure someone made a mess of the last show. I wonder if we shall go back to refit, and what sort of tanks we shall get. I wouldn't mind something big and tough with a great gun which would reach the Hun tanks. Honeys are OK for recce and strafing, but not for attacking anti-tank guns and tanks, except under ideal conditions.

My lads are cheery now, but they have been very browned off and difficult. I can soon tell when they are cheerful again. Our favourite joke is to talk as if we were at home: 'Going to the pictures tonight?' 'Who's going to cut the bread?', etc. This country is tiresome enough, but lack of food and the requirements of life make it pretty hard. They are very earthy. They do not seem to have the power to rise above it with a laugh and yet they will go on and on through anything as long as they get what they think they are entitled to have. Nothing makes them madder or less inclined to fight than unfairness or someone else being better off. It's too much to rise above those things!

Oh! Leslie. What are you doing? What are you thinking? Will my dreams ever mean anything? If God grants me my life what am I going to do with it? But there is more to be thought of than that yet. You and England are not safe from danger. We must accomplish that. We will, O God. We will.

3rd February

A night march of some thirty-six miles in filthy dust, but with a moon. We brought up the rear of the whole brigade, which made things a little easier.

Another stay-put day however, but wind was bad and we have no shelter yet. I had tummy trouble and could not sleep, and then the brigadier decided to make a speech at 3 p.m. which broke up the siesta! So hard to make out how the campaign is going that the brigadier tried to explain a bit. Everyone rather mystified and worried that someone was making a balls somewhere. It certainly does seem an odd sort of war where the territory doesn't matter a bit; only the destruction of the enemy's forces counting.

Our supplies are wonderful and rations now very good. I gather the Germans have a good show running in their leaguers, with mail and papers and food, from accounts of chaps who have escaped. One officer overpowered his guards and drove a lorry away! We have had porridge and mixed veg and a lot of tea, milk and sugar. How I love porridge. No sooner had we received orders for the night march and leaguer, and were packing up, than the order suddenly came for the composite squadron to hand over all its tanks to the new regiment. We had a very great rush round piling all our squadron kit on to four lorries, as it was getting dark. However we did it OK and then drove to El Adem to join the regiment which is reforming.

There we found, at 1 a.m., the mess with food and drink all laid on, and Bing and Stephen and Joe Radice in bed. The latter back from Russia. Lucky man, he has been all over the Middle East already and had a lot of fun. I should love to travel a bit more. This desert is very wearing and a strain, and also far from dull at times. So we are to have the American tanks. Oh, well, never mind. Everyone has an equal chance in whatever sort of a fight you get into.

February 4th

The coldest and most miserable night I have ever spent, followed by a wicked wind and sandstorm in which we had to collect nineteen miserable Honeys and get them ready to move off by tomorrow morning. 4 Troop were lucky. I have quite a good tank, and it has a brand new wireless which Bradley is very pleased with.

Depressing enough, though, trying to sort out all the kit and lack of kit in a continual sandstorm. No rest at all, but took off all my clothes and powdered myself. Got hold of a bivvy tent, luckily. They are very nice and I spent a most pleasant night. We all had a lovely dinner too, and lots of drink. Chianti, beer, whisky, gin, anything. Felt much better.

February 5th

No move today, so a chance for a mighty wash which we all had in the mess tent. A lovely day too, and all much better and happier. Fired all our guns in the afternoon to the accompaniment of bombs continually falling on the aerodrome. Saw a bit of Jerry but he dodged the fighters all the time in the clouds.

I found a bit of paint and Mounsey put 4 on my turret and the good old squadron name 'Sunloch' and also 'Leslie' on the top, which I can see all the time. So we are all set for another go, and slightly rested. One real day of peace makes all the difference and I have plenty to read too. John T.-W.'s sister is in Tobruk as a driver! John will see her, I think, today. Poor Peter Frankau is not too good. He has gone off on the *Somersetshire*. He may lose one or both his arms. That last would be awful indeed. I hope that will not be so. Very sad to pack up his and Spud's kit today.

February 6th

A lovely night and now a lovely hot day, but still cold in the wind. We halted for a brew up at 9 a.m. and are still here at 4 p.m. Lying in the lee of our sheet the sun is like England, and closing my eyes I can hear a lark and insects buzzing. I might be anywhere. Occasional artillery fire in the distance to remind us. Am enjoying another book, D. du Maurier's *Frenchman's Creek*. Managed to wash my hair in a little water, but it has dried rather soapy. Never mind, the sand is out of it. Sudden news and orders after dark. We are to join a column, just C Squadron, for a raid on the German advance between Tmimi and Gazala! Everyone very pleased as it is a good role for us Honeys. A busy time indenting for kit and ammo as we get priority. Then bed.

February 7th

Plenty of time to get organised and set off to the RV. Of course I lead again.

Typical brew up when we get there. No brew for half an hour, then when we do brew we have to move in the middle of it and eat as best as we can as we go along. We join up OK, but lose the fitters and one tank through breakdown. Good time for brew when it gets dark, but a job to get in position in the leaguer. A wonderful sunset. German armoured car sighted, and Very lights. We are very close to them, so we do a night march in the very dark for a few miles. Very difficult job. Only three-quarters of an hour guard and a good night's rest but with our boots on. Too many suspicious lights.

Sunday February 8th

An extraordinary day of peace in the midst of war. We sat all day with armoured car patrols buzzing about, and Jerry and us shelling each other—we trying to reach his anti-tank positions in a wadi.

Always at a moment's notice, but able in the end to feed very well and shave, with the uncertainty all the time of having no definite answers. Plenty of air activity but nothing reached us. We are in 'Currie' column. The commander came up at tea time and said he was sorry we had had a dull day, though he had thought of sending us against the guns in the wadi!

We had a lovely afternoon. The sun is getting really hot now and there has been no wind. Sweaters removed all round! Sat and listened to lovely music and wrote to darling Leslie. What strange contrasts there are. We are lucky today. What of tomorrow? We always hope for the best.

6.30. Into close leaguer where it grew very, very cold, with wind, and it was a job to get settled.

February 9th

Very cold, but sun. Came upon several Italian tanks abandoned, which our RE blew up very merrily. Terrific firing of all sorts to our left front, and I thought we were going to have a lively morning. However it was only the Free French firing at our FOO. Throughout the rest of the morning we tootled slowly south and 'home' to the regiment after a good lunch brew up. Our return was greeted by a camera man getting impressions from all angles of tanks returning from the front!

Lovely to be in open leaguer again with the mess tent and all the comforts. On a good spot too, and the weather very good. News tonight mentioned our column as the most important of the three operating, and said that an artillery duel had resulted in the withdrawal of the enemy!

Coles pitched my bivvy again and our dinner was heightened by making our rum issue into rum punch, although the primus blew up and nearly destroyed the tent and all. The RSM who arrived with the issue said, 'There is rum for every man who has been on the exercise.' 'Exercise!' said Bing. 'Mr Bumpass, we have been on an operation, I would have you know!' I hope we go out again. Much better than being a cog in a huge divisional machine, and I have confidence in a man like Colonel Currie who is his own boss and quite unhampered.

A nice little packet of mail waiting for us, with airgraphs from Pa of Christmas and one from Leslie who got the silk stockings, etc. which I sent from Cape Town.

February 10th

A lovely warm day when it was possible to wear a pullover again. Nice to laze about and read and write. Slept on my bed out in the open in pyjamas.

February 11th

The worst brigade scheme ever. Lasted from 7 a.m. when control didn't net in for three quarters of an hour. Messed about all day and the squadron never found the brigade at all and had to give up and brew up on its own. A dreadful shambles and very tiring. A lot of air activity all day which we missed, but when we returned we had three bombs close and a bit of machine-gunning on our left. We prepared for the worst but no one came. Not a sign of our aircraft.

Another wonderful dinner and our drink supply is doing very well. Dick Ward has been to Tobruk today and so I hope he turns up tomorrow with some more. Got him to send off a cable to Bob. I didn't mind the expense as I do want news of him from himself. Both Pa and Leslie have written about him.

February 12th

Not so good! Luckily we do not move today for I am feeling pretty rotten with some form of stomach trouble and spend the day in my bivvy trying to sleep it off. Feel better in the evening and able to join in the meal as usual.

February 13th

Feel much better, and porridge for breakfast! Can hear just one small singing bird like a blackbird as the sun gets up. That is a really cheerful sound which brings back so many memories, especially of my visit last March to Mother at Minehead, for every morning as I walked to Far End House for breakfast down the lane, there was one particularly cheerful thrush singing from one particular tree. George let me stay behind today from a regimental scheme, so I sat reading and trying to write a poem. I promised Leslie one last February I remember, and I never wrote it. I will send this effort on an airgraph if it is good enough!

> **Sonnet**
>
> I wrote at school and college labouring
> To set my moods to verses savouring
> Of ill-cooked dishes wasted and returned
> With comments curtly penned and rudely spurned
> By third year critics of a freshman's brain.
> Discouraged then I did not try again

Thinking my muse had fled and Mars held sway.
A year had passed to bring me to this day
Talking together in our dim lit tent
Breaking the silence of the desert night
Am I deceived or does my muse relent
As memories gather round the candlelight?
And thinking thus its dying flicker seems
To form the fireside embers of my dreams.

Some Arabs and camels came by before lunch, and with cigarettes and biscuits I managed to make it understood that I desired a ride. Whereupon with much laughter a chap leaped upon an old she-camel towering miles into the air. It made the most horrible noises which were very frightening, so I insisted that for me it should be made to sit down in the approved fashion. There were worse complaints at this, but I jumped on and nearly fell off as it got up. However I enjoyed my ride, except I had no means of guiding the beast.

February 14th

Lot of air activity lately. Alex Barclay got a bit of bullet in his nose, which had bounced off his turret. Various lorries have been strafed round and a plane was bagged yesterday afternoon which we all saw. Today someone got two Stukas. On our return one rash fighter came over us and received a hot barrage which forced him down. However, we were not without danger as some of our keen Browning gunners fired at a very low angle and bullets flew about the camp! Padre came in with some airgraphs, and a talk about tomorrow's services. However, as we sat down to dinner at 6.15, a message comes from RHQ that forty German tanks are thirty-five miles away and that we are at fifteen minutes' notice to move! Dammit! It is pouring with rain and I should loathe to go off now. I hope we get a service tomorrow before we are forced to move.

A dreadful tragedy—yesterday evening an old biplane came over, which was easily shot down. It contained the Wing Commander attached to Division, who was killed.

Sunday February 15th

We moved all right! With all the usual hanging about and nervous tension. However, it all came to nothing and the great move after a long halt for conference only resulted in a brew up! We remained all the rest of the day and night quite comfortable and at leisure. Only mail for me was a second parcel from Mrs Mathers. Very useful socks, ointment, Ovaltine tablets and chocolate which we wolfed immediately. Have lent George *Lorna Doone*. Books are very short. I have now made the acquaintance of Jorrocks. An odd chapter now and again is very entertaining, but huntin' people must appreciate it more. Hope we can either get some more books or go back to Cairo! The brigadier said another action would finish off the brigade. It's odd keeping on waiting for action again. I am very glad to have made its acquaintance, but I think I have too high an imagination. Want some more mail now. Our little tanks are not much use. When we hear the Germans have twelve tanks it really means something, and I don't think we quite have the confidence we should. However, we are all cheerful, and don't mind being used properly.

February 16th

Met a very pleasant Lieutenant Charles of the HAC, whose guns are next door to us. We had a long chat and a drink of whisky. I showed him my tank and its limitations. He agreed but said the division's name was pretty well mud at the moment, as the infantry had said to him. Chaps are OK, I think, but somehow the higher command couldn't have been up to much. Charles lost his RAF brother at Msus, and he and I both heartily agreed about this war. He doesn't think much of the regular army, and I don't quite know myself whether I could stay in the army or not. Heard from him that my friend Armitage from Oxford fencing days, who was with us at Christmas, was killed at Wadi Faregh.

February 17th

Sitting, sitting, and the gunners digging and digging, while we all wait for the enemy to come. It is very boring and depressing. This afternoon I sat inside the tank while the others played cards in the bivvy outside, and tried to read *Diary of a Nobody* by George and Weedon Grossmith. Very clever, but not very suitable to my mood. Got some quite good music on wireless though, but always uneasy about the batteries. Found my only outlet in writing to Leslie. Gosh! How I think of her, and how happy it makes me. However, I am so uncertain about the future that I feel gloomy again. I am far too apprehensive. I always be a dreadful thing. I do so desperately want to get back to Leslie, but I do realise that is no good going back if the job is not done, and someone has to be lucky and someone unlucky. I can only put my trust in God and get on with it. I think my finger is on the trouble. I have neglected God and His comfort. I can and will pray to Him with a new spirit. Padre came today and I hope for a celebration of Holy Communion for fresh strength and a new sight of God and all those I love.

> Let never day nor night unhalloed pass,
> But still remember what the Lord hath done.

February 18th

A very good night with a short guard from 5.10—5.30! Having erected our huge tent affair yesterday for the rain, we slept in it, and it made a great difference having a head cover. Also I dared to remove my trousers as it didn't look as if we would move in the middle of the night. News better, though Singapore gone—Rommel's light forces have withdrawn, so it seems. I wonder what we shall do now? Added some oatmeal to my frying sausages and bacon and enjoyed it. We hadn't enough water for porridge. Received a nice airgraph from Cousin Edith with the rations last night. News of photos arriving and Leslie writing to say she liked hers.

I lay in bed and thought of Leslie just as I was getting up for guard. It would be 3.45 in Stanway and she would be sound asleep. Would she think of me at all today? I cannot tell. Hope Padre comes today and manages Holy Communion. With a bit of initiative he would have nipped round already, but I suppose it is very difficult for him.

Listened to Bruce Belfrage on the Home and Forces programme this morning as he prefaced the news with a few records and one of Arthur Askey's and then the news itself with Big Ben, followed by a resumé of today's programme. Should be excellent if our batteries can stand it. Feel much better now. It's odd how one's moods fluctuate.

I wonder what news of Michael L.C. I bet he doesn't write such nonsense as I write sometimes.

An odd fact about the desert I must record. Most areas we see have been so fought over or camped on that there is always a lot of remains to be picked up, some useful, some mere rubbish. We had no spade on this tank and we just happened to stop for two minutes in one spot on a march, and there on the ground I saw a spade! Also, where we are now I have got a pick and shovel, a tin of graphite grease (invaluable and unprocurable) and tent pegs of wire which fix our bivvy nicely.

Army Commander General Ritchie came round yesterday. We were all prepared but he drove straight by to one of the gun pits.

John T.-W.'s sister was out the other day, driving a big noise the sergeant-major said. A splendid show and most welcome for John and interesting for her, but dangerous. Supplies running low again. Hope Dick Ward can get some food in Tobruk again, and I do want a new pair of desert boots. Rubber soles are grand for stones but Stephen said he had already found them hot. We all want to see the dentist but until we are in a rest position again nothing can be done. Luckily no one is actually suffering, but we all have twinges. Things have cleared up enormously. The mess lorry has arrived and the tent has been pitched and the Germans have gone away again! Horrible wet afternoon, but a rum ration and a fairly good bivvy and a game of cards kept the chaps cheerful and I am quite happy again now. The mess has provided a splendid lunch and an even better dinner, with Chianti. Letter cards have come, but no more letters. Stephen and I and James had a great argument about Christianity and the war. Our conclusions cannot be set down now. I am very sleepy and must do a guard.

February 19th

After the rain it has turned bitterly cold. Luckily I had the comfort of my little bivvy, but I couldn't take my clothes off after guard. Far too cold to do it outside and no room inside. Had some odd dreams, about General Alex and Pa fighting the 2nd Armoured Brigade, and also visiting Stanway House for a sort of 'do'. I enjoy dreaming on most occasions. Far too cold to wash yet at 9 a.m. but everyone rushed for the 'throne'—that great erection (sanitary!) which the mess insists on planting almost as soon as the tent. It is the only possible place to perform, today at any rate, *and* it has a seat pinched in Benghazi! George is washing all over in the tent—a very spartan exhibition and example. Row comes over from RHQ and installs a telephone. We wish we could ring up home. RHQ could put us to

Brigade, Brigade to Division, Division to Corps and Corps to Cairo, and there you are!

Just getting ready to go to Holy Communion at RHQ. We have a bottle of cherry brandy left. We must open it after church and have a little sponge cake to go with it (perhaps). Bing is reading *Goodbye West Country*, thinking H. Williamson rather an ass. I'm not sure I don't think him rather objectionable at times, but Bing and Co. are not immersed in the H. Williamson lore as Bob and I are. We are H.W. fans in many ways, and find his little oddities and whims very like our own. Gosh! what fun we have had in the West Country, and intend to have again someday. Two-hour interval for mess truck catching fire (luckily extinguished before either the lorry or my suitcase went up) and church services quite well attended by all ranks and supporting arms. John T.-W. came back for some cherry brandy afterwards and we had a long chat. One point. Captured German intelligence summary stresses the fairness with which British and Australians treat prisoners, and bringing it to the notice of all German commanders. Good sign that, especially after the excellent way Copper and Sgt Cockwell and Co. were treated. I found it hard to be unpleasant or brutal as I have never experienced ruthless attack. I like the Germans as a whole, and when fighting feel no more than the normal keenness to 'fix' them. What about this war then? I will never agree that it is not worth fighting, though some people wonder whether the working classes would be any the worse off under German rule. That is dangerous doctrine. People like Stephen and I have a somewhat different view to our men. I think we are fighting for the Oxford way of living. In England already there are many necessary restrictions on liberty (many due to the war only and therefore not permanent) and I do not imagine England ever being entirely free of any control, but I am quite sure German or Nazi control would not be beneficial or tolerated by the majority of English people. The whole question is very, very large and I cannot discuss it here, but I do not want to return to a National Socialist England. I have described many times what I want. Perhaps I am selfish and thinking entirely of myself and how nice to marry someone (I daren't say more than that!) and live on the same plane as before though perhaps not on the same scale, and if money permits, pursue the same occupations, or shall I say relaxations...? In this sector we are the nearest troops to the enemy and yet we are happily reading and writing and sitting down to lunch once more. When will the next 'move now!' come? Never mind, I won't discuss that or be morbid, but I will try and be ready. I don't think I shall feel as bad this time as last, when I had an attack of 'back to school' and 'dentist' feeling. The further we dig in, though, and the more comfortable, the harder it is to move. Grand to get hold of *Goodbye West Country*. Just come across Compton Mackenzie's lovely prose in *Guy and Pauline*. Must tell Bob to read it. Sent him a long cable the other day. Must have news of him soon.

February 20th

Lay awake for a long time last night, wondering whether to undress and get right into bed, remembering all the time that I had to go on guard at 1.20. Finally fell asleep and only got right into bed after guard. A very difficult process in my tiny bivvy where I have to do everything either outside (which weather does not permit now) or in a prone or supine position.

While we stood to at 6.15 a.m. I heard the little whistling bird again and Pully whistled back at it. The rain stopped and the red watery sun came up in a real tumultuous, disordered, angry sky which made the desert look sullen and forbidding. Against this I heard another note. The watery whistle of a bird sounding just like a Norfolk wader. Memories of Cley and Blakeney came flooding back. What a world of enjoyment, laughter and friendliness that small bird represented to me. Bob Langton again, and the very essence of England, the warmth of large fires after a cold day on the salt flats (or in the Hinksey lanes for that matter), gun-cleaning, large meals, dim lighting, laughter, books, cold bedrooms but warm snuggly beds.

Canteen has come today, with chocolate. Chaps all very pleased. But more thrilling, the mail. A lovely rambly letter from Leslie, from Stanway Oct. 27th, and one from her mother on the same date and an airgraph from her of Jan. 12th. She is a great one and I love her. How beautifully she always writes, and how sensible and sympathetic she is. Her letters made me feel quite sad for a moment. She described a certain birthday party when Stuart Cooke came. That was when I met her first properly and when we both felt her presence so strongly that we remarked on it afterwards. But she treated us all alike, unconscious of her charm and uncaring for anything but fun and everyone's happiness. How I love her, and what pleasure I get from her mother's little words about her. Oh! God! Thy will be done. Do not let me shirk anything out here, but if I might be worthy of her, how dearly I would love to return.

February 21st

James of the infantry came in to drinks after dinner. He had quite a lot to say and it made an amusing evening with someone fresh to talk to. James went off this afternoon to Tobruk to get more food and drink and odd things for us, like desert boots and ink and pipes (some hope!).

It was my time to go off somewhere but I somehow didn't really want to go by myself. Rather a tiring desert journey and all the rest of it. I would like to have gone with James though, just to see the place, but I also wanted to sit about quietly and write letters and read. Very pleasant occupation really.

Sunday February 22nd

A lovely misty early morning and I could dress again in the open. It grows hot now as we wait for church parade. A cheerful morning when one feels like singing. Not a breath of wind or sign of hostility. A thought strikes me that it doesn't really matter when we move off or what we do. The job has got to be done and those who come through, come through. There can be no thought of war dodging really, and soon I think we shall be able to advance and deal with Rommel. We regard him rather affectionately, I think. We all admire his great military skill, and by talking of fighting Rommel we identify the whole German success with his brain and personality. He will be interesting to meet after the war, unless we can capture him. Somehow it always seems odd to me that people and nations can ever be friends again once committed to war against one another, for real war seems the ultimate peak of hatred from which there can be no reconciliation. You don't kill your adversary unless all other negotiations have failed, yet after trying to kill him you can be friends again. We must be thankful for it, though.

Cameraman at work during the church service, and enemy planes overhead. As we came away several bombs dropped a longish way away. Butterflies and dragonflies and other flies(!) now appear. Strange weather for February! The roar of planes overhead now. We all rush out with glasses, so I go too now. . . Yes, Italian Macchis, but flying very high and only on recce.

2 p.m. It is such a lovely peaceful afternoon. George has fallen asleep over his book, Joe is reading, there is a distant sound of muffled voices and insects buzzing, like a Sunday afternoon in any home in England in

summer. I could almost suggest a game of tennis. I will go and sleep, I think, and then write some more letters. How odd it all is. I find it hard to believe but easy to understand. Rommel is not advancing and the desert is so large that we are a long way from him.

Someone is busy this afternoon, though. Sunday has been our fighting day before now. Last Sunday we were moving out, expecting action that day or next. Now there is a week's training programme out. Just like Saunnu over again, but I hope that the resultant clash will be different. We were a long way down on Rommel's ground. Now we are playing full back on the home ground. Our defence is strong and our attack developing.

The BBC said on the wireless last night that Rommel was scared of attacking. I rather doubt it, but he may be, but all the same I think that is a stupid thing to say. Very cocksure and self-satisfied, almost insulting.

Still reading Henry Williamson. Love his country bits and most of his philosophy, but not his politics. Must write to him, I think, but it won't mean anything to him. Thousands write to him. Why do I like him? I don't know, because he is rather a rude, moody, queer man, and yet he captures the spirit of the West Country in a wonderful way which has communicated itself to Bob and me in some manner. Like his novel-hero, his other half in fiction, Willie Maddison, I wish he was more natural, less analytical and simple. He is too sharp and clever, without enough human sympathy I think. I wonder why I bother to write about H.W. Yet I am a devotee of his country lore and the West Country is in my bones. Shall I ever forget my first visit to Sampford Brett with Mother last March? Darling Ma, it was her last visit, and she so looked forward to going there with me. I loved that day, and yet what an effort it was for her to go.

February 23rd

Nasty accident. Pullyblank burned his face and hands adding petrol to a tin fire. Bradley dealt with him very well and we got him away quickly to Doc and to ADS. Burns are horrible things and he was in great pain, but a few weeks rest should do him a lot of good. I have old Smart (thirty-seven, specs and grey hairs) driving me now. He is a Welsh milk-roundsman and very pleasant, but quiet and rather distant. He misses his Welsh pals. On a scheme this morning with Bing in command we were suddenly ordered to attack some 'enemy' tanks.

For a few moments we didn't know quite what to do and my crew immediately loaded up. However, we soon realised that they were our friends in front. Italian fighters over again, but they give us a wide berth as they know we can hit back. They are very contemptuous of our friends nearby, however.

Rather a stir at the moment as a chap, Kershaw, has disappeared. He was on guard in the middle of the night and has not been seen since. That was two days ago! I can imagine lots of horrors.

James came back from Tobruk yesterday with lots of tinned fruit and choc and things for the canteen, but no milk. Got me some more desert boots which are very comfortable. A *Daily Sketch* comfort box arrived today with writing paper, soap, sweets and scarves. All very welcome. I do wish those knitted garments had their histories on them. I wonder where the scarf in my hand was knitted, and by whom? A dear old lady in a semi-detached house in a suburb immediately comes to mind. So unlike Army issues, every one is different in colour, shape, size and knitting.

Unfortunately, but maybe luckily for him, I never got Pullybank back. When he had recovered he was posted at base to his old unit of the Royal Tank Regiment, the easiest thing to do administratively: or maybe they were very glad to have such a good soldier back again. I was luckily able to locate him again in 1987, and he wrote to me telling his story:

I joined the 1st Battalion at Knightsbridge and was cut off several miles behind the enemy lines, and had great difficulty in getting back to our own lines.

I was still a lance-corporal but a Tank Commander. I had a crew of new men who were top-rate chaps and we did have great difficulty in doing the job, as the Tank (a Honey) had no wireless and no internal communication; string was tied to the driver's arms and up to me in the turret, this was the only control I had over the driver as to what I needed him to do, but worst of all was that I was completely out of touch with the OC or any other tank and was therefore completely in the dark as to what was going on; this eventually proved to be the knocking out of my tank and one man's leg taken off. I just did not know what was going on.

After I lost my tank and crew I rode on a lorry, it was utter chaos. I got to El Adem airfield and stood around bewildered. A lorry (British) came up to us and out jumped two Jerries. We were told by a huge sergeant-major (German) to line up. There were then about sixty or seventy of us of various units. By the SM's English and command of drill orders etc., I am sure this German NCO had served in the British Army.

We were marched up an escarpment and into a German leaguer, again the SM's command of drill orders was perfect and given in English. We were given an order to wheel and kept going until we were in a large circle and told to sit, meanwhile four MGs were put around us. We had no water or rations but must give credit to our captors they did not do anything contrary to the rules of war, indeed they were a very friendly bunch, they did not take away any matches or personal items, but could not help with water as they were in the same boat, having none to give. The only thing that was wrong, guns, 88s and various anti-tank guns were mixed up with soft transport including ambulances and did in fact expose these guns when sighted by three British tanks, but Honeys had no chance against 88s and withdrew.

We sat there four days and on the fourth evening the Germans suddenly mounted up, but left the MGs. We all thought 'this is it "shot while trying to escape,"' but no! The last lorry picked up guards and guns and went off with these words, 'Cheerio, see you in Cairo!'

Anyway, after getting water from a broken down lorry's radiator, we four of us walked miles through the blue in the right direction we hoped, and were picked up by the 4th Indians, questioned by some brigadier and then off to TDR Camp.

I will carry on this story at a later date. I kept no notes so I have to rely on memory, but it's very vivid.

So indeed he did, in five more graphic letters, describing actions across North Africa and up Italy, surviving without a physical scratch, but at considerable mental and physical strain which has told on him in the course of years.

7

Tank Delivery Troop

February 24th

Consternation! Colonel and John came over and say I am to command the 2nd Armoured Brigade Tank Delivery Troop operating from Advance Division Workshops to the regiments. This is General Lumsden's idea, and I have been chosen to command the first party to go off!

With hindsight I realise that this was an admirable idea; part of the belated concept learned from the Germans of the possibility of the quick return of tank casualties to battle. I am able to quote from two excellent papers by Lieutenant-Colonel D.E. King, MIEE, REME, entitled *The Survival of Tanks in Battle*, and *Tank Maintenance in World War II*, which deal with past, present and future problems of AFVs (Armoured Fighting Vehicles):

There has never been a time when a tank holed by an armour-piercing round [Like mine. MH] was 'killed' in the way described by many historians of the tank battle. There will of course be a limit to the availability of trained tank crews. The trend is, however, for the equipment damage to exceed the rate at which human casualties are suffered in conventional war.

Several episodes in North Africa revealed that successful tank recovery after one battle could decisively affect the balance of the next. In Rommel's attack on Tobruk on 30th April 1941 he lost 17 tanks on an Allied mine-field: but 12 were recovered and soon put back into battle. Two months later the Allies claimed 'kill' of over 100 German tanks, but after the failure of Operation Battleaxe, the Germans possessed the battlefield and were able to salvage all but 12.

We had learned the lesson of the need for the quick recovery of immobilised tanks in World War I: but by World War II the lesson had been forgotten: and there were no armoured recovery vehicles whatever (AFVs). But by 1941 our REME commanders were aware of the urgent need to get tanks out of battle and repaired as close by and as quickly as possible.

My job was to get repaired tanks back to the appropriate units as fast as possible. Of course REME were not particularly helped in their

resolve by many of our tanks simply having broken down, and most of the overall tank casualties being so difficult to maintain. Unfortunately the British between the wars had not learned like the Germans the need to produce heavy engines for AFVs, nor to insist that the designers made reliability and ease of maintenance their first priorities.

February 24th (continued)

Very sad to leave the troop, but Edward Lydall will be up soon to take over. Besides, this is a step up really, in spite of not being in the front line. Sorry indeed I leave our very happy mess but it cannot be helped and really I shall enjoy the change and new faces and places for a time. Colonel says I am to stay a month, but wonder what a month will bring forth.

Reported to Brigade with my Bays chaps in my own 15-cwts with driver and Coles as servant and all my kit. Horrible sandstormy day and so only went as far as B Echelon. Ben Hough I found installed in Brigade ACV, looking very much king, or rather boy-king, 'rather unhappy and lost!' At B Echelon had a very good reception and all was lovely. A nice meal in the mess and a chat to Pete Willett, Tiny Blair, Jerry, etc. Also a good read in *Bedside Esquire*. Heat being felt now and night hot though pleasant. Chaps all fed and contented. A good lot I think.

February 25th

After getting pay books and rations and clothing we all set off to find our destination thirty-five miles away. Went via LRS and Battle HQ. Very impressive. I have never been on my own like Tony, Dick and Co. who are quite used to it. Felt a bit nervous about finding destination but gave myself plenty of time. A real hot summer day. Went via El Adem aerodrome and all the wreckage. Dreadfully depressing this 'troops-inhabited part of the desert', and dust filthy. Stopped for lunch just south of Sidi Rezegh battle area and by a wrecked Italian tank and burned up Italians smelling horribly. I am used to this sort of thing. Much more impersonal horror than poor Freddy Minks.

Arrived OK at Division Workshops and got my men settled in. Terrific wide area and about two miles to the mess. All the officers very nice but quite a different type from the Bays. All of them hearty and cheerful, with a nice mess in a big Amriya tent. I think I shall get on OK here, but there are a hundred questions I want to ask. This is my

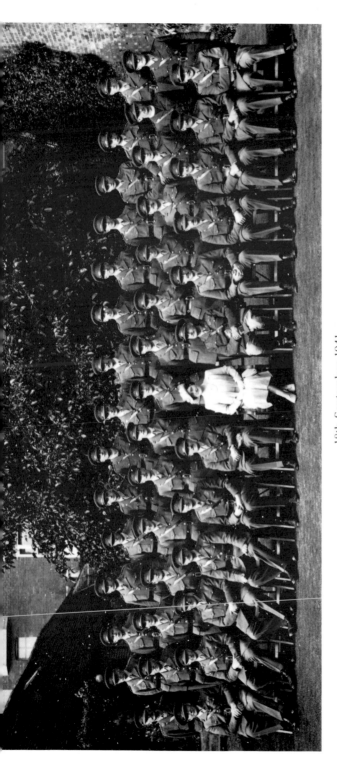

18th September 1941

Her Majesty The Queen, Colonel-in-Chief of The Queen's Bays, with her officers in the garden of the Ailsbury Arms Hotel. Marlborough. Wiltshire.

Tom Draffen (author's C.O.) on her right

After the Battle of Gazala John Knebworth wrote in what sadly turned out to be his last letter home, dated 20th June 1942: *"The outstanding feature of the fighting has been the Colonel. For coolness, steadiness and judgement he was exemplary, and an enormous help to everyone."*

CAWNPORE 1936

The officers of the 1st Battalion, The Loyal (North Lancs)
Regiment, dressed for their favourite sport; the idea of their C.O.,
Lieutenant-Colonel J.G. Halsted, seated centre in topee, with
shotgun.

THE SOUTH WALES DISTRICT MEDAL

Red on gold with a light green ribbon.

Papa with the two-pounder at Woodbridge.

The Oxford University Revolver Association, 1940.
The author is second from left.

I was proud of my light tank at Oxford: but thank God I didn't
have to fight in one as some Bays crews did. "*Good enough against
tribesmen, but no chance against the Panzer divisions in 1940*"
(From *TANK* by Macksey & Batchelor, Macdonald, 1970).

IN MEMORY OF
FRANCIS NEVILLE HALSTED
D.S.C., D.F.C. FLIGHT COMDR. R.N.A.S.
LOST IN THE BLACK SEA OCT. 1920
GRANDSON OF JOHN HALSTED OF ITCHENOR
ARTHUR FITZGERALD HALSTED
FLIGHT SERGEANT R.A.F.V.R. KILLED
IN ACTION MAY 1943 GRANDSON
OF HENRY HALSTED OF CHICHESTER
ROGER HUBERT HALSTED
FLYING OFFICER R.A.A.F. KILLED IN
ACTION DEC. 1944 GREATGRANDSON
OF JOHN HALSTED OF ITCHENOR
ALL DESCENDANTS OF WILLIAM HALSTED
OF WESTERTON IN THIS PARISH
WHO DIED 1732

In St. Peter's Church, Westhampnett, Chichester.

Squadron-Leader B.H.D. Foster. D.S.O. D.F.C. and Bar. 1951.

Bob Langton ready for an expedition – in his faithful 1933 Morris Ten-Four Tourer.

GOVERNMENT HOUSE, ALDERSHOT, 1939

H.M. King George VIth visiting his Expeditionary Force General Officers on September 9th, 1939.

Left of H.M.; General Broad, Brigadier Halsted, General Alexander.
Right of H.M., General Dill, General Lloyd, Brigadier Percival.

1937 — 1987
SILVER MODEL OF A CRUSADER TANK

Presented to Her Majesty Queen Elizabeth The Queen Mother by past and present members of The Queen's Bays and 1st The Queen's Dragoon Guards, to mark her 50th Anniversary as their Colonel-in-Chief, St James's Palace, 19th February 1987.

The P.M.'s visit to the Bays in February 1941, with Lieutenant-General Martel, General Sikorski, General de Gaulle and Major-General Noons.

Impressing our gallant allies.
How Pullyblank crossed the River Wey: just.

TIDWORTH, 8th August, 1941
The President's Representative Mr. Averill Harriman accompanied
by the Prime Minister and the C.I.G.S. presents us with American
Stuart M3 Light Tanks (Honeys).
Papa, Major-General J.G. Halsted, MGA Southern Command,
is over General Alanbrooke's right shoulder.

Below: Churchill inspecting Honeys.

See page 203

'C' Squadron Grant crews brewing up.

At El Alamein, Douglas MacCallan of 'B' Squadron lends a
hand to replenish his Sherman tank with shells.

Driver Wilson on Maintenance.

Troop Leader on the guns, James Cumming.
Sun compass on the left, stele folded down.

Joe Radice.

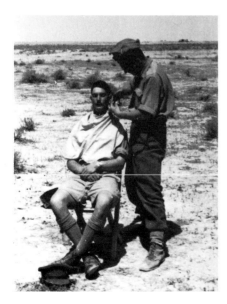

Keeping up appearances: L/Cpl. Bradley plies his trade.

L/Cpl Bradley of a quiet morning!

The mess, and hungry officers.

Tinned pears, while dug in.

Jimmy Cumming (left) who survived unhurt, and Stephen Christie-Miller, who was killed at Alamein.

Squadron orders.

Sermon on the Sand.

LEADING TROOP
In a Crusader. You may see one of our later Crusaders with a
six-pounder gun in the Tank Museum at Bovington, Dorset.
The 1st Armoured Division insignia, a White Rhino, is on it.

Here a sandstorm approaches

'C' Squadron officers.

Bardia plage.
George, Stephen, Joe and Jimmy

An improvised wash all over.

Doc inspecting a 'throne'.

Better than a bivvy!

Michael looking grim.

Such was Joe Radice's caption on a copy he sent home!

20th CENTURY FOX STUDIOS, HOLLYWOOD
Off the set of 'Lifeboat'.

Alfred Hitchcock, John Turnbull, Talulah Bankhead and M.H.
Below: Cary Grant, John Turnbull, Terence d'Abo and M.H.

CITY HALL, NEW YORK CITY, 21st September 1943 M7 Day.
American Locomotive Reps., Mayor La Guardia, Major McMasters
(U.S. Ordnance), M.H.

OLD NEW ORLEANS RESTAURANT, WASHINGTON, D.C.
Tony Wigan (BBC), Janie Phillips, M.H. and Annette Ebsen (Press).

Major-General Douglas H. Pratt
Expertise and responsibility

'Party Activist'.

"User angle" and "fraternisation"
Photo and caption by Tim Wimbush.

Christmas

in
New England
-1943-

"PAUL REVERE'S RIDE"
BOSTON-LEXINGTON-CONCORD
APRIL 18, 1775

Michael Halsted

One of the author's five journal covers (and illustrations within) done for him by Don Hougham, the Staff Draftsman.

Our Colonel-in-Chief Queen Elizabeth the Queen Mother, with us again on the occasion of the new regiment's Tercentenary Celebrations, at Wimbish, Essex, on 28th June 1985. Tom Draffen is on Her Majesty's left.

THE ANATOMY OF A TANK

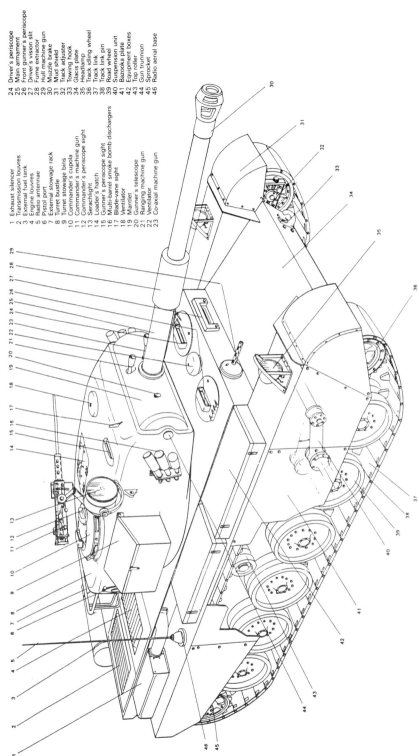

1 Exhaust silencer
2 Transmission louvres
3 External fuel tank
4 Engine louvres
5 Radio antennae
6 Pistol port
7 External stowage rack
8 Turret bustle
9 Turret stowage bins
10 Commander's cupola
11 Commander's machine gun
12 Commander's periscope sight
13 Searchlight
14 Loader's hatch
15 Gunner's periscope sight
16 Multi-barrel smoke bomb dischargers
17 Blade-vane sight
18 Ventilator
19 Mantlet
20 Gunner's telescope
21 Ranging machine gun
22 Ventilator
23 Co-axial machine gun

24 Driver's periscope
25 Main armament
26 Front gunner's periscope
27 Driver's vision slit
28 Fume extractor
29 Hull machine gun
30 Muzzle brake
31 Mud shield
32 Track adjuster
33 Towing hook
34 Glacis plate
35 Headlamp
36 Track idling wheel
37 Track link
38 Track link pin
39 Road wheel
40 Suspension unit
41 Bazooka plate
42 Equipment boxes
43 Top roller
44 Gun trunnion
45 Sprocket
46 Radio aerial base

From *TANK* by Macksey and Batchelor. Macdonald. 1970.

SHIP TO SHIP

MARCONIGRAM

SHORE TO SHIP

Prefix	Handed in at			Date Received	
Number	No. of Words	Date handed in	Time handed in	Service Instructions	Time Received	By

To *From Commodore*

H.M.S "Repulse" will pass slowly
though convoy today to allow troops
to see her at close quarters. She will
pass up between columns 5 and 6 leaving
"Mendoza" at 1630.

See page 36

Our special Correspondent was Oliver Woods, who joined The Times in 1934, won an MC in the tank battles of the Western Desert, and returned to the paper after the war, rising to the position of Colonial Editor and finally to Chief Assistant to C.D. Hamilton, Editor-in-Chief of Times Newspapers.

◆

FURY OF TANK FIGHTING

From our Special Correspondent
WITH A BRITISH ARMOURED UNIT, LIBYA, NOV. 23.

The battle of the tanks in Libya is still going on. The Germans are fighting furiously to destroy the British tank forces and to break through the ring. The British are fighting with equal fury to prevent them.

The tank battles are an affair of sudden onslaughts in unexpected places. Essentially, the fight is between individual tank crews and victory goes to the crew of the tank which sticks the exchange of blows the longer. For sheer cold heroism, there can have been little in this or any war to surpass that of those British tank crews who, with lighter guns and less thick armour, have stood up to and fought off time and again the massive German medium tanks, armed with a gun twice the size of theirs.

One cannot be everywhere at once, and I decided to go in search of our unit with American tanks which were reported to be fighting hard. Finding a tank unit in the desert is not easy. They move all day and at dusk go into close laager wherever they may happen to be.

Eventually their supply echelon was located and headquarters reached just as they were about to move off in support of another unit which was heavily engaged. Already the American tanks had been thrice in action within 36 hours, mostly in the region north-west of Sidi Omar. They were first attacked by 60 tanks on the second evening in the campaign. The Germans were outnumbered and eventually withdrew from the action.

Meanwhile, however, Rommel had brought the bulk of his force from Tobruk to join up with the force based on the Bardia area, and the American tanks had to face next morning an attack by a large number of German tanks. The action which ensued was, on the British side, heroic and successful. We were pushed back a couple of miles, but it was the Germans who eventually broke off the action.

Where the [German Mark IV tanks] were in action the fight must have been something like that between a terrier and a mastiff. In this case the terrier took a good few wounds, but also inflicted many, and the Germans broke off the action. They attacked again later, but this apparently was only a diversion. Von Rommel had decided to switch his force westwards in search of some easier prey.

A tank unit on the march in the desert is an impressive sight. The tanks in front, Command vehicle, and headquarters transport were not visible, but the formations behind them with their high turrets dipping and rising as they cruised on the uneven desert surface and their signal pennons waving in the breeze looked for all the world like a great fleet of destroyers...

See Diary of Friday December 12th (1941):

We had missed the great battles officially described as the second Battle of Libya: and we were witnessing something of the sacrifices in men and machines. Soon we would be advancing through grim remains on the sands themselves.

Note Oliver Woods' comment on disparity of arms.

14./5/42.

James.

Stephen

Edward

Michael

George's charicatures.
See page 163

FINE RECORD OF THE QUEEN'S BAYS

HARD FIGHTING AT GAZALA

An account of the doings of the Queen's Bays in North Africa was issued last night by the Ministry of Information.

After a long and splendid record of successes with the Eighth Army they were represented in an armoured division in the First Army, and were involved in heavy fighting in the central sector during the first week of May.

In the Battle of Gazala, during their service with the Eighth Army, the Queen's Bays were engaged for 19 days in continuous fighting against an enemy vastly superior in numbers and weight of armour. On June 12, 1942, about seven miles north-west of El Adem, they were attacked by 45 German Mark III and Mark IV tanks. Though they themselves could muster little more than half this total, less than half of which had equal gun-power to the enemy, the Bays held off the Germans till the afternoon. They then withdrew north-west after covering the retirement of the Royal Horse Artillery, which had given them support, by the skilful use of a smoke screen. They spent most of the night shooting up enemy motor transport, and early next morning set forth to engage a German force of tanks twice their size to the east of " Knightsbridge." With the help of a score of Matildas of an Army Tank Brigade the Bays held off the German attack. On the last day of the battle of Gazala the Bays, with only a few armoured fighting vehicles, tackled 30 German tanks, and, with the help of the Royal Horse Artillery, knocked out 11 of them.

On June 14, 1942, when the battle came to an end, the Bays were left with only six tanks still running, and they left the battle area for refitting. Less than two weeks later, now reformed with a squadron of the 4th Hussars, the regiment went forward under Major Lord Knebworth as a mobile column operating 30 miles south of Mersa Matruh. On June 27 they shot up an enemy column of 2,000 M.T. Three days later the column found itself well behind the Axis lines south of Fuka. Our forces operated eastwards alongside the enemy and shot up their motor transport, including several staff cars, one of which was laden with American cigarettes and 12 gallons of water —a welcome windfall. During the evening they beat off an attack by German Mark IIIs and through the night they passed one enemy leaguer after another in their journey to rejoin our lines. Next morning they were in an uncomfortable position, for only eight of their 16 tanks were available for immediate action, and they were still 12 miles behind the enemy lines. Their sheer boldness deceived the enemy, however, and they rejoined our troops at 7.30 a.m. with but one truck lost during the tour through enemy lines.

From *The Times*, 10th June, 1943

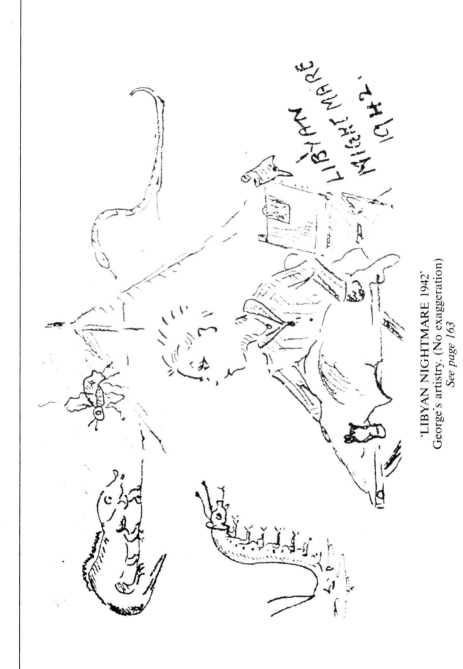

'LIBYAN NIGHTMARE 1942'
George's artistry. (No exaggeration)
See page 163

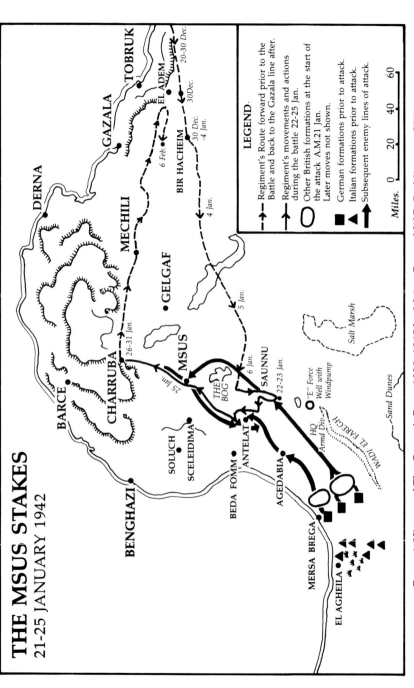

THE MSUS STAKES
21-25 JANUARY 1942

TOBRUK

GAZALA

EL ADEM

20-30 Dec.

30 Dec.

BIR HACHEIM

30 Dec.
-4 Jan.

6 Feb.

4 Jan.

DERNA

MECHILI

GELGAF

5 Jan.

BARCE

CHARRUBA

26-31 Jan.

MSUS

25 Jan.

6 Jan.

THE BOG

SAUNNU

22-23 Jan.

Salt Marsh

BENGHAZI

SOLUCH

SCELEIDIMA

BEDA FOMM

ANTELAT

AGEDABIA

"E" Force
Well with
Windpump

HQ
Armd Div.

WADI EL FAREGH

Sand Dunes

MERSA BREGA

EL AGHEILA

LEGEND.

→← Regiment's Route forward prior to the Battle and back to the Gazala line after.

↑ Regiment's movements and actions during the battle 22-25 Jan.

◯ Other British formations at the start of the attack A.M.21 Jan. Later moves not shown.

■ German formations prior to attack.

▲ Italian formations prior to attack.

⬆ Subsequent enemy lines of attack.

Miles.

0   20   40   60

From *A History of The Queen's Bays, 1929–1945* by Major-General W.R. Beddington, CBE,
Warren & Son, Winchester, 1954.

The Campaign in North Africa

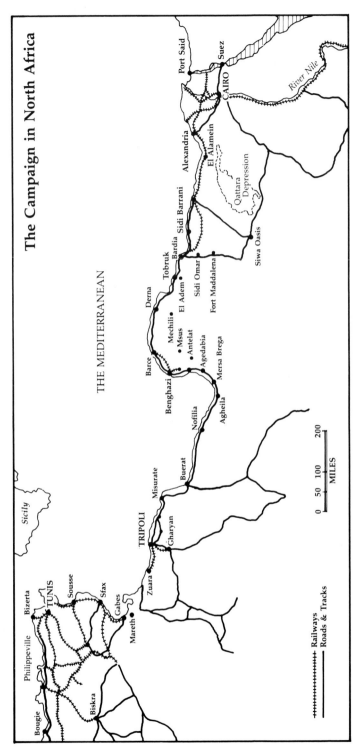

From *Tanks in Battle*, Sphere Books, 1972.

first job on my own and I have administration and everything to do. My official title is OC Brigade TDT! Found my way back from the mess to our leaguer and discovered my bed fits exactly into the back of my truck, so able to undress and sleep in great comfort.

February 26th

Never so busy since Amriya, and a horrible sandstorm all day, practically blotting out the camp at times. No shelter anywhere except in back of truck. On the go all the time. Took over five tanks at once and also had the task of running round interviewing everyone about pay and rations, and it all takes time. However, all went well but tremendous talking about my job and what the whole position is. Lieutenant Colonel Cooper (Tubby) A&Q came over to see me and he was very helpful. I have quite a good job to do and seem quite the final authority. It is not the simple task quite that Colonel Draffen outlined, but I shall soon get things going.

Not a chance to write a letter at the moment and I felt quite tired this evening, so retired early. Had to sleep in the major's truck as mine has petered out. Anyhow quite the best place to break down, outside the mess and not twenty miles north-east of Bir Dammit!

February 27th

A glorious hot day with slight breeze. I would love to be at the seaside. Busy all the time, but the men OK and happy, and no grumblings so far! Much helped by the arrival of a Stores lorry for me from Field Park complete with corporal. OFP Officer quite amenable (only a 2nd Lieutenant like self) but rather grammar schooly and needs being very polite to!

February 28th – March 4th

Would you believe that I could be so busy as to have written no letters, read no book and written no word in my diary? Well, I have, and it's meant dashing around all the time seeing to odd jobs and running round the tanks. No Ordnance seem to approve of TDT as they are merely snoopers and worriers to them. Everyone comes and gives orders and counter-orders, but I try and plod on to get some tanks fit to fight in.

I have an office and a phone laid on now. A table, and files and paper, all scrounged from the desert. My office-cum-house is a three-ton lorry frame with a big tent top stretched over it. Nice shelter from the wind, and phone is most helpful.

Mess is quite nice but I don't like the two-mile drive back in the dark after dinner, but I have been OK so far with the moon. The one dark night Coles luckily heard me and flashed a light. Of the mess now: Major Peebles is a very pleasant family man from the motor trade. He has good sense of humour, very considerate and understanding. Digger Lees is rather an old codger, obstinate and not too helpful even though he was with us at home. Adjutant Campbell is an ex-guards ranker, thorough gentleman. He is quite funny at times but a bit of an ass. He confided in me that he was a 4½-litre Bentley, long-hair-brushed-back, suburban-hotel-and-club-frequenter! Bill from the Middle East OCTU, very nice and helpful and a good fellow. George J., the baby! Quiet, short, young but a huge sandy moustache. Very nice. Gets all the odd jobs thrown at him and never complains. Born in Russia and brought up in France, his English is still only 80 per cent. I enjoy the wireless in the mess very much. Everything lovely till the rains decided to fall.

Tried to go off to Q Control to meet Peter Ling, but rain pouring down and desert getting very messy. Hated thought of going in open truck. Luckily Jones arrived in his Dodge just as we were leaving and I took courage and phoned Brigade saying we wouldn't be coming under the circumstance as Jones was very gloomy. All the afternoon it poured, and my tent, which was only an inner lining began to leak horribly. We packed ready to evacuate and caught the drips in tins as well as possible. Very, very, depressing as we sat around able to do nothing but wait for more water to come in. Cpl Coppen, back from a scrounge, let me have another inner sheet which I threw over the top, and that kept the water out for a time. It eased off and we went to bed wondering.

March 5th

Woke up at 3.40 a.m. with a mouse on my bed and water pouring in on my clothes. Sat huddled miserably till it grew light and then 'it were 'orrible!' There was a lake outside and all the men were flooded right out and soaked. Only the lorry covers kept it out and all the men huddled in there. They managed to make some tea on a petrol cooker, and I managed somehow to pay them out as Roddie wanted the acquittance rolls urgently. I had to wade up to the 9th Lancers' lorry.

Managed to get an M3 started and went up to the mess through the water and mud. No mess remained, only a pond, as the tent had been dug right down in the ground. Somehow the good old servants managed to provide a meal, and then Wilson, Cpl Garforth and I floundered back via the flooded cookhouse in the pouring rain and managed to get some tea, milk and sugar. 'If only the rain would stop,' we kept saying. 'Then we could do something. It would give us a chance to dry out a bit'.

At last it cleared a bit at lunch time and we surveyed the situation for a while and got up to lunch in a Honey again. Dark, ugly sky still and a heavy squally wind blowing, so we decided not to try the mess again. Returned to our island home, which appeared to be nearly submerged. Spent an hour with a spade trying to divert the floods round the side. Luckily the rain stopped and my bed remained dry. Felt so miserable by then that I crawled into the tent, took off sopping boots, socks and trousers, hung them up and crept into bed, thankful to have a bed dry. Lots of the chaps will have to stick the night out in their wet clothes and bedding. Gosh, it was nice to be in bed, but I was still fearful about the rain and so we stacked all the rest of the kit in the truck which Wilson had pulled on to dry land with a tank. Coles, Cowburn and Wilson have done fine work. Wilson, who is an ordinary business man who ought to get a commission, is quite a friend of mine now, and a great support. There is more in this job than one might imagine.

We had a peaceful night, I am glad to say, though one shower of rain early on made my heart sink!

March 6th

All evacuated safely to a nearby bit of higher and stony ground, and the sun came out, with a wind so that we could dry our clothes. Luckily my telephone kept going, so there was 'business as usual'. Peter Ling came over from Brigade to settle some points, which saved me a journey. I don't like travelling about in the desert, though I must go to Tobruk one day and also to the regiment to see them.

I am very happy now in my'office' with Wilson to do the clerking and Coles the domestic duties. Young Cowburn, my driver, is a grammar school BA, but for the moment I hold the commission!

I don't know how things are going up at the regiment, but at the moment life is delightfully static. I hope Jerry leaves them alone, and also the General! I sent Bing up a note the other day, via a tank returning. I hope he thought it was funny, because I did.

March 7th

Haven't been so comfortable for ages. A lovely hot day, starting with mist. Quite a lot of work with new tanks and new arrivals. Able to sit down this afternoon though, and write up this diary. Now our lorry is back from Tobruk but no luck, no food again, or drink. Third time lucky I hope. I must go and see them about the new chaps coming, as they don't seem to have brought any with them.

What lovely letters I've had. From a number of kind people. I hope I shall have time to answer them. Nothing from Pa for some time now. Silences do make one a bit anxious. When I can sit down to answering I shall have a lot of fun.

A very nice one from Phyllis Edwards. Just the same as ever, though I seem to have dropped her like a hot or cold brick. Joanna still very friendly and I still feel very much for her. Roslyn is growing up too, and Brian is now taking her around a bit. I expect she will be very much altered when I return.

Talking of girls, I must write to Lynette Ryall of Cape Town again to see if she can send one or two *Esquires* and *Lifes*. They are far the best to read out here. I like the American college pictures with all the happy co eds! My last evening in the squadron I showed George some pictures of the girls I liked the look of, and clothes too. His taste agreed exactly with mine. I showed him Leslie's photo then and he was most interested. I am so proud of that photo. D.L. received some portraits of his wife and baby son the other evening and he passed them all round. I showed them Leslie's photo too, and they all approved very much.

March 9th

Another day has fled by. Have broken the ice and done a bit of desert travel today to the RASC. Both units which I knew on the boat. Major J. and Major K. No difficulty in finding them as only a journey of five to ten miles. I have a silly fear of being lost in the desert.

Found a German PZKW III. Very interested to see it, but it was burned out inside. A lovely gun, though. That's what we want indeed. Very busy day chasing tools, inspecting men and tanks and fixing up to draw rations and all the sort of administrative jobs which I have never done before, but I am learning. It is great fun. Finding it rather a bore to go chasing up to the mess every meal time by car. Chaps not very thrilling I'm afraid, so I am thinking of having my meals with the men when we start drawing our own rations. I never stay long up there and love to return now to my little shack under a lorry frame. Wilson has done very well, and as a grown-up business man is a great help to me. We have scrounged quite a lot of stationery for office work and made some files, etc., and quite a show is now running. Luckily the chaps love it and are doing fine. They have actually built a cookhouse of wood and corrugated iron, all found in the desert. Their mess tent is fine, with a grand table and all, and Dudbridge has turned out to be a first class cook, and is greatly helped by the oven they found in the desert. I think you could find anything if you waited long enough.

March 11th

Graham arrived at last. He is very nice and a Cambridge chap. All the lads very pleased as they have had great success in Tobruk and so am I as they have brought me whisky and chocolate. Horrible fear tonight as rain threatens, and quite a heavy shower at 5.30. Wilson, Cowburn, Graham and I sat drinking whisky and chatting between business and *Men Only*! Then I joined the chaps in their pub when I heard the singing and laughter going strong. I was announced as 'orderly officer' and I roared out 'Any complaints?' which was received by a shout of laughter which was a good start. Luckily I remembered one good long army story which Roddie Campbell had told in the Ordnance mess. Of course I had to get on my feet and I think it was quite a success. Then I listened to some excellent poems by Cpl Howard, the usual sentimental home-ballad type. Then some cowboy songs from Cpl Birley, and I returned gracefully to bed. But horrors! Rain at 1.05 hours! Had to lie miserably in bed with torch and candle waiting for the drips. And they came—pouring in. I thought we were in for a night of it as Tobruk news was two days of rain for RASC information. However, there was a lull and I went out in my pyjamas and with Coles' aid put an old truck cover on top as an extra. However, we slept in peace as no more rain fell.
Beer had his bed in the office too.

March 12th

Determined to go up to Brigade and Regiment in spite of threatening rain. Got Coles to pack the truck all ready and then set off, having settled with George Finch the PMC that in future we would feed by ourselves as the mess is so far away.

We had a shock on reaching the Bir to find that there were floods all round. However it was only surface, and by slipping and sliding we got on a bit. It then looked like rain and I nearly turned back but on going on a mile or so found it quite dry, and so sailed along a very clearly marked track all the way to Rear Division. Then a bit of a job finding the cross-roads by B Echelon but got there OK and reached Brigade after two and a half hours good going. My confidence considerably restored as regards desert travel.

Slap up lunch in the mess with Peter and the brigadier, talking business all the time. In fact I talked business for about three hours after I had met everyone remotely interested in my job. Especially one colonel from a cavalry regiment. A real live wire, with a determination to get things done. I told them all my troubles and put forward my suggestions as forcibly as I could. I can only hope from now on.

Then to the regiment. It was just like going back to the old school. I was very well received and told my story to John T.-W. and the colonel, who invited me to tea which I enjoyed, meeting Alex Barclay, Tony Dean and all. A very cheerful atmosphere pervading all round, and everyone very comfortable and settled in. Much evidence of good things, as Jackie Harman had been sent down to Alexandria executing a mass of private commissions very skilfully. During tea I mentioned that I had not found my Herbert Johnson hat which Harry Spencer reported had arrived in the field minus packing. The colonel then confessed that he had it, and Lindley had the chinstrap! I got it back all right, and very pleased as such hats are expensive and impossible to get in this country of course.

Then up to the squadron, where there was great fun and games. All in the best of spirits there, too. They have a wireless now, pinched from an old tank. I thought we soon would. It was nice to see Edward Lydall again. He is almost as lucky as Joe, having had a month in India by the fortunes of war. Spent a long time with my troop. They weren't quite so happy with Edward, but a change over is always difficult. Pullyblank is still away, but Bradley and Swire in great form. Secrecy forbids me to describe much of what I saw, or all the news I heard, except one most cheerful piece—Spud is a prisoner. I am so very glad because he is safe now even though we are all having such a jolly and peaceful time at the moment. Also Peter Frankau is so much better. Also the other Peter has recovered and becomes a colonel, and goes to command a regiment. Good luck to the regiment. He is charming and also will do them very well. I hope to hear of them again.

I found a dinner party laid on. Major J. McDermott and Robin Dunn had been invited, and they were great company. It was lovely to chat with James again and chaff Auntie and Joe and be chaffed by Bing. And what fare! Menu as follows: tomato soup, chicken, cauliflower and roast potatoes, fruit, lobster salad. Gin, lime, lemon, whisky and port. Many stories of war and chaps' adventures, which went on till quite a late hour. Then in came some mail by hand from Peter Sykes who had flown up, delivered to him by John Knebworth who had brought it out from England, having returned from the USA and having written to all officers' families. James had another letter from Grannie and George's lovely Polyphotos from Nettie of herself and young George. I was most interested in these and found once again that my taste, or whatever you like to call it, is very much akin to George's as I picked out one of the ones of Nettie that he liked best. I think Nettie is charming, and as for young George—Gosh! How wonderful one day to look at the photo's of ones own son, and wife. . .

Having seen J. McD. and Co. safely into their truck and on their course—I'm sure they were not in a state to worry about the bearing that they had so carefully worked out beforehand—we all dispersed to bed. All except James live in bivvies near George now. James offered me a share of his big sheet with the mates. It was the mates that rather put me off, so I slept very comfortable in my truck. I loved showing James my photos.

March 13th

A lovely day of sun. Started well with a good breakfast of grapefruit, cereal, eggs and bacon. Had to leave early to get all the jobs done and get home in good time. Did not want to go a bit, and yet once on the way warmed to the job again. Took Bradley to B Echelon to do some hair cutting and there met old Peter Willett and got a book off him—*Kipps*—and some airgraphs. The journey via my calling places was easy. One moment we came into a little patch of green, a tiny dip filled with flowers which smelt lovely, and bees hummed about us. We stopped and picked some and felt quite homesick. I must send some home pressed in a letter. Such was my urge to get back to camp again that I would not stop and have any lunch. I am like that—it is very stupid—just the same as when doing motor cycle trips I would not stop. Then my front springs went, and I began to wonder. My throat was quite dry but we managed to crawl and crash along. We met one

John Sydenham having his lunch on the track. I told him our plight so that at least someone would know and send out a search party. I should have loathed a long march on a hot day. But we made it. Very glad to get back at 3 p.m. Immediately sat down and ate a tin of Bartlett's pears. Just caught Tiny Blair on his way back to the regiment. He was very cheerful, too, and just as keen for a chat and a buck. I hope I don't get left here longer than a month. There is much I cannot write, though.

Sunday March 15th

Very pleasantly ensconced in my little tent provided by kind DADOS. Nice to have Graham with me. He is very cultured and uplifting. Rather theoretical, a little prim, a Baptist, but a good sense of humour, companionable and keen. Had a surprise letter from Leslie the other day, also from Libby, Uncle Arthur from Durban and from Bob at last. He blamed me too, but it was an old surface mail letter. I must send him another cable. He enjoyed taking out my 'sweetie' as he called her. A wonderful letter from Libby. How tremendously she has come on in the last year and as pretty as Jim and I prophesied. She is sending me a Polyphoto. I sat down and wrote a long letter card in reply.

She is a dear girl and has a love of books and poetry and the country which so admirably fits in with my ideas. She is becoming rather like Leslie but is much quieter and less society-minded. A girl who lives very simply and happily with no money and three brothers to knock and be knocked and also educated, with the same slender means.

Wrote to Lynette Ryall at Cape Town this evening, or rather finished off a letter which intended to ask for some copies of *Esquire* and *Life*, but which became sentimental and asked for a photo of her and therefore the effect could not be spoiled by asking for magazines containing photos of females, etc!

March 17th

A horrid summons from the Adjutant recalling Cpl Brownhill and Wilson. Very sorry indeed to lose Wilson. He is a real friend now, and I felt quite lost and miserable when he had left. On his bright suggestion I sent a note to George telling him again how sad it was and could he possibly spare him? I don't suppose anything will come of that as he is a tank driver and needed at the moment as James has taken some experienced chaps with him on a course to the base. I'd very much like to have gone back to the base but I am having my change of air here, I suppose. I hope Cowburn will be able to manage the office. Wilson has got everything completely organised and ran the show very well.

Graham, Cowburn and I spent a subdued evening in the office. I'm afraid its not going to be so gay now, but never mind.

March 18th

Went out with Freddie Godfrey in his truck to look at some shot-up and bogged Italian tanks. Bodies luckily had been removed a short while ago and buried near by. These tanks had fought to the last, so it seemed. Nothing left worth having, as we came too late. How depressing a ruined tank is. No fear of booby traps on these anyhow, but there were rounds still up the spouts of the guns.

Then we were redirected to some small Italian tanks a few miles way. Arriving there we found eight little two-seater Fiat-Ansaldo things. One was OK apparently abandoned in a hurry, but the others were all burned out and all but one contained charred remains of the crew, sometimes one, sometimes two. Little death traps they looked. I should hate to fight in one. There was nothing worth burying so we came away. Just as we were driving off a rabbit got up and we had a tremendous chase as I kept on firing with my automatic. Finally he went to ground under a tank between two bits of track, and not even the combined efforts of Oscar (the dog), Freddie and I could get him out—so we handed it to him, and returned to lunch. I couldn't shoot him then but we went back to have a look at the one good tank with George Fround and found the rabbit still there. George got him out at once with the aid of a jack and we let him go again. George decided that the tank was worth towing in so Freddie and I went back for a Honey. Got hitched up all right and started for home with the engine firing occasionally as Freddie put it into gear. However, when turning slightly, Freddie's view was obscured by dust and he didn't pull the correct stick with the result that the Fiat was wrenched across by the tow rope and cannoned into the back of the Honey, damaging the idler wheel so that it was immovable. Freddie was cut under the nose and had a lucky escape.

We were in a nasty position then, having damaged a tank which was at twenty-four hours notice to move up to the front. Freddie and I walked back two miles to camp in half an hour, got his truck and rushed to find a transporter in Workshops. There was none, so we had to beard Major 'Digger' Lees. They were sympathetic and John Siddle told us we could have a new idler wheel. Just as we were getting it and preparing to take bedding out to the chaps by the tanks, a large transporter came in, and we rushed to offload his tank and persuade the crew to come to our rescue with only half an hour of daylight. Those transporter chaps are good and we got the Honey in, and the Fiat at the back, but we had to walk two miles in the dark in front of the transporter to guide it to our leaguer. All was well then as we gave the transporter crew a good meal and a sing-song and some whisky in the big tent.

Graham was away at Tobruk so I slept by myself, rather wondering if I should think too much of dead men, but I was only bothered by mice during the night.

March 19th

A rather tiring day of fruitless effort trying to change the Honey's bogie wheel. What made things worse was the arrival of the recovery section who removed all the old shattered Honeys so we couldn't take an old bogie. We also had to waste precious hours replacing the broken differential off my 18-cwt on the old one on the dump so it could be towed away. Late in the evening I took full charge and enlisted Q's aid. He went to the blacksmith and in half an hour before dark we had done more than all day's effort. I gave him twenty-four ·38 revolver rounds, which are like sovereigns nowadays.

March 20th

Success again, and I can breathe more freely. It took until the evening with many a hitch and worry, during which I had visions of touring the desert for spares or tools. In the end we, or rather Sergeant Menzies and Cpl Birley, had the new wheel on. Not only that, Andrews and Co. got the Fiat-Ansaldo to work and we have been proudly touring around with our own flags on it. It is a great little toy—hardly a war machine it seems, and odd that it now gives such pleasure to the driver when once to drive it must have been nerve-racking. However, I still enjoy driving tanks. Even the derelicts that are brought in here are rather grim, though. One can judge what was hit by the shell holes, and often there are charred bones. Graham is just back from Tobruk with some good things to eat and some clothes for the chaps. Jerry is flying very low overhead and there is another air raid over Tobruk. Our mouse is out again and wants a biscuit.

I have been trying to write to Leslie and Mrs Marshall for their parcel of books and Cousin Geoff for his magazine. Even though things are much more cheerful, I don't think I can do it tonight, somehow.

I've just finished *Kipps*. It's splendid entertainment, and now I wish I had seen the film.

Sunday March 22nd

No call to go away this time so looked forward very much to a Holy Communion Service at 4.45 and so went down with Graham and found Bill there too. Sad to say, no Padre turned up until too late and chaps had to go off to tea. I buttonholed him though, and he promised to come to TDT at any rate on Wednesday.

March 23rd

Cpl Birley found some beer at the Recovery Section and as they hadn't any money we managed to muscle in on quite a lot and that was the signal for an evening party to which I was invited. Sergeant Edwards having brought back some whisky from Tobruk, it was a regular orgy run of course by the irrepressible Cpl Garforth.*

Everyone had to take part and sing or tell a story, and it went on and on, and they would put whisky in my beer. When I tried to go they sang 'For he's a jolly good fellow' and I had to stay longer. When I finally got away, I was able to walk back but only just! I am sorry to say I was sick before finally and dizzily lying down. I have a very weak stomach and head I'm afraid, and lessons die hard to live up to when so much is expected of one.

March 24th

A very grim day. Awoke feeling terrible and hot and thought I was really ill. Found the heat due to the weather. A tremendous wind began to blow and it was very hot. In fact it blew very, very hard and from the south, and a horrible sandstorm resulted. I stayed in bed until 11.30, and feeling better got up, but the wind continued. It was awful, quite paralysing and so hot. The office, being a poor erection and facing

131

* Alas killed Goubellat Plain, 24th April 1943.

the wrong way, almost blew away and anyhow the sand made it quite a shambles. The dreaded khamsin has started!

March 25th

Saw a Dodge arrive and thought it was Peter Ling, but it was Stephen Christie-Miller and Edward Lydall. Edward to find out the state of some tanks. Stephen to take over from me! Quite a shock but I soon got over it, and really do not mind a bit. Life has been very pleasant here, but I am quite happy to go back as I enjoy it there and I think I shall enjoy it still more now I have been able to see the regiment, indeed the whole show, in perspective. Spent the rest of the afternoon trying to get the best out of the workshops. Bill was very helpful and put me on to the right chaps to get my glasses (field) repaired, my boots altered and a Browning mounting for my Cruiser.

At last electric light in the office as I write this, only today have I found a battery lying about. There are a lot of things lying about here and there. Contemplating selling my Luger to someone for £5 to go towards a camera.

A lovely letter from Libby's aunt Polly Stevens yesterday. Hers are far the best and now I found myself thinking more and more of Libby. A great little girl really. Her charm is her country simplicity, yet she is a school prefect now, and quite brainy, loving reading and poetry as I do. I think I shall send her my other spare photo, though to be sure it is very poor—I wonder if Cousin Edith has that spare big one?

March 26th

Last day at TDT. Spent the morning running around in the truck with Cpl Coppen scrounging stuff to take back, such as material for a bivvy and other oddments. Also running errands for Sgt Menzies and Co., who were struggling to get the Cruiser on the road. Spent the afternoon, or rather intended to spend it, in domesticity, but just as I was preparing to wash my hair, back came the Cruiser all ready for the road, roaring along, and I couldn't resist going out for a run to try the guns. So we ran out to the little group of Italian tanklets and shot at them.

The area round Workshops has cheered up a bit lately with the arrival of many flourishing Bedouin camps complete with flocks and herds. The animals make queer noises at all hours but they are friendly and comfortable noises. The women when visible wear bright clothing, mostly red, which provide a treat for the eyes. Cpl Coppen and I drove up to within a respectful distance of one caravan and watched them all going along, and was concerned to see that even the smallest mites had to toddle along, and very few rode asses or camels.

Before sundown we went over to the Arab camp with a small sack of sugar and Parrish with his guitar and whistle, and Cpl Birley with his Italian rifle, Cpl Garforth and Wigmore perched on the truck and Graham and one or two others. After a good welcome we got down to business which was mainly conducted by a young and rather educated-looking chap who thought he was standing no nonsense. However, I wasn't either, and I finally insisted that the rate of exchange would be one handful of sugar for one egg. Eggs appeared mysteriously from under garments of the women or from old men's folds, and I knew there must be plenty in spite of assurances to the contrary and demands that I should hand over all my sugar at once for about five eggs. In the end I got thirteen eggs for all the sugar. They didn't like the guitar a bit, but the children laughed and enjoyed the whistle.

Luckily I had no farewell ceremony to go through at TDT, so after tea I retired for a final bit of letter writing at the office.

March 27th

Back to good old Charlie Squadron. A lovely day and everyone very cheerful. My bivvy fits nicely into Stephen's vacated hole in the ground, and is not nearly so bad as I thought it would be after the tent. All the greenery in the valley is so nice and the flowers actually smell sweet and whole atmosphere is one of peace and quiet and rather reminiscent of Ogbourne. There is quite a lot of stuff to learn up and make notes on, but I shall soon be *au fait* with the fun and games.

March 28th

Quite a job to get up and stand to at dawn. However it will help to bring me back to the operational way of life and I don't mind that a bit. TDT was bad for my discipline but I find my outlook changed a bit. I can tackle this squadron life without a thought or a qualm now, and the main bogey has vanished. The 'Move now' horror has been overcome, I feel, and I don't mind travelling now half as much. I have begun to adopt a rather more philosophical attitude to this war and action. Going over to inspect my tank, I am very glad it is a Cruiser, but I'm not fussy nowadays. However, I must get Mounsey to paint it with the usual signs and insignia.

Just as we were finishing breakfast I heard a burst of violent MG fire and looking out saw men running and then a fighter plane coming straight at the tent. I shouted 'On the floor' and we threw ourselves on the tent floor which luckily is below ground level. Two planes went over firing—they were gone in a second, but in these few moments we all hoped for the best and then got up laughing and dusted ourselves. Very little damage was done. Three of the crew of one of Joe's tanks were slightly wounded. They left the entrance of their bivvy where they were washing up and lay down at the far end of the tank, but a cannon shell or something peppered them. The fourth member lay below ground on the floor of his bivvy and was OK but his battledress jacket above his head was riddled! What a breakfast surprise! Excitement No. 2 came when we were out a few miles from camp and saw two planes bomb somewhere between B Squadron and HQ. Huge columns of smoke rose and it looked quite bad. On our return I found two had dropped within thirty yards on either side of Sgt McGuinness and Co., but they were quite unharmed. A very lucky escape, especially as they live on solid rock which stopped the bomb from penetrating more than six inches. Now we shall be able to convince the Doc that we cannot dig latrines there! Good old Four Troop, in and out of it again.

Sunday March 29th

Nice to go to Holy Communion again. This time at HQ where afterwards Tony taught me a bit about astral navigation. Padre gave me the books I had asked Massey to bring up from the base, and Douglas and I looked at the pile of *Sketches*, *Tatlers* and American magazines that Tony had brought back from Alex. Lucky chap, he has been around quite a bit. I am very much looking forward to going on leave. I particularly want to buy a camera, having sold my Luger to D.L. for a fiver.

It is hot but there is a wind blowing that flaps the tent. Everyone else has started to rest and kip.

Here goes! . . .

8
Respite

March 31st

George said (while sitting in state just outside the mess tent), 'Would you like to go on leave tomorrow?' He didn't need much answering, and so I hoped for the best, but is still hung in the balance till lunch time because he nearly went himself! I was determined to take the chance in case a push comes off. Spent the evening seeing what people wanted and telling them the glad news. James is back now and is sharing my hole in the ground for the time being. It is very pleasant having him to talk to in bed, and he had a jolly good time in Cairo during his course. He gave me all the tips and wrinkles, but he was not very hopeful about the opposite sex.

April 1st

John Knebworth and Peter Gill and the leave party embarked on a 3-tonner for Capuzzo at 7.30, after inspection by the colonel. I could not bear to go in the back so I alternated between a perch on top of the cab and inside it when the others felt like changing seats. Am quite happy about desert travel now. We passed Sidi Rezegh and all the grim ruins for miles. What a bloody looking place, and what a mess some of the tanks were in. Went through Bardia too, and it looks a hell of a place to capture among the rocks. Arrived 5 p.m. Transit camp mess full of *Lifes* which we devoured, then slept.

April 2nd

The desert train arrives alongside the camp where a small black notice board serves as a station. It pours with rain as we climb into the dirty, noisy, evil-smelling metal cattle trucks and prepare for a tiresome journey, with or without air strafing as the case might be. It was a beastly journey. Truck too bumpy to read properly, next to no food or comfort. However, by some amazing means I managed to sleep balanced on two valises against the side. Spent the last hour or so standing in the open on the AA gun truck with a couple of South Africans. A meal was laid on at railhead and I got the rail warrants OK after the RTO had rung up someone higher to ask authority!

Then settled down in an ESR first class with a South African captain Roger, and his SSM. Both very nice and we had whisky and a long chat till we slept. I only woke up at Amriya and then when it got light. Also met a Lieutenant Tewfick Fanous of Egyptian Army who invited me to call some time. He might be useful.

April 3rd

Marvellous to see the lovely green of the Nile valley and all the trees and sights and sounds of the Delta. How different I feel though, this time, to when we first went up. Now I take it all in my stride.

Cairo at last! 8.35 a.m. After finding the time of the train back I went straight to Toc H via Shepheard's, where I dropped Peter Gill. Met the sub-warden, Gordon Turvey, who said he could just fit me into Alan Cowling's room as he was ill, and that I was just in time for breakfast. I muscled in on that, looking very odd I'm sure with all my desert kit slung round me. During eating Gordon came and chatted and we got on to people out here and he asked me if I came out with Michael Halsted! From then it was simple.

Spent the whole of the day in an odd way. Having got all my clothes from Massey at Abbassia, I walked and walked and walked all round the shops just in the same old aimless way. Had tea in a lovely open-air garden advised by James C.—Groppi's. In the evening went to eat at St James' with Peter Gill and suddenly saw sitting there Hugh Finch and Toby Graham from school. Marvellous, and didn't we have a good dinner. Then on to the cinema for a very nice Gary Cooper film, *John Doe*.

April 4th

Cairo is quite a pleasant spot. Much better shopping than Alex. Took me quite a time to find my way all round about, and I spent most of today just dashing around and getting things done. Had a very pleasant lunch with

Hugh at the OCTU in the famous Kasr-el-Nil barracks. Once a lovely place, then a Guards' mess. All very impressive, and I was greeted by the colonel and given a drink, which rather overawed me. I think I have rather lost my social nerve!

Spent a long time buying books for the squadron. It is an awful job chasing round shop after shop trying to find what you want. Bought a camera for £10. Think it will do well. Also from same shop and nice French girl, bought *England is my Village* by Flt/Lieut Rhys, who was later killed. I think I shall very much enjoy it as a complement to *Fighter Pilot*, and I hope it will help me with my own ideas. The trouble is that I am too restless to settle down to write.

Wandered round Shepheard's and the Continental this evening, feeling rather frustrated and not quite knowing if I wanted a bint or not and wondering what I should do.

Met Gus Ballingal at last. He has the MC and escaped after Antelat. He took over from the troop of 11th armoured cars Stephen had shot at, and afterwards chatted to, and was at Cherruba. We wished we had known. Anyhow, fixed up a cabaret party for Tuesday. With him was Richard Wingfield-Digby who I used to meet at the Suttons' parties at Coopers, their Eversley home. Later on I wandered on to a snack bar by myself and had a couple of sandwiches and then went to the cinema. Saw a lovely short called *Sounds of Britain*. Main film was of Mickey Rooney and a very pretty girl, whose screen acquaintance I had not made before.

Sunday April 5th

Shared my room with a very nice gentleman corporal of SA Medicals and Sub-Lieut, Fleet Air Arm, who was at Oxford. We all three went to 6 a.m. Holy Communion at the Cathedral. It was beautiful. The lovely garden and flowers seen at sunrise, the silhouette of the cloister arch and windows of the chancel with the lights behind was most impressive to a wanderer from the desert. How much I enjoyed the service too, and the walk back along the fresh-smelling streets, with everyone coming to life.

Then changed into old shooting clothes—oh joy, shouldered gun and cartridges in old Pa's, or Pa's old, pack and went round to breakfast with Hugh at Kasr-el-Nil. I could write for ages about this day's shooting, but I will not do it here. I am writing a special article which I hope to send home to *Game and Gun* shortly.[1] Luckily Hugh had a car so we drove sedately if noisily to pick up Nevvi the Shikari, having left the lunch behind once! Then I saw my first view of the Pyramids in the morning sun. The setting was much more beautiful than I had imagined. First because I thought of the desert there being rather worse than Amriya, secondly I did not expect them to be so close to such lovely green countryside, nor the Mena road to be so modern and good. Their size impressed me, too. We drove by lovely canals and villages and palm trees and past where Memphis was and by the Step Pyramid of Sakkara, beyond to other pyramids and by a little waterworks hut of some sort. Here we de-bussed among the swarm of boys avaricious, quarrelsome, talkative but keen. It was very hot, the going rather hard, but it was fun in spite of my bad shooting and other troubles. The main one was the danger of hitting men, women, children and beasts hidden all over the place among the tiny fields, all busy at some task or other. Quail lie very close, so that we had to walk closed right up and comb every bit of the area to get them up. I think we mostly shot too close, and a curving going away bird is about my worst anyhow! Beaters kept up a high-pitched whirring noise repeated alternatively by groups, rather irritating but quite effective. For lunch we had plenty to drink so that it was hard to move afterwards, but we actually shot a bit better. Total bag 31. What a job we had getting away and paying them. It is hard to remember that the average *fellahin* only earns 5 piastres a day in the fields. We managed to shake them off in the end though, and stepped on the gas for home where we had a bath and got clean and cool and all met again for dinner at Shepheard's, which was most pleasant. We sat in the red music room and watched all the dancers and I felt I so wanted to dance with someone. The mood did not pass but nothing could be done there, so we moved on to the Dug-Out where I looked around for a partner. It was not a very hot joint and not up to much. Unfortunately the only girl I spotted as any good at all simply would not dance, not even with anyone. However, I had recovered by the time I got home. Gosh! How I like to see a bit of skirt, an arm, a leg, hair and all the rest of it.

April 6th

Felt pretty tired after all the exertions of yesterday. Also quite recovered from my repressions. Spent the morning at Gordon's desk at his typewriter, purporting to polish off my correspondence and get that load off my mind, but no luck. I got on to the typewriter and nattered away to Bob Langton till it was time to go and lunch with Hugh.

Then he took me to Gezira Sporting Club. It was a great treat. What a wonderful place it is, with polo and every sort of game. What I like best was sitting having tea on the terrace by the swimming pool and watching the form. It was a real tonic to see everyone enjoying themselves normally. Gus Ballingal was sitting there, and one or two pretty girls, too. Oh dear! Never mind. There isn't really any chance to do anything in these few days. It was nice to see them. That evening I bought tickets for the cinema but went to Doll's Cabaret with Hugh. I couldn't resist going but it wasn't very good. The only interesting thing was the presence of some Russian officers which was announced on the mike and we all drank toasts. I went over and had a drink and a handshake!

April 7th

A very satisfactory morning's shopping. Contacted a Col. Childs about going up in his staff car which we heard was to go back. However, no luck as he was returning too. It would have given us an extra day. What a pity! Spent a lot of money on books. My choice as follows:

1. Nonesuch edition, Lewis Carroll
2. G.A. Birmingham Omnibus
3. *Peregrine Saga*, Henry Williamson
4. *Testament of Beauty*, R. Bridges
5. *British Life and Thought*
6. Prayer Book
7. *England is my Village*

and one or two others. I could have bought and bought. It was difficult to stop—I hope I have time to read them all.

Lunch with Peter Frankau whom I met at Shepheard's. It was splendid to see him again. He looks a bit shot up, and his right arm is still useless. He was lucky not to have it off. He happened to know the surgeon at Tobruk very well and persuaded him to leave it on till he got to the base. The wizard surgeon patched him up. He expects to go to South Africa and then home! How lucky. He was doubtful of taking the opportunity but I told him to seize on to it. It is amazing how eager people at the base seem, so loathe to remain there and wish to go forward! We had a long yarn and then I left him and went to the dentist at Abbassia. Captain Findlay was really excellent. I had four stoppings and injection for one. I hadn't had an injection since the great tooth extraction day in 1936 followed by a pilgrimage to the GPO, Mount Pleasant for the Arab dagger from Papa! It all went off very well though, and my mind is at rest now.

After a visit to Sgt Reynold who holds the fort at the base, I went to the Grand Hotel to meet John Haigh, now an RAF pilot at Gambut. Going down the street the night before I thought I recognised the face lit up by a shop, and called out his name. He responded! I was amazed. He was just as dour and sinister as before but school was very vivid in his mind. He was actually writing a book about school!

Then on to dinner at Shepheard's with Gus. We had a lot of fun and chat and drink. Then we went on to the cabaret at the Continental. It wasn't very good but it was better than before and anyhow Peter Frankau turned up which was excellent. Gus has a nice little Morris car just like Stephen's at Ogbourne but much better condition! Gus' MC in the paper this evening!

April 8th

Most of the day spent packing up and returning my clothes to Abbassia. But I had a lovely lunch at Gezira and watched the polo and swimming and tennis. Poor Hugh has his eye on another rather famous girl Ann, a very charming colonel's daughter who looks very decorative on a horse. Met Peter Gill at 5 p.m. at the station, where a milling throng gathered for the desert train. Luckily got a good seat with an Australian observer. He had a wonderful collection of Leica photos of his squadron.

Then began our great trek back to the regiment. First night at Amriya, arriving 10 p.m. A very good show running at their transit camp and glad not to spend a rumbling night in a train.

April 9th

Uneventful journey to Matruh. A very nice spot and another even better show running. Met M. and Capt. J. of the armoured cars. Maxwell has the MC now. Also a doc of the Surrey and Sussex Yeomanry 177, who is Edgar Seward's brother. Edgar was secretary of Oxford Rifle Club and he's a great shot too. Also met Jim Ashton of Divisional HQ and friend Captain Butler. Jim speaks of activity at the front. Hope we don't find ourselves chasing a battle in lorries. We hated the idea of facing a fourteen-hour journey to Capuzzo in a cattle truck. Luckily Butler came to the rescue and offered his truck.

April 10th

Lovely not to have to get up at 4.30 a.m. with the train party! We left leisurely at 9, with lunch in the NAAFI canteen at Sidi Barrani, reaching Capuzzo at 3.30 after a most interesting run up Sollum Pass. What beautiful sea and bay from 600 feet up, but what horrible hinterland. Think of the hundreds of miles of lovely coastline, ideal for coast resorts if the land was green.

Spent the rest of the evening writing letters at last. Had a wonderful letter from Libby the other day which made my heart beat faster. She is marvellous really and an excellent writer. She tells me all her thoughts and I feel her thoughts are very similar to mine. She loves the country and reading and poetry, and all the simple and beautiful things. I wrote three air mail letter cards as a serial, a thing I have never done before, but by luck the IO at the camp gave me several of these much-prized letter cards. I felt more and more sentimental and began to think more of Libby. I have asked for a really good photo. In fact I am getting rather mixed up. Another very good letter from Roslyn the other day. My word, she is growing up now, and doing fine work as a nurse.

A very loud display of fireworks at the railhead tonight. Jerry dropped magnificent flares and we saw him come in to bomb. No damage done but we, standing outside the tent, heard one lot whistling and went flat on our faces!

April 11th

A very tiring and boring journey over the most bloody desert from Capuzzo to Tobruk transit camp, where another good show running by South Africans. Met SSM Harris in a truck but he hadn't room to take us home. Hope Jerry H. can spare someone tomorrow morning. Told by Harris that messes are back so I shall go up to the war.

Sunday April 12th

No sign of a truck so I spent a very pleasant morning writing letters, as I got some airgraphs off a NAAFI truck parked outside the camp. Now I am fairly up to date with letters so I can go back ready for anything. After lunch, at which we met some amusing gunners, I rather wondered whether we should attempt to get back to the regiment by hitch-hiking, or wait till the lorry came today or tomorrow. However, my conscience was salved by the arrival of Sgt Empringham. We had the most horrible ride I've ever had in the back of a 3-tonner, taking just under two hours with sandstorm included! Arrived at B Echelon and had a mad scramble to sort out my tank kit in the storm, and there was a lot to do with all my Cairo stuff and books, and no more to be taken up than would go on a tank. Got going at last and reached the squadron at 6.15. Nice to see them all again and I enjoyed telling them all about my trip and showing them what I had brought back. I would have brought masses more had I been supplied with cash!

Quite a change to bed down in the open again with Wilson and Bradley and Swire, but I really quite enjoy being back and I don't mind the idea of flaps a bit. I seem to have missed the main ones anyhow. I really think I have the desert buttoned up and I feel ready for anything and not apprehensive about myself any more. James agrees with me that he too feels far less precious and important than he did. I used to think that it would be awful if I didn't get back and that someone would be missing something. Now I see rather differently, and merely feel like a small cog in the war machine which wouldn't matter a bit if it stopped. How glad I am James is here and very sympathetic. It is essential to have someone with whom to share one's secrets and confidences.

April 13th

Got really sorted out and ready for anything, and began to get busy with my camera too. I hope for good results. Had a chat to John T.-W. about regimental photographer, and then the colonel came round inspecting the tanks very minutely in a 'cleanest tank in the regiment' competition. We were not in the running! I am very lucky. The mess has now arrived again, and I am back in my little bivvy again, and we're all together again, which is so nice—I can now have more books and things out, but I am grateful for the scurry yesterday—it made me revise my ideas and repack quickly.

April 14th

Went off with Joe and selected a reasonable patch of desert to turn into a football ground. Then we set to work conscripting a working party and soon we had quite an army armed with shovels and matchets hacking and digging all the rest of the morning. Made the acquaintance of John Lentaigne of the Rifle Brigade who sent some chaps to help and I arranged a match with him. Slept soundly for two hours in the afternoon and dreamed about an old lady at home!

Turned out and tried to play football without much success, but the ground is quite playable. Henry Sherbrooke came to dinner and was quite amusing.

April 15th

I must say I enjoy this life, but it's awfully bad for us and after a time becomes very wearing. Spent a very pleasant morning just sitting, reading and writing.

I am awfully pleased with my Nonesuch Lewis Carroll. There's a delightful Oxford atmosphere about his little things. His illustrations in *Symbolic Logic* bring back many memories of Mr Brewis and Pass Mods and all. I like his particular 'donnish' humour, and of course I have never appreciated *Alice in Wonderland* and Co. as I do now.

A very successful football match v the RBs. Hotly contested, but we won 2−0. No air attack or alarms I am glad to say, but it's no good worrying about things anyhow. We would never play football at that rate.

John came to dinner, and I found him very nice indeed. I was amazed to find he was at Eastacre in '30 and '31. He also lives at Uckfield and knows all my Lewes friends, Sturgises, Boyles, Ponsonbys and even Phyllis Edwards who sent me a very nice Christmas card the other day.

April 16th

The start of another khamsin but it didn't come to much. However, after dinner when I tried to write a poem, I couldn't, nor could I continue with my article, so I went to bed rather negatively!

April 17th

A real khamsin today. An amazing hot wind, exactly like a hair blower dryer full on. Sweat simply dries up on you until you get out of it. Tents and bivvies like ovens, water in petrol tins almost boils, and so drinks are not very quenching. Movement impossible after midday but flies dreadful.

143

John Lentaigne gave us a grenade demonstration which was very amusing and we learned a lot and got over some of my fears of explosives! A lively evening when the sun and wind went down. Extraordinary that we can have a bath and change for dinner, and sit out in the dark looking at the moon, smoking cigars and listening to music in the FRONT LINE. So much for a lull in desert warfare!

A most amusing chat with James and Joe about women! I will say no more!

April 18th

No more khamsin—instead a wind from the north. Coolish, but rather paralysing sandstorm. Managed to write a sort of poem which James and Joe approved of, so I will send it home. BBC news mentioned khamsin for two days hampering operations. I should think so! I've never experienced anything like it. It has to be felt to be believed.

HOPING

What is the use of growing sentimental
When there is no one near to share the stars?
Music only accentuates our yearning.
Our spirits mounting, slide to earth again
Dampened by the uncertainty of war.
When shall we wander by the streams again
When marvel at the broken line of hills—
Beauty denied us in this wilderness—?
Will our homes be changed; how shall we live;
What chance of realising our desires?
These questions are unanswerable and still
We think of them. Again we ask and still
Derive no comfort. Only Hope is left us,
And our memories indelible
In mind and eye supplemented
By mail and treasured photographs.
'Hit hard and keep on hitting'—(motto!)
Our consolation is annihilation:
Our occupation seeking to destroy.
We work with iron and ammonal,
We do not kill professionally but fight
As citizens, part and parcel of our land in arms.
Our inspiration springs from our desire
To live as we have always lived;
Waiting the cue to turn our tools

To trowel and mortar, pen and paper,
Construction not destruction.
Social services, equality of chance
No stranglehold of callous class indifference.
Happiness and prosperity, not greed and gain.
When shall this come to pass?
Are we deluded, dreaming of Utopia,
Or shall we reap the benefit of lessons learned?
Shall we remain together as in emergency
We stood and called ourselves united?
If not, we fight in vain, at home, abroad.
We could not live a moment on such ground.
Onward! Our strength is real and just our cause.
In God we trust and striving still,
Can do no more than what we believe
Our duty and our best.

Written one night in the mess tent (18.4.42).

Sunday April 19th

Holy Communion at 8 and parade service at 10.30 with Bing taking the parade and reading the lesson. Managed to get quite a few letters written and a welcome afternoon kip! Very nice letter from Lynette Ryall from Cape Town. Took a lot of answering. Gosh! She is the prettiest girl I have met in my life. I wish I had seen more of her. I wonder if I shall ever see her again? Oh damn! The same old question. We know nothing, we can do nothing.

April 21st

Met a chap from another regiment who was at Blackdown with me. Quite a hearty party in their mess followed by some drinking in ours which was all very satisfactory. George and Edward have gone away so we are a small party under Bing.

April 22nd

A move back today and another regiment takes over our positions. A very busy time digging our lorries in, and many of us have blisters. Am living on my tank now, which isn't a bad change. Wilson is a splendid cook and does it all for us with a finish. He produced a wonderful Welsh rarebit yesterday, which James shared.

145

April 23 – 25th

A most pleasant three days just reading and writing. I got a lot of routine letters done and also some longer better ones. At last managed to get my article on Sakkara Quail. Took great courage from reading about Ernest Hemingway who rewrites his paragraphs or chapters or bits many, many times to get the effect if he is not satisfied. I find I have to write a rough copy first, which may be very bad. I then try and prune and improve. One very hot afternoon James, Joe and I sat in the tent and wrote dirty or doubtful limericks, rhymes and clerihews with Bing asleep on the floor! Another evening when the sun was just on the decline George Rich and Jojo came over for a drink and a chat. Suddenly we looked out of the tent and saw a huge wall of sand two or three hundred feet approaching rapidly. We could see nothing through it at all and yet we could see both edges very clearly. Tanks in front of it were silhouetted in the most grim and foreboding manner against a russet brown wall. We got quite scared, never having seen anything like it before, and chaps ran for their vehicles and others for their gas masks. We just sat by the tent, hanging on to the guy ropes and wondered!

The wind came in gusts from the north-east when we had had a south wind nearly hot all day and now the wind was cool. Well, it hit us but it wasn't so bad. It didn't take the tent or the lorry away as we feared it might, but it filled the air with a thick choking dust and we couldn't see five yards. This went on till it began to grow dark, when the wind eased and the sand lifted until only a blur was left in the gusty moonlight night.

April 26th-27th

A big scheme which I can't say much about except that the first day we bummed along and the second day we had a bit of a fight with the C.O. Blue sparks came out of my earphones when my navigation went a bit awry. It was quite fun but we broke down three miles from our destination. A Recovery took me in and the chaps slept the night by the old machine. A German M3 was nearby, completely wrecked, but I got a 50mm shell to polish up as an ornament.

Gradually my inner self is becoming reconciled to war and I'm beginning to develop the 'get at them spirit'! I wonder what I shall be like in the next show? Life is pretty good at the moment so I won't bother too much. I have plenty of books to read and plenty to write about if and when I can get my mind going. I can see that there will be much more chaff than wheat, though!

April 28th

After a day and a half of medical inspection, kit, arms, etc., and bath parade in lorry covers sunk in pits (my invention, ha! ha!) a party of us set off for Capuzzo with Joe, Stephen and James. We didn't do too badly on a bearing but had a bit of a job finding the spot after being round the ridotta[2] and seeing the cemetery again. Gosh! what a terrible place it is. I no longer feel depressed by it now that I have conquered the desert. I can go anywhere, I hope, without feeling anxious. Very nice to see George and Edward again. We are in a very comfortable mess and there is a chance of a bathe tomorrow. Good! A lovely hot day with a cooling breeze and no dust. Ideal!

April 29th

Talk about idealism! We piled into a lorry after lunch and set off on a sixteen-mile (one hour) mainly bumpy journey to Bardia. It is a little battered town perched high on top of the grim rocks, with all the ruins of war stretching behind, but below the beautiful blue Mediterranean stretching away to Greece and Italy. Alas, the Royal Navy have battered the little church and municipal buildings and rows of white houses into mere shells. On the walls of some are soldiers' drawings, many of them most amusing, one in particular depicting the old lion in full flight pursued by a plucked and scrawny-looking eagle!

When I walked to the edge of the cliff and looked down into the bay, the contrast in desert view took my breath away. It was the colour of the sea in the bay—a deep, deep translucent blue edged sharply in broken white. The sun was shining from dead behind, straight on to the bare brown rocks which reflected the light right down through the water, which was dark blue in the deeps, shading to pale Cambridge or bird's-eye blue as the white sand came up to the surface. To the west I could see the same cliffs and white sea edge, and above me the battered attempts at battlements. It did not do to think on the desolation beyond that, so we all descended the steep, precarious footholdings down to the shore and the rocks.

It was most pleasant sitting and swimming and talking and taking photographs. There was a wonderful 'monsters hole' round the corner where every wave roared up and splashed heavily over the edge, and the ebb sucked back gurgling and shushing. As we walked slowly and regretfully up the cliffs again, my heart turned over as I thought of my last bathing at home and all the pleasant befores and afters, and when shall we be bathing at home again, and who with?

A lovely mail today. One good letter from Sage, one from Joanna, a charming one from Lynette (Oh dear! Oh dear!) and two letters and an airgraph from Roslyn, more and more complicated! But it is very pleasant. My word, we are doing well in this mess, and having quite a bit of fun. The most excellent food and drink, and radio too, suits us all. I have at last met Stug Perry, a really charming man, and I find George Errington and Thomas. I am quite content listening to them. Life is not so complicated with them. I somehow feel we are a rather serious lot, especially J. de G.T.-W. alias Pin Head, alias Otto! Of course it makes a difference if it is your pals who give the orders.

May 6th

I've not been neglecting this book, only there's nothing I've been able to say except that I have been too busy to write letters for some time! Parties of chaps have been able to go to the sea to bathe, which I call enlightenment. I really didn't expect it!

We've been fighting the weather mainly. A second khamsin, and just lately days of horrible wind and sand making us all feel bloody. However we've had Lord John Knebworth to keep up our spirits, and he really is enormous value. Sgt Smith has come back with my photographs which are luckily a success and there are many demands for reprints. I hope the next lot are as good.

NOTE

[1] 'Sakkara Quail' appeared in *The Field* of 19th September 1942.

[2] Italian for Fort or strong point.

9
Battle

May 14th

Rushing around in circles again and ready for anything! We've got our General Grant tanks now. I feel quite serene this time and don't mind anything that may come. We're fighting a war and must not jib at anything. What horrors others are cheerfully undergoing. There is no sacrifice we must not bend to. Nothing is too much to give in this war.

It is very pleasant in the mess tent this evening. What fun we all have together, but perhaps George gets a bit tired of our schoolboy tricks. Last night during a little horseplay round our bivvies before going to bed, George came out in his pyjamas with a large stick! We all keep our tempers remarkably well, I think. Edward is a very good addition to the mess and Dick is very pleasant too. Now I realise why Billy at home admires James so much. 'Auntie', as we call Stephen, is a bit variable in her moods. I think 'she' hates the army more than most and takes a little longer to rise above it!

Flash!

10.40 p.m. Edward and James playing a paper game. Stephen writing out our orders. George drawing caricatures. They are really awfully good but not likenesses in the portrait sense. He has managed to capture a chief point in each of us.

Now we are ready for bed and the morrow. Once again war.

Sunday May 17th

It doesn't seem a bit like Sunday, because we haven't had a service to put us in the right frame of mind so that we feel like no work for the rest of the day! There's a lot of work to do today and too much leeway and haste to make up, I suppose. I enjoy it when there's plenty of work to do, but all the same we are living rather on the edge of a volcano! I really don't mind a bit this time except that I had one sudden moment of absolute misery and hopelessness when I felt I wanted to run away. That is all over now, it only took about a minute anyway. I think we are all pretty confident this time, but none of us like the idea. Who does? We are all sitting quite happily in our mess tent which never fails to find its way up. I have my little old bivvy which I won in the obstacle race at Southdown School in 1933. Wonderful how it has lasted.

We are all drinking a bottle of whisky provided by Edward who is going off to Brigade. We've all been talking about England. Lords, Henley, Eton and Harrow and all the rest of it. What a life we all led then. How about the Germans! It is a pity we have to fight them really, but others have suffered and others will suffer more unless we can clean them up.

But we are ready to show what we can do. What an extraordinary life we are leading. How normal we seem in our mess, we all sit and talk, like undergraduates. Shall we ever have so much fun again or shall we stay in the desert for ever! Talk veers from England to the war and back to Marlborough and those heavenly days. Well, I can't end on a happier note—the Oxford days and Leslie and all the fun.

I think I shall send this diary back to Cairo while there is a chance before I may lose it. I am happier now, having sent a lot of my stuff back to Cairo—I live ready for an emergency and I am emergency minded. I hope I live as myself—and then?

I wonder . . . what . . . will . . . happen . . . to . . . us . . . all.

In leaguer the night before last I dreamed about Mother. Quite a long dream I had. I woke up the next morning and suddenly wondered why. And then it came to me all in a flash. Mother died on May 15th last year. How well I remember it all, and I have the diary where I wrote my impressions among my kit at Abbassia. They were days of Gatwick Airport, Leslie, Joanna, Royal Naval School, Margo and Tilford, tennis and all the rest of it. Father writes about Mother's tombstone. I have left it all to him, and never thought about my loving Mother again. Isn't that rather odd, considering that I owe all, I repeat, all my life and happiness to her?—I do not exactly forget her, for I feel her presence always. I am afraid it is the same with God and my prayers. How often do I forget. Oh! Lord! I must remember! Why do I neglect God except in my hour of need? Bing reads his bible every morning. I carry my Bible everywhere, but do I read it? No! I do not—I will try and I will pray.

May 18th

One of the most lovely music nights I have ever spent. From 10.30 pm, I have been sitting alone in the tent listening to a programme by the BBC theatre orchestra. Lovely songs and tunes that made me feel so sentimental and longing for a definite conclusion of the war. I wrote to Polly and Libby and Leslie as I love these the best. It is strange here on this battlefield where wrecks of many tanks and lorries and bits of what used to be men lie scattered all over the area. The ground is cluttered with shell fragments and pocked with shallow shell holes which make little impression on the sand. But the desert is the same again. It does not change. It is not even eerie. There are no remains of a dead world, no ruins of a great civilisation now ashes, only a few remains of men who fought passing by. Just a few incidents in history which are chronicled and disappear. But not in the hearts of the tortured wounded. Not in the hearts of the bereaved families, not in the make-up of the warring nation which has lost more seeds of a strong future generation. I can stand gazing at the stars, and feel nothing of the horrors of the El Gubi battle. Are there ghosts here, I wonder? No. I should think the dead even would leave this deserted nothingness. What of my thoughts? They are of the future. How shall we fare in the next trial of arms? What will be our fates as individuals? Shall we live or shall we die? Shall we half-live perhaps? Shall we return to England, to Cairo or go to South Africa for six months as Peter Frankau has done? Shall I live to love and who shall I love? These questions go on and on and there is no answer save in time.

I sit by the phone waiting for the word that may possibly come tonight, that will set the ball rolling once more. The 'Move now' that will set us trembling and sweating and trying to be brave and nonchalant. Trying also in our machines of destruction which we are genuinely attached to and treat as our homes and our pets, trying to exterminate the menace to our happiness. Unless we fight to the end, no more of all that we love.

High sounding words! Goodnight all.

May 19th

I must write on a subject that is much on my mind these days when everyone is waiting, waiting, waiting, in the shadow of Death. Isn't it odd how we are living? So very, very strange the way we are living. Never have I experienced such great uncertainty. We are not frightened, nor do we show any signs of apprehension—much. I am sure, though, that the other hearts must sink occasionally when the latest news comes in. It is the moment of beginning that we find hard, but it must come soon. It is better that it should come so as to reach a final conclusion all the sooner. But I have derived much comfort from what I have read today. I have kept Lewis Carroll up in the desert, in spite of my fears that I might lose him. In his preface to *Sylvie and Bruno*, he says, among many reflections on death: 'But, once realise what the true object is in life—that it is not pleasure, not knowledge, not even fame itself, that last infirmity of noble minds, but that it is the development of character, the rising to a higher, nobler, purer standard, the building up of the perfect Man, and then so long as we feel that this is going on, and will (we trust) go on for evermore, death has for us no terror; it is not a shadow but a light, not an end, but a beginning!'

Then there is General Smuts' speech to South African troops—a wonderful lesson from an obviously great man. Perhaps the *Grey Steel* by Armstrong was unfair, but I didn't think much of Smuts. All the speech is good but this bit I will write down:

> You are going to face danger, hardship and sacrifice—perhaps death itself—in all its fierce forms. But through it all you will gather that experience of life and enrichment of character which is more valuable than gold or precious stones. You will become better and stronger men. You will not return the same, as you will bring back memories which you and yours will treasure for life.

7.20 p.m. Certain maps have arrived again! I say again because they were issued earlier [See Dec.29th]. Then they were issued in the moonlight.

8.20 p.m. Came back into the mess after paying out squadron and found everyone much more cheerful, in fact quite hilarious! We all had a very good dinner and then played Consequences and 'Weekend suitcases' and tried our hands at limericks. It was quite amusing and we got a good laugh out of some of the allusions but they weren't all exactly clean! Not nearly so clean as our last game at Giof Ardun. Its odd that we haven't played since.

May 21st

They are now asking for volunteers for the Indian Armoured Corps. I think George got rather a shock when I gave him my name, but I do think it would be a great opportunity to prove one's power of leadership if any. Also to help in the construction of what will be a great force. Look how marvellous the infantry Indians are, and I think they are a fine race and theirs is a great country. I wonder if I shall be able to go. I do hope so. What a chance, too, to see more of the world.

May 22nd

Huh! Colonel says he will only recommend one officer whom he can spare but names are to go up to him. We are on the eve of something, I think. Scheme is cancelled and we are to be ready for anything. Great spate of letter writing tonight, both because of the move and because of the welcome mail that suddenly came after dinner. I've written to Sage and Libby and Lynette. Oh dear! What am I to do! I ready [sic] for war this time. We'll crack them, we really will.

May 23rd

General Lumsden here today. Very very nice and spoke of Pa. I send this to the base with Coles for safe keeping.
Cheerio. The battle is almost on.
Or is it?

[*July 14th: I have found the remains of jottings of the next few days in my little old pocket book. Now I copy them out here as a continuation of May 23rd.*]

May 23rd (continued)

I really was delighted with General Lumsden's visit. He was in the best of form and chatted to everyone very gaily and confidentially! He was particularly nice to me when I gave him a demonstration. He chatted about Pa and said what a good 'Q' officer he was and how hardworking he was. I wonder what he will get in the end, I hope perhaps that South Wales District will be preparation for a Command. His career's far from over yet. Bing knows me (and it is becoming a nickname) as 'Old Ballsteds's son!' I must tell Pa, he would be very amused. I am always introduced as my father's son which makes me

153

very proud. I do hope I can be worthy of him. His advices are well worth following.

Sunday May 24th

We move thirty-three miles in a sandstorm. Rather sad to pack up the mess but we've had a good time and I wound up by writing a mass of letters all round, but principally to Leslie and Libby. Good news from Pa, at last, about his job in Wales. Lots of fishing offers and he's going to live in Lady Herbert's house. Charles Robathan's written that I must not expect myself or Leslie to be the same when I return. I wrote back to say that I was coming to realise that and now lived with an open mind, hoping for the best.

A charming letter from Mrs Lees at Cape Town and Lynette writes again in a delightful fleeting mood. I am hoping for something more from Leslie yet. I am quite happy with my correspondence at the moment. Bing and Co. make great fun of my writings. But they are very different from me in that respect. I never see them writing much. James least of all.

Phyllis Edwards has joined the WAAFs, after deciding to stay out of uniform. I wish I could see her.

Here we are, waiting and waiting for our fates. Looking at it objectively it is nothing really. Men have fought and died for much less, and I must not look at it so gloomily. I am getting better, I think, and hope to face it this time with complete calm. After all, what is our regiment out of the world's armies, and all is over and done in a very short while. Individuals are nothing, and I am worth nothing to my lovely English country unless I am prepared to sacrifice all.

May 26th

I've spent some of the day reading *Jill Somerset* by Alec Waugh. In fact I read the whole book. It was jolly good especially as the day was most boring and hot and windy. It was all about a family growing up and marrying with the Great War in progress. I enjoyed some of the problems presented and the philosophy of Life in the Shadow of Death and War. I'm all right, I think. It has taken a long time to get straightened out in my mind. I wonder what everyone else thinks? I believe they are all very much alike. They all get the same sort of sinking feeling at signs and portents and messages and rumours, etc. We all get over it though. I hope this time that I shall be able to go all out at it. As for humanitarianism—well, that depends on opportunities as they present themselves. Let them come. We can trounce them this time.

May 27th

The battle is on.

9.40. Sitting on my tank ready to move and listening to heavy shelling on the left. I wonder when we shall be in?

[*July 14th: That was the last thing I wrote in my diary in the desert. Now I am sitting in the smoking room of the hospital ship SS Tairea, steaming down the Red Sea, and I will write the ending of my visit to Libya when I was hit in the first engagement and missed thereby the days of battle, chaos and hell when George and Bing, Stephen and James and Dick fought their way back to El Alamein and finally Cairo. Then they came and saw me!*]

In a moment the word came to pull off our sun shields and move off southward. What a relief to be rid of those horrible shields. We took no care of them this time, but ripped them off and drove away leaving them lying on the ground for good.

James was leading and I was on the right of George with Sgts McG. and Savile following well. After a mile we halted and troop leaders all jumped out and ran hastily to George as ordered before. In a moment he gave us the news and dispositions of some of our own unit who were in action and one lot in particular who had been fighting an enemy tank force and were reported just going in to finish them off.

As soon as I could reach my tank we were off again and after another short run the far outskirts of a battle seemed to be before us. Over the air came orders from the colonel for information by recce patrols and we all swept the whole horizon with our glasses. Rather like a row of cats with their backs arched and tails erect. George ordered us to form a line facing right. We did this and sat listening, and watching, and ready to fire. I passed the tin of sweets round and we munched away.

Then—the enemy in sight, four to five thousand yards to our right front. They appeared as a black mass of moving and stationary vehicles. Apparently they were two united columns being joined by some more.

I could see a good distance all round and looked at our brigade set out in battle formation and I could hear a lot of the direction on the wireless.

It reminded me of an olden day battle. Both forces sat facing one another and we waited breathlessly for the opening move.

I saw some Cruisers and Honeys in action in front. They seemed to be having a running fight as I watched the flashes from 2-pounder guns but I couldn't see the opposition through the haze. Over on top of the ridge in front there were three tanks burning. I took a photo hurriedly, but fear they were too far away.

My glasses were glued to the little ridge in front; we feared an anti-tank position and the arrival of some enemy tanks. I felt confident of meeting them in the open this time.

Then the gambit is ours.

We are ordered to advance in line against the left-hand edge of the mass in front. Here we go then, Stephen, James, Joe and I, Charlie Squadron at them again.

It is very hard to see the opposition clearly. I see one of our OP's in front near a wrecked Mark VI. A moment later Tony drove past me to search for any dead or wounded members of the crew. He is out in No Man's Land now, climbing around this tank with its gun pointing aimlessly skyward. He does not bring any more away, so perhaps they are all safely clear. Then the gunner OP tank runs round to our flank and we advance a moment later.

Targets are hard to pick out in front but I order Swire to fire on several black shapes and the smoke of shell bursting obscures them. Cannot see if any damage done.

No fire returned yet and George orders us to close the range and make for a point in the right hand end of the enemy's mass. The mirage is clear now and I can see what to shoot at and get Swire on to some guns and lorries. Jerry opens up on us now and then anti-tank shells whip past us with sharp cracks. They keep so low on the ground that their flight can be seen by the swirl of sand just below the projectile. Very uncomfortable feeling that one may come inside at anytime. A very satisfying target in front of us. What a change from range practices. Once more we are at the real thing, rather like an important football match after weeks of practice games. No tank stops yet. I glance along the line on either side but all is well. I give a cheer on the internal communication set, which probably blasted Swire's and Wilsons's ears, when I see one of his shots blow up a full petrol lorry. Then horror! We have four rounds of HE left and still not on top of the enemy. I report this to George on the wireless and get the answer that we are all in the same boat.

All right! Don't fire any more, Swire, try your Browning gun Allcard, we are in range now and we may be able to keep the anti-tank gunners on the hop. Gun firing well and the line rolling slowly on to the Jerry line. Then—a terrific crash and a cloud of smoke inside the tank and driver Wilson reels sideways, An anti-tank shell has come through the front. We are stopped now and without another thought I nipped out of the top and thought of getting Wilson out and away while the going was good. Loader Mounsey came out through the side door, then a shell landed and made a nasty mess of him. Poor chap lay screaming on the ground, with his legs almost in ribbons. I could do nothing. I turned for morphia to Bradley who was out behind the tank but that was the last thing I did.

I felt a great blow on the face and fell on the ground unable to see or do anything but wave a hand feebly in the air. There was no pain but I felt just helpless. A few minutes later a tank drove up alongside me as I could hear and I felt someone picking me up. I did what I could to assist them getting me on to the back of a tank; one foot hurt very much and I could just see with the one eye the end of my left boot removed and a gory mess there instead. The pain became too much for me then. I could feel some of the time what was happening to me but I knew nothing of the people around. I remember asking to be taken to the ambulance. It was comforting to have seen the good old Doc chugging along with RHQ in his scout car, followed by his ambulance. All I wanted then was to keep still but it could not be so.

For hours and hours the ghastly bumping went on. I could see nothing, but by feeling about me I managed to raise my head off the blanket by pulling up on my arms. I remember trying to keep quiet but I could not. At last we reached help and doctors once again. I felt I was in a tent. I heard South African voices and the voice of my own gunner—then on the road again. I had no conception of pain before this. It cannot be described. If only I could keep still. If only I could keep still.

A drink from a water bottle tasted better than any other drink I have ever had. We stopped again and I was told I was at Mersa Matruh. I heard two voices I recognised. The padre whom I had met before when going on leave, and the other was a squadron leader from

157

another regiment whom I had often met. Luckily he was not very bad. It was still black all round me. Then anaesthetics. I felt myself in an ambulance again driving to the landing ground. I just remembered the country I had been over before when we just arrived, but couldn't do much thinking. What a smooth journey that air flight to Cairo was. Then hospital and quiet. For some days I felt I just couldn't live a moment longer. I couldn't sleep or eat but I could drink and drink. My first meal was ice cream. I couldn't see it and could hardly believe it. I remember saying to the nurse, 'I'll pretend I'm having dinner at Shepheard's', and she laughed.

I will say no more of hospital details. That I am now Home and well again is a great tribute to the Medical Corps. No one could have worked harder or with greater understanding. From the moment I became normal I had the greatest faith in those who were looking after my troubles. They were all so very kind. From the colonel and matron downwards. Imagine my delight to be given four presents on my birthday by the matron. What a strange coincidence that the name of the sister in charge of my ward is well known in Oxford. And whose voice should I first hear when I arrived and could not see, but that of Joe Fison the late curate of St Aldate's! Who should come to see me but three old members of my college!

When at length I could read with my one remaining eye, I received the most wonderful letters from home and especially from my Father. What a help they were, and how happy I was when visitors came along. Among the visitors was the husband of a lady I met in Cape Town. I could give him first-hand news of his family.

Then who should turn up but Joe, who had been wounded the same hour as myself? A shell entered and burst inside his tank. In spite of leg wounds he stayed in the fire amid exploding ammunition to try and extricate two other members of his crew, but they were dead, and he had to give it up. But that was not the end. There were three ambulances together, with Joe and I in one, but nobody to guide us to the nearest Main Dressing Station. In one ambulance which contained Gordon, there were nine men piled in it when it should have only contained four. The German doctor had been working with our own when we had captured the position and we carried some of his men too. To guide us to help, Joe insisted on being pulled out of the back of the ambulance, and propped up in the front with morphia and a compass. And so we had driven until he was exhausted. Then by luck someone else took on. He managed to steer us round two German leaguers without attracting their attention. They were the advance units which had penetrated our lines. We had been bumping, bumping all night, travelling roughly north-east. At dawn we hit the main Tobruk-Bardia road and by great luck found a South African Casualty Clearing Station. From there I was passed to Mersa Matruh and some went to Tobruk. Five men died on that first journey. By luck I was not one of them. I needed help very quickly and to Joe I owe my life. I could only thank him and give him my binoculars which are so essential to the desert. Joe was going back to the regiment, but I was not. [Alas, dear Joe died of wounds two years later fighting with the French Resistance.].

10
Return to UK

Miraculously I soon became a 'walking wounded'. I was fitted with my first glass eye satisfactorily, and I didn't lose it down the plug-hole as another officer did his. It was early July 1942. None of us knew what was going on outside in the way of the Great Flap. Rommel was about to enter Egypt. There was a great burning of documents, and evacuation plans of which we hospital patients were to become part.

Just before I left the hospital, who should turn up but George, Stephen and James and the colonel himself. I was overjoyed at seeing them but I hated the thought of leaving them. They seemed part of my life. I listened to the story of their fights in the retreat to El Alamein and then watched them regretfully as they made their way back to their truck and off to the desert once more.

When the time came to move us I remember being put back on to a stretcher while being dressed in uniform and railed smartly to Port Said. As I was being carried along the quay I saw my baggage, still amazingly intact, going past me on a barrow. It's not fair to say that RAMC stands for Rob All My Comrades: but I had lost my silver flask out of my blood-stained haversack, which I still use. Valuing my possessions I got off the stretcher and saw that my tin trunks and other impedimenta were actually loaded on board. From that moment I never went back to bed for more than very short periods. I felt it was a miracle, I could only thank God and the medical profession. One thing I was able to do was to organise a sort of ship's radio station; and act as a disc jockey and play requests from chaps who were bedridden or at any rate worse off than I was. The chaps who were specially worse off in the prevailing circumstances were those with limbs or trunk or neck in plaster of Paris. At least twice while steaming down the Red Sea the heat and stink and irritation of their skins built up to such an unbearable level that the ship was turned round and sailed against the wind to get some air down below to ease the poor chaps' misery. My diary, or more strictly pocket book, for 1942 doesn't tell me much over this period, but I do seem to have been able to go ashore at Mombasa on July 26th and visit Padre Cribb at the Seamen's Mission, and eat and drink at Shanzu, 'Dad's Place!', and to execute a few commissions for fellow passengers: cigarettes, plain chocolate, etc.

My pocket books over these years contain dreadful stories which I would be ashamed to reproduce, but one or two still make me laugh, as does the odd note. For instance some wag spotted the fact that if you go through the *Manual for the Handling of Captive Balloons*, and substitute the word 'wench' for 'winch' the results are hilarious. I find in my little books dates or references to activities (shopping lists, etc.) which allow me to be pretty accurate on chronology. And from entries throughout I can build up lists of books and pieces of music or tunes to which I am now glad to be able to refer. More important are the names of friends. How vital friends are. Friends plus health equals happiness: even without health they equal happiness.

By August 10th we docked in Durban, and we were sent up to Pietermaritzburg (Sleepy Hollow) by train, to Oribi Military Hospital. Natal is very beautiful and the views alone did wonders for our morale and health. When I was settled into a bed in a ward, the officer in the next bed said: 'Oh, Halsted? We had a chap of that name in the 63rd—poor devil, I'm afraid he's had it. Any relation?' I quietly replied: 'That was me'. It took some time to convince him: but that made me realise how terribly lucky I had been, and I thanked God again.

Then I set about enjoying the town of Pietermaritzburg, which was handed me on a plate by several kind residents. There was one in particular, Josephine Thorpe, who set about making my life marvellous. Today she does fine work in the Durban Institute of Race Relations.

When José learned that I was in the middle of my history course at Oxford she arranged for me to study in the Natal University College whenever I felt like it. Here I did go sometimes, but of course in a desultory fashion. I felt at home again though, using the library. José took me up to the magnificent Howick Falls through the Valley of a Thousand Hills, and to the famous public school Michaelhouse. What a wonderful land to be educated in. My idyll came to end about September 1st when the next batch for repatriation were moved down to Durban again. Here I was lucky to be able to meet several close members of my family whom I had long hoped to see. They were the descendants of my great-uncle Charles who went out from Sussex in the Boer War with Kitchener's Fighting Scouts (the Knife, Fork and Spoons).

We then embarked on the SS *Orion* which had a good turn of speed, about 14 knots, and was allowed to make the voyage unescorted. Well, we made it. My diary contains notes of deck games and other entertainments such as housie housie, deck quoits, competitions and a band. The days passed easily. A fellow passenger was Roy Farran, the author of *Winged Dagger** and a very brave cool calculating officer of the SAS whose exploits were well known to us. We were nervous of him as he was pretty aloof, though of course we admired his courage and capability. It must have been Roy's example which made me go in for some unarmed combat lessons. But I gave them up after my instructor had me over his head splat on to the deck. I could do with less risk just then.

We docked at Southampton and were taken off to Horton Emergency Hospital near Epsom, and firmly put to bed to be sorted out. I was nearly put straight down for psychiatric treatment because when a young doctor in a white coat and a stethoscope came in to deal with our batch, I cried out 'Come hither Puck!' The effect was fun. The doctor was J.P. Hopewell who had been Puck to my Oberon in the Bradfield College production in the Greek Theatre in 1938. He is a Harley Street man today.

In fact, and this is another of the wonderful things that have kept happening to me, I was sent to the Military Hospital for Head Injuries, which was of all places in the requisitioned Ladies' college, St Hugh's, Oxford. I had come up to my beloved Oxford for the second time.

St. Hugh's is an admirable brick-built institution of the 1920's period, and was a very comfortable hospital inside. I had never penetrated its portals while an undergraduate though I had admired several inmates. There still remained much of a college atmosphere I now felt, rather than that of a hospital. I received marvellously skilled treatment from Brigadier Hugh Cairns and Major Jack Angell-James from Bristol, of later Ear, Nose and Throat fame. Here is their final report on me:

REPORT ON LIEUTENANT J.M.G. HALSTED

This officer received a shell wound on May 27th 1942, with the following injuries:

1. Destruction of the right eye

*Reissued in paperback, Grafton, 1988.

2. Wound of the left side of the nose, with injury to the left fronto-nasal duct.

3. Penetrating FB in right temporal lobe. this was not large, and the examination of the central nervous system showed no neurological signs resulting from it. (See attached x-ray report.)

4. Wound of left foot.

5. He was also unconscious for the great part of the first 24 hours after injury.

He received the following treatment:

1. Amputation of 2 ½ toes of the left foot.

2. Evisceration of the right eye and subsequent fitting with an artificial acrylic eye.

3. Puncture of removal of pus from right antrum, followed by opening of the antrum through the canine fossa and removal of numerous polypi. A wide opening was made into the nose beneath the inferior turbinate bone, and the cavity was packed with proflavine and sulphanilamide gauze.

4. Plastic repair of the left fronto-nasal duct.

5. The above plastic repair could not be performed until his septic tonsils were removed.

6. Treatment of facial acne by penicillin ointment.*

The results of this treatment were satisfactory, and the officer returned to duty Category B in May 1943.

S/d Hugh Cairns
Brigadier
Consultant Neurosurgeon.

Military Hospital (Head Injuries),
St. Hugh's College, Oxford.
15 May, 1943.

I was thankful for what was done for me, having had a shell fragment through the back of my nose just missing my left eye but cutting my right optic nerve, and breaking up into small fragments which remain in the back of my right eye socket and skull. (Maxwell Lyon eviscerated the dead eye.) I had also lost two-and-a-half toes of my left foot, but the surgeon in Cairo mercifully (who was he?) was able to keep half of my

*One of the first uses of penicillin ointment by Sir Alexander Fleming, I was told.

big toe; and the whole foot healed up so well that I have never noticed the loss over nearly fifty years. I wish I could thank him. I have been able to march anywhere, and to enjoy Scottish and Highland dancing round the world for thirty years while in the British Council.*

The last months of 1942 became an idyllic interlude for me, even though my life was based on St Hugh's Military Hospital and bearing in mind all the time that others were fighting the war overseas or being bombed at home. My first very cheering visitor was my father, then General Officer Commanding South Wales District, with headquarters at Abergavenny, Monmouthshire. He said I looked a bit battered. Papa himself, as I more or less gathered from him, had been pushed out of the way to Wales by powerful persons whom his uncompromising rock-solid honesty had upset. But he made the best of it, and there were rewards, thanks to the great kindness of Lady Herbert with whom he was billetted at Coldbrook. She became a very sympathetic friend to both of us. Papa was allowed to fish to his heart's content on the Usk at Llanover, which he did until he died: and he had a delightful Staff including Major, later the famous actor, Andrew Cruikshank, to whose younger daughter Harriet he became godfather. He also had some fine shooting, thanks to Colonel Godfrey Llewellyn of Tredilion Park. I was a very happy frequent visitor, especially as the colonel had a delightful daughter, Wenks, who was so good to me. Papa said his job was an easy one. He certainly was a success and very popular. Before he left to become (at last!) Vice-Quartermaster-General at the War Office, which he said was *not* easy, he had a medal 'struck' which he called the South Wales District Medal. This was awarded to persons who would never be eligible for an official medal, such as ladies who worked long hours in the staff canteens. Papa's Staff Colonel Ash-Moody secretly got hold of another of those medals and it was awarded to Papa, with these words on the reverse: 'We shall not see his like again.' Heart-warming for us both.

Soon I was fit enough to take up with old friends again, and to make many new ones. I have nearly all the names and addresses of the time in my diaries. If any of them read this I'd love to be in touch again. Those I have managed to meet have proved so rewarding. For instance, while at St Hugh's I discovered that the beautiful Blenheim Palace and Park at Woodstock had been commandeered by MI5: and that about the place during the day, or billeted in Keble College (which had become

*See the RSCDS *Journal*, October 1987: 'Reeling round the world'.

a reverse of St Hugh's), was a band of attractive, intelligent female personnel. Somehow I obtained a pass to at least the Park, and through friends based on Home Park Farm I was given a very happy time which undoubtedly contributed to the healing of my body. It was my heart which was pierced by the fabled dart. A visit I made a little further afield was to my old school, Bradfield College, where I was welcomed by the Headmaster, Colonel J.D. Hills, MC, MA, and his very sweet wife Lady Rosemary. I thought John Hills was a splendid chap, but I couldn't guess then how happy the outcome of my visit would be.

From Oxford I had access to another aspect of Britain at war: another community and an inspiring one—the RAF off-duty. As I whirled round the countryside (how, I cannot recall) with one delightful female companion or another, we would meet fighter or bomber pilots relaxing in various bars or hostelries. Their audacity on the ground sometimes left me gasping and feeling a naive dimwit, which I suppose I was. At least I learned how to relax, but not how to handle popsies! I admired these 'Brylcreem Boys', as one called them to one's peril. (What a heaven-sent piece of free advertising that was for the firm).

I began to understand how they became attuned to fighting in the sky and on their own. I could not have managed either. A mutual favourite haunt was The Bear at Woodstock, which was admirably and tolerantly run. We heard a number of encounters re-fought, or as the chaps would say 'lines shot'. I would have a few strips torn off me in return for being a 'skulking malingering brown job' etc., etc.

I didn't mind a bit. Their spirit pervaded Oxfordshire and the whole British population. Their small temporary airfields gave new status and new life to many a beautiful limestone village.

One little interlude was my temporary transfer for some specialist treatment or other to the Lutyens home of Lord and Lady Jersey. The palatial house was cushy for us patients. St. Hugh's was cosy, but Middleton was a dream. The bathrooms had gold-plated taps, and the shower cubicles had one-way mirror sides, looking outwards.

A more significant and poignant transfer was to the Plastic Surgery Unit at the Victoria Cottage Hospital, East Grinstead, headed by the famous (later Sir) Archibald Macindoe. One of his staff repaired the hole of the shell splinter entry-wound at the top left inside corner of my nose. The wound scar was soon almost invisible: marvellous. But how close a shave that was to losing my left eye as well as my right—a fraction of an inch . . . Amazing work was done at East Grinstead on the very badly burned air crew and others. I saw some ghastly-looking sights when men had flaps of skin growing on their faces of extensions of good skin or from other parts of their bodies. I don't blame the poor chaps being very sensitive about being seen by relatives and others, particularly girl friends. Richard Hillary, the RAF fighter pilot author of the famous book *The Last Enemy* was a patient at East Grinstead for a long time as he graphically described. I know how grateful he really was, but I could never understand the brutal way he sometimes treated his nurses. But then I was never in such an agonising state. I admired his courage, and I thought the girls were saints. I was very sad that Hillary, like Guy Gibson, the Dambuster, insisted on going back to active flying, and was killed. So was Guy Gibson. What a shame after such bravery and suffering. Strangely, at the time of writing this (April 1988) a book has just come out called *Mary and Richard*, by Michael Burn.* Mary was Richard Hillary's lover, though twenty years older than him. She married Michael Burn four years after Richard's death: and Michael Burn has selflessly arranged for the publication of a packet of his late wife's love letters he found among her effects fourteen years ago. They are very moving. *Mary:* 'You have left me rich in the memory of fulfilment of love.' *Richard:* 'It's only with you all the anger goes and I'm at peace.'

Back in St Hugh's a remarkable act of kindness gave me a reward of vital importance to my post-war career. I had come up to Oxford again, so to speak, still as an undergraduate on the books of St Edmund Hall. Teddy Hall was a small, and always will be an intimate, friendly college. I knew the Vice-Principal, the Reverend J.N.D. Kelly, DD, very well, and he knew of my situation. When it became clear that my brain at least was unimpaired by the efforts of the Afrika Korps, John Kelly took up the task of becoming my tutor in the field of Political Science. He regularly came and sat by my bed for tutorial talks. I could hardly believe it when one day I set off on foot from St Hugh's in my uniform, with my gown worn over it, to the Examinations Schools in the High to sit an examination. Later I received a formal letter from the Vice-Principal informing me that by virtue of the work done to date I had been awarded a War Degree. Our splendid Principal, A.B. Emden, the 'Abe' of course, wrote to me informally as follows: 'Congratulations on being the first undergraduate to my knowledge to have been awarded a degree by the Hebdomadal Council without doing any work for it.'

*Published by André Deutsch, 1988.

But I had got it! And Papa was pleased at the news. He stumped up the Masters degree fee without a murmur. Once again life had been kind to me.

Life's next contribution arrived at St Hugh's on a stretcher, bringing, though I couldn't know it at the time, further permanent good fortune. The bearer, or rather the borne, was Major John de G. Dill, son of the future Field-Marshal. I had never met John before but I had heard a lot about him from Papa and envied him. General Dill was GOC Palestine in the late thirties during the Arab-Israeli hostilities. Papa, had gone out to command the 1st Battalion the Loyal Regiment (in which there was the remarkable Major, later Field-Marshal, Templer). But General Dill, who knew of Papa's administrative abilities from Staff College days, took him on to his staff. John Dill, who was at Oxford in those years, was able to go out to Palestine in the vacations and have quite an exciting time: but I was too young to be allowed to go.

John's wife Heather was a FANY, and she was able to visit him sometimes, so I got to know them both. As a result I was honoured by being asked to be godfather to their first-born, a daughter, Rosanne. As Rosanne grew up she became a delightful woman, a caring, loving and entertaining friend. The touching gesture of John and Heather's has given me years of pleasure to this very day. Now came another almost incredible, certainly unforgettable, stroke of fortune. My turn had come to serve under Field-Marshal Sir John Dill.

Part Three

British Army Staff
Washington DC, USA
June 1943 – June 1944

11

'Gaberdine Swine'

Field-Marshal Sir John Dill headed a relatively unpublicised branch of the army, the British Army Staff/British Supply Mission, Washington DC. Its function, important if unglamorous, was to administer our side of Lend-Lease, which was to obtain from America all the variety of stores asked for by the British Government. Every Allied government had its own Supply Mission, and like ours had its variety of sections or directorates, such as Raw Materials, Food, Weapons and Equipment. Our AFV (Armoured Fighting Vehicle) Supply Directorate III was at this time headed by an old friend of Papa's, Major-General Douglas H. Pratt, its task to procure various types of AFV's for the different theatres of war. There was a technical staff, both civilian and military, with long experience in tank design, and also officers of various ranks with up-to-date battle experience sent over for shorter or longer periods.

It so happened that at the very moment when St Hugh's medical board passed me out of hospital Grade B, Douglas Pratt needed a GSO III (General Staff Officer, Grade 3, a captain) with tank fighting experience who could be spared from the front to advise on tank design from the point of view of the crew: what the Americans call 'the user angle', a very sensible provision indeed in the manufacturing of almost any product. I got the job. So straight up to London, back to Huntsman's in Savile Row for a beautifully cut gaberdine uniform, to become another 'gaberdine swine', as the desert troops unkindly called the Cairo 'base-wallahs'. I seem to have managed the odd dinner-dance in Oxford or London: but I spent my days dashing about between the War Office, outer London and various specialist centres such as the School of Tank Technology, Chobham.

I learned that I was to travel out in the company of, and as an unofficial ADC to, Major-General A.H. (Alec) Gatehouse, DSO, MC. He had been a tank officer in World War I and Commander of 10th Armoured Division at Alamein:* a tremendous chap to whom I became

171

devoted. So did the ladies—instantly. He was ruggedly handsome with wavy grey hair and a bushy white moustache. The ladies fell about. He picked them up. He wore a Royal Tank Regiment beret, and told me to wear one also, which I did, with a gold-embroidered Bays badge. This headgear was necessary in order to make us easily recognisable by the American public as British. We were briefed that because of the size of America and its distance from the war it was necessary for our small supply force to 'wave the flag' as best we could, and to travel widely to show that Britain was in the war too. We were also told that it was necessary to convince Americans that our presence in the USA was not a waste of their money. On our journeys and on meeting counterparts or friends, both military and civil, we should talk positively, and one might say, more boastfully than a normal reticent Englishman would respond when asked about his part in the war.

From early June 1943 I was on stand-by. On the 8th as usual I rang the War office: on the 9th I entrained for Glasgow. Departure was from Gourock again but what a contrast to the troopship *Empire Pride* in the convoy of September 1941. I was in a dream, but it was real. There was a launch waiting to take General Gatehouse and Captain Halsted (with the general's golfclubs) out to the *Queen Mary*, to belt across the Atlantic unescorted for five days. We had four thousand German prisoners of war down below. Not my responsibility, luckily, but they gave us no trouble. The few men and women fellow passengers with interesting special jobs ahead seemed lost in the vast spaces. We had two cinema shows: *Waterloo Bridge* and *The Great Dictator*. Suddenly the Statue of Liberty glowed green and gold in the sunlight as we slid past the *Normandie* lying on her side. She had gone on fire and toppled over with the weight of water. But she was soon made ready for service as an aircraft carrier.

Charming Red Cross ladies met us and we were driven to our respective hotels: the general to the Ritz-Carlton and I to the less expensive Hotel Benedick. Wandering up Fifth Avenue in the early evening, I was amazed at the high standard of window dressing in the famous stores such as Lord and Taylor, Bonwit Teller, Peck & Peck, compared with our Selfridges and Liberty, even in peacetime. I was told there was a dim-out, but I couldn't believe it after blacked-out London, until I peered up and made out the vague shapes of many extinguished illuminated signs. Air attack was not feared but Allied ships quite far

*See B. Horrocks, *A Full Life*, Collins 1960, P.118.

out at sea had been sharply silhouetted at night in the glow of peacetime lighting, making them easier targets for U-boats beyond.

My shipmates were all for a variety show that night but I was able to telephone Lady Herbert's nephew Arthur Gammell, a lawyer on Broad Street. As a result I made my first subway journey. I was struck by the simple payment system—a nickel into a turnstile post. But I had to get from uptown to downtown New York. A kindly traveller came to my aid. An Express to 14th Street, and the rest was easy—until I lit my pipe. Horror and gesticulation all round, and a very subdued British officer! Arthur Gammell, a Bostonian was certainly the funniest man I have ever met. He wore a hat turned up all the way round and spoke in a sing-song voice through clenched teeth and without a smile. He didn't need to crack jokes. He rang the bell for his secretary and (typically of all executives) asked her what I should do until he was free for dinner. She advised the RCA Building and the Rockefeller Centre: and piloted me to the right subway line. It was 5 p.m. and rush-hour. The impatient crowd was trying to go faster than the trains. I became wedged tightly in the corner of a car and could hardly breathe. I managed to squeak out that I needed Grand Central Station and a gruff but kindly soul jerked his head at the right stop and out I scrambled. In the Rockefeller Centre the complexity of shops, offices and eating places made me think that one could live a whole life inside without ever coming out. No Rockettes for me, alas.

Arthur Gammell took me to dinner at the 'very exclusive' Racquet Club. After dinner he left me with three 'well-known' club members: a stock-broker, a racing man and the director of a drinks firm. They plied me with questions and brandy and would not let me go. Then the brandy began to have more effect on my hosts than on me; and I managed to extricate myself without them noticing. This American campaign was going to be a tough one, I thought. Indeed it was to land me back in hospital in England after a year.

I kept a diary going because I hate to be unable to recall facts: the most important being the names of so many people who have been good to me over the years. In America it was astonishing and heart-warming how many hard-pressed men and women in wartime jobs bothered with me at all. Some were friends of friends, such as Michael and Esther Wright. Michael was Councillor at the British Embassy. They had previously been posted in Egypt and Esther had come to see me in hospital in Cairo. My arrival in Washington DC went like this: '*June 17th*: Lovely parlour rail to Washington DC. Passed Baldwin loco factory (they made

173

tanks). Met by Major Toby Farnell-Watson (RTR) and Freddy Fisher (Royals). Rushing round office after reaching my hotel. Cups of tea. Dinner, General and Mrs Pratt. Terrific talks. Ursula (girl friend at home and friend of Wrights). Storms.'

Nowhere else in the world could I have lived days and nights in such a whirl, in such excitement, in such a contrast to the desert I had left a year before. I never got into the office properly for over a fortnight, but then luckily for me, and for them, mine was more of an outside job. I began with three days getting administered, dealing with baggage, bank, signing the Embassy book etc., and dashing round Washington, eating and drinking at various hotels and bars, meeting the most hospitable people almost hourly, and accepting their invitations. All the way along keeping an eye out for girls. I only had one eye but no problem. 'People curious of my badges of rank.' 'Beret causes some excitement.' I hadn't needed any money in the desert, but now I realised that I was going to need all my pay, and the daily allowance of $8, which I thought magnificent. But of course it was minute. I was never broke, but I could never repay a fraction of the hospitality I received throughout the country.

It was my first experience of an office. We operated from a small house on 19th and K streets, and I soon had digs nearby at 19th and N. Our generals, Pratt and Gatehouse, set the spirit, and created a cheerful, informal, hard-working atmosphere out of a mixed bunch of English, Canadian and American civilian staff with British service and civilian executives. Our American ladies managed to survive their bosses, and the language and customs gaps were soon bridged. They only once complained strongly, when we couldn't stand the heat of the new phenomenon, air-conditioning, and opened all the office windows. A fur coat protest followed. One American secretary in another mission complained to the papers that her war effort was only making tea for British officers. She didn't realise how important that was. I had a real treasure of an assistant in a charming English girl, Cecilia Rogers, calm and wise; and a very funny American girl secretary, Mary Lee Chase from Vermont, both older than I was. The *New Yorker* of 21st August 1943 reported that an American secretary, when asked to call a certain British major, had received the reply from his office that he had gone to the UK.' 'Oh,' she said in a hushed tone, and turning to her boss, said, in a voice throbbing with womanly sympathy, 'He's dead.'

The supply officers worked very hard and, and in emergencies, long hours, tough in the summer with Washington's damp tropical heat. All our requirements began in our Ministry of Supply in UK, who first tried to obtain the items through Home or Dominion sources. Failing this they went through the United States Munitions Assignments Committee who first had to see: 1) How urgent was the operational need; 2) How was the state of US production and supply of the item; 3) How much did the US Army require; 4) How much did other allies require. A fairly cumbersome but logical process. There was remarkably little US/UK friction. There were battles over items in critical supply, but I watched these overcome swiftly and quietly.

The highlights of the work were the processing of interim demands in the form of urgent cables from a theatre of war. The US MAC would deal with these as spot requisitions or direct cash purchases from the British dollar fund. On getting the items, our Ordnance Branch in the States would work with the US Ordnance or the manufacturers, and make arrangements for the packing, marking, moving to port and shipping, or air-freighting if small. The record time between the receipt of a demand and the delivery to a theatre stood at three days. The most notable success was the combined US and UK Ordnance staffs assembling and dispatching the first load of Sherman tanks given readily by President Roosevelt to Winston Churchill for the Battle of Alamein; and managing to repeat the delivery still in time when the first shipload had been sunk *en route*.

Of the cavalry, Humphrey Sykes, IXth Lancers, a charmer, was a very hard desk worker and had few diversionary compensations. But Freddy Fisher and John Turnbull (Capt., MC, XIth Hussars) and I were swanners, as was General Gatehouse—in the sense that he was sportingly understanding and co-operative in following to the letter the policy that the few British officers in the USA should be encouraged to travel far and wide. Sometimes John and I were allowed to travel long distances on what in normal circumstances might have been called flimsy excuses.

Before I got settled at my desk I was off to Detroit with the General to meet our senior tank development officers, Brigadier Ross, and Colonels Berkeley-Miller and Smith. They were all very good value. We had a large Ordnance contingent in Detroit. Here tanks were made for us by Ford, Cadillac and General Motors; and certain series had to have (for a period at least) 118 modifications on those going to the British army. By day we were out at the proving ground at Flint, testing armoured cars and tanks as fighting vehicles. To mount up we were given white overalls and wooden steps, to our great but concealed amusement! There was royal accommodation at the Statler Hotel, and one evening a dinner at the Detroit Club. I appear to have been asked what sort of girl I wanted, and according to Freddy Fisher, replied: 'More fun than the one last night.'

We were very impressed with the Sherman tank which, after the Stuarts we had had was a dream of a vehicle almost beyond our imagination, with a good weight of armour and a 360 degree turning turret with a 75mm gun. In fact it had taken the American foundry industry several years before they could cast a tank turret capable of accommodating even this size of gun. I heard later that despite the technical advances and the speed-up of the American automotive industry which could have produced a better tank in time, the Joint Chiefs of Staff decided to invade Europe with the Sherman. Later models were required to take even a 17-pounder gun: a bit of a difference from our 2-pounder!

My morale went up when Brigadier Ross produced a letter for me from Ursula at home; and the best day was in the company of the Davidson family of General Motors, first at the Milford proving ground, then at their beautiful home at Grosse Point. I was now beginning to feel the strain of being in the public eye by day and part of each night, meeting so many people, executives, engineers and secretaries. But I was catching on as to my PR role, quite new to me. I sat in on the Ditzler paint plant dispute, met workers from Continental Motors and viewed the city's housing scheme. I ended up with a police captain and his detachment after a race riot which did not touch us, and heard their views on the problem.

I suddenly learned in Detroit that I was to go on to Fort Knox, Kentucky, with Colonel Tony Pepys of the Royals, as part of a team of observers of American armoured force training at their centre there. There was a muddle over our plane so we had to go by train, but a Major Fonda met us at Louisville from thirty miles away, with a shrug and a grin. The Fort Knox set-up was very impressive and the accommodation of a high standard in beautifully laid out grounds in what looked like English countryside—and, rare they said, English summer weather. I could cope with very many 'kind and courteous' officers, 'laborious hand-shakes and effusive greetings'. But conversation was sometimes a bit difficult. However, I soon had a British supporter—and no one could have been more welcome. It was Major McGill, RAMC, our Bays doctor who had attended me in the desert! So there was a medical 'user angle' too. Avoiding an

Enlisted-men's Dance, we went to a film and then out into a lovely
night: 'stars, frogs and crickets.'

The next three days of training were realistic, with live bullets
in some schemes and a 'German' platoon.

Back in Washington DC., Independence Sunday, 4th July, gave me
new friends and an undying memory. I went to St John's Presbyterian
Church (known as the President's church) where the Revd John McGee
was the minister. He and his English wife had been missionaries in
China. They invited me to iced coffee afterwards, had me to lunch
and offered me a room at a very reasonable rent. What kindness! The
eldest of their three sons, John, had been educated in England, and had
won the Rugby School poetry prize at the age of sixteen. He went on to
Yale with a scholarship: but the war decided him to join the RCAF. In
September 1941 he flew a Spitfire from Digby in Lincolnshire, where
he wrote the now world-famous poem:

HIGH FLIGHT

Oh! I have slipped the surly bonds of earth
And danced the skies
  on laughter-silvered wings;
Sunward I've climbed,
  and joined the tumbling mirth
of sun-split clouds,
  and done a hundred things
You have not dreamed of
  wheeled and soared and swung
High in the sunlit silence,
  Hov'ring there,
I've chased the shouting wind along,
  and flung
My eager craft through
  footless halls of air.
Up, up the long delirious burning blue
I've topped the windswept heights
  with easy grace,
Where never lark,
  or even eagle flew
And, while with silent, lifting mind
  I've trod
The high untrespassed sanctity of space,
Put out my hand and touched the face of God.

The next day was my birthday and my first day in the office. It
was terribly hot and humid and I had to change my shirt at lunch

time. When I got home I had no mail and no company, and despaired of a party. But I just went out round the main hotels until I found one! I wrote: 'Learning American ways of necking, etc. Good band with good old tunes.' This wasn't an unusual activity of British army staff off duty. It was well worth wandering from hotel to hotel. One of the very best evenings was at the Mayflower, when our presence caused an impromptu get-together at the piano with Groucho Marx and Lucille Ball. I love Groucho still.

There were very nice British service girls on our staffs whom we all appreciated, including the home-from-home atmosphere they exuded. But in time I had the companionship of three specially delightful American girls to whom I remain grateful and whom I do not forget: Laura Beatty, Rosemary Baldwin and Janie Phillips. There was no mucking about with them.

Back to work: to that office of offices, the giant Pentagon building across the Potomac river in Arlington, Virginia. It was built for the war and housed 30,000 staff. I would nip across on business whenever I could. There was Janie Phillips, a sixty-cent lunch, a barber, and a free US Army dental clinic, part of Lend-Lease. So was the famous Walter Reed Hospital back in the city. Here I would go occasionally, with full confidence, to have my wounds looked at.

Life in Washington became wholly enjoyable. Pleasant digs in the good company of several other officers; drug store breakfasts and sometimes suppers. We learned what to ask for, and how to ask for it: 'Minced ham on whole wheat toasted.' Not: 'Well, um, yes a couple of pieces of toast.' 'Oh, honey or jam will do.' 'Ah, have you some er. . .' That brought the sharp response: 'Why don't you say what you mean?' New British arrivals were easy to spot. They wanted ice-cream with all meals; but their 'Ah, bring me an ice', would be met by a blank stare. I got tired of having to eat vegetables off separate dishes, but was told it was bad manners to transfer them to my meat plate. I enjoyed all dessert pies, especially 'à la mode', except pumpkin pie. Ugh! But I didn't dare refuse it on Thanksgiving Day. We got tired of gaseous American canned beer, but we did find a 'Musty Ale' at Harvey's Sea Food Restaurant. The Americans are artists at seafood. We missed puddings, and like Shackleton's men at the South Pole we dreamed of suet pudding and treacle. But the American ice-cold milk drinking habit was very acceptable. American army mess 'dinner' at 5.30 p.m. was not.

One unvarying bright spot throughout my tour was the efficiency of the Bell Telephone Company. I 'called up' places from the office anywhere within a six-thousand-mile radius of Washington without a moment's delay and with consistent clarity. What was important to me was I could always telephone privately within a few minutes of wherever I was, from many a bar or drug-store, without any of the hassle, dirt, draught, smell or risk of infection which the use of one of our British call-boxes may entail, if it has not been vandalised. I often spoke by telephone to Mr Del'Agnesi, manager of the Waldorf-Astoria in New York. The General would buzz me on the intercom: 'Michael?' 'Sir?' 'Book me into Waldorf-Astoria please, this Saturday.' 'Right, Sir'. 'Mary Lee, please . . .' 'Ah, good morning Mr. Del' Agnesi. Yes, for General Gatehouse. Yes the suite again please.' A change from Burgh-el-Arab! My General had a way with him that I much admired, apart from his patience and understanding. There was a story that, soon after his arrival, he bought himself a blue Cadillac, and found he had used the whole of his special allowance, not just the settling-in sum. The Treasury was not pleased. I was also pretty sure that for a time he knew the glamorous Latin-American starlet Maria Montez quite well.

I evolved my own occupations in New York which were less fraught. For instance I used to search the downtown gun dealers about 4th street, looking for caches of machine pistols and the like, of suitable calibre, which I would list back in Washington for possible purchase for shipping to Europe and the Resistance. I was able to enjoy my small arms interest most actively between New York and Washington, at Aberdeen proving ground. Here I used to go to examine specimens of captured German tanks or Russian tank samples. I would also handle many a pistol, Colts or Smith & Wesson: and was once even asked to demonstrate the Bren gun. Luckily I could.

My great New York City day was a gift from Alec Gatehouse. American Locomotives produced the successful self-propelled gun, 'the Priest' to us, the M7 to them: and they telephoned to ask for a British representative to attend their M7 Day celebrations. The General sent me. I was put up and dined at the Ritz-Carlton, and next morning was driven by their chief executive Angus Chisholm to the City Hall to meet the famous Mayor La Guardia, 'Little Flower'. The Eighth Army was equipped at Alamein with three types of self-propelled artillery: 'the Bishop', 'the Priest' and 'the Deacon'. The Americans couldn't see the point of our custom of naming our war machines, but they soon caught on. I was no hero, and I hadn't fought at Alamein, but I had to face a crowd of military and civilian executives and talk about the war in North Africa and our use of American Lend-Lease tanks and guns.

The only awkwardness was when I was queried for having no medals. The truth was that my Africa Star ribbon had not yet reached me: and anyway our system of awards was different from theirs. I was presented to the Mayor, who was tiny: but he had power, and New York City was under his thumb. He stood no nonsense from anyone, gangster or politician. I could feel his restless energy. He spoke impatiently in short, grunting sentences. It took the combined efforts of all the press and the officials to persuade him to descend the great City Hall steps and climb up on to a Priest. He stood on the gun platform frowning like a sulking child, tapping the armour with his fingers in impatience. No one seemed to care a hoot what he felt. They only wanted pictures of him on an M7: good publicity for American Locos. I tried to look affably British. Suddenly the Little Flower was bundled to the ground. With 'Well boys, lets get back to work', he darted up the steps and disappeared into the gloom behind the pillars of the great portico. I was then given an informative and detailed guided tour of the city in a big sedan: fascinating. Next I attended a formal American Locomotives luncheon at their offices in Times Square. I think I was shovelled on to a train back to Washington, sometime in the afternoon. I don't remember.

Back in Washington I did my best in the office, met as many Americans as I could—not all girls, but they helped—and accepted as many invitations as I could manage. One was tempted to come up to expectation and be terribly British. Certain officers couldn't help being so. One of them boarded one of Washington's admirably fast, frequent, clean and efficient trams, for which one could pay in tokens one bought on board, and said to the driver: 'Give me a dollar's worth of those things please'. The shocked driver could hardly restart his tram, and the other passengers went into a Bateman style reaction. A better story comes from an American. An elderly lady wishing to alight from a slowing tram darted from door to door. As the driver applied his brakes he called out: 'Either end, lady, they both stop'. I was taken to one ball game. I enjoyed the sporting excitement but I couldn't get the hang of it. You can imagine what the Americans thought about cricket. Once I was a member of a BAS cricket team which had permission to play against another on the green patch behind the White House. It was fun receiving puzzled interest and mockery too!

I was taken to a National Symphony Orchestra concert at the Watergate—an ideal summer setting for listening to music. The water carries the music with a soft mellow accuracy across to the audience. The stone seats are rather hard, but any little discomfort is forgotten. Alternatively, one can drift along or moor in a canoe, an even pleasanter way to listen to more popular music, such as Frank Sinatra whom I heard when I went with a girl-friend. But I dared not risk an international scene by possibly making a nonsense with the canoe.

I was very struck by the constant sound of music as one moved about the city. At home there was little more to hear than 'Music While you Work': but everywhere in the States radios were constantly tuned to local stations. I was very irritated by the radio commercialism. The stations were all sponsored except NBC (National Broadcasting Corporation). I decided to make use of my position and visit one Washington station, WMAL. When I complained to Sam Diggs, who seemed to be the leading light, that programmes changed every five minutes, he said: 'Well, Captain, the American public will not listen to any programme for more than a quarter of an hour.' I was incensed by the short, scrappy news flashes. 'We listen to all the news,' I said priggishly. 'But you are closer to the war,' rejoined Sam.

One day I was astonished to receive an invitation to luncheon at the British Embassy with Lord and Lady Halifax. He was a great man. The criterion is 'the greater the humbler', or vice-versa if you like. Lord Halifax was quite ready to talk to the humblest guest as if she or he was the only person who mattered. I enjoyed the lovely purpose-built Embassy and gardens, and listening to the conversations of more senior guests. 'What a programme in front of the Halifaxes', I wrote, 'six major speeches, three minor, one radio, on a trip to the North-West USA and Canada.'

I got a trip to Canada—without a care in the world. General Gatehouse was invited to address the officers attending war courses at the Royal Military College in Kingston, Ontario. 'You really need an ADC, sir, don't you?' 'Yes, I think you should see Canada.' We went by overnight train via Montreal. The RMC is attractively situated in Fort Frederick on a peninsula all of its own jutting out into Lake Ontario, with Fort Henry across on the mainland. The forts were built to guard the mouth of the St Lawrence river in the war of 1812. While I was there I was thrilled to see a display of the Northern Lights: points of light hovering in the sky and flickering, due to movement of the polar ice.

The general's lecture was a great success: so were the two afternoon fishing trips with Colonel Hurley which the general had asked me have laid on. I am not really as keen a fisherman as Papa was, but I won the ten cent fish weight kitty by landing (on a spinner) a four-and-a-half-pound bass. My impression of the RMC was that they rightly held firmly, but not rigidly, to tradition, and that they were very efficient, keen and kind. We were very well treated. I think our stock went up when in the mess we heard Winston Churchill speaking in Quebec.

We left by car for Toronto, 160 miles along the lake, in order that General Gatehouse could meet the Chief of Police, General Draper, under whom he had served in tanks in World War I. It was a great reunion. A terrific lunch was laid on in the Chief's private suite in the Royal York Hotel where we were put up. General Draper had taken over at a very rough period in 1927, and cleaned up Toronto, as we heard when meeting the Mayor and the press at police headquarters. I was made happy by being shown the Chief's firearms collection—and very envious. Then we were driven by police car to the airport and back to Washington via New York, over the storms.

In Washington I was lucky to find a lively, tolerant and sympathetic friend in Tony Wigan, the BBC correspondent (who alas died in 1983). He was very highly thought of at Broadcasting House as I have discovered on reading his obituary in *Ariel*, the BBC Staff Newspaper of August 31st 1983. He was the first professionally trained journalist to join BBC News. He paid me the great compliment of taking a lot of trouble over me: from inviting me as crew on his sailing boat on the Potomac to memorable evenings at the Press Club. There was one particularly hilarious evening with Red Skelton. But once I nearly broke up a firm friendship. We were sailing in nicely to our mooring at the highly professional Washington Yacht Club, when I carelessly let go the main sheet. So there we were, two cack-handed Britishers, so it appeared, disgracing their sacred anchorage.

A winter sport in which I achieved another downfall, literally, was the BAS Indoor Skating Club. One of the keenest and most competent members, and an official through her skill, was lovely Jennifer, daughter of the Holmeses of the British Embassy. I fell 'bonk' for Jennifer, and although I couldn't skate wormed my way on to the committee to be near her. The first time I had to make a public announcement on the ice with the club in full session I fell 'bonk' − on my behind! Another lesson of life! I did better on a non-slip stage. I joined the British Players, and took the part of Harold in J.B. Priestly's *Laburnum Grove*. The Jewish community kindly lent us their centre. Mrs Roosevelt, to our consternation and delight, came to a performance and met us all afterwards. We were able to give £100 to British War Relief.

A PRINCETON WEEKEND

I had the honour to be selected as one of the eight British army representatives who, together with Royal Navy and RAF 'teams', attended a weekend course at Princeton University on 'America'. This was one of a series they ran as a result of similar courses on Britain initiated by Oxford and Cambridge for American personnel. Our party included the women's services, and this caused a stir at Princeton. The next issue of the Princeton Alumni weekly carried the caption: 'Co-eds for the weekend'. Although the atmosphere throughout was light-hearted, the various subjects were covered seriously, and from our side we had been told by our Mission's liaison committee that it was our duty 'to learn something about America, it's history, etc'. We were a good group. We got on at all levels, everyone was articulate and able to speak up, either in a small group of 'natives' or in a public session. We were under the nominal leadership of Guards Brigadier F.A.V. Copland-Griffiths, DSO, MC, from Tunisia: a striking figure with a highly developed sense of public duty, and humour.

Our first evening was more hectic than expected—beer and ham sandwiches with members of the faculty in the Nassau Club. Nassau Hall was held as a British post in 1776, and taken by Washington at the battle of Princeton the following year. Half the time we were in total darkness, since the area was going through air-raid warning practice. This situation suited the university secretary who knew his way around the bar in the dark and chose the blackouts to refill our mugs more frequently than others could manage. We finally staggered off to bed, and the brigadier picked on me (why?) to wake him at 07.15 hours, as he said he had no mechanical aid. I had a disturbed night, but called him on the dot. He was already shaving, the cad.

The main street of the pleasant little town of Princeton divides the town from the university. The campus has an English public school atmosphere. Many of the nineteenth-century buildings are a good imitation of some of our university buildings, but none so bad as Keble. The two-day programme arranged for us was comprehensive and interesting. There were lectures on such subjects as 'The changing North-East', 'The Solid South', 'The Isolationist

Mid-West', and 'American Policy'. The next day American literature, painting, music and architecture were covered. One evening was a formal dinner, on the next we split up as guests of professors and their families. After this occasion there was a concert by the Budapest String Quartet, which I thought made a good end to the day. But no: the student friends I had made on my staircase the evening before, after I had passed a Pernod-drinking test, invited me to an Orgy. 'Wow!' I thought, 'At last!' But alas, it wasn't quite what I hoped. There was lots of champagne but lots of propriety! The whole weekend was worthwhile and memorable. The atmosphere, indeed the whole concept was due to their outstanding President Dodds who took such a personal interest in us and went so far as to tell us that we could consider ourselves honorary alumni of Princeton. I am proud to be associated with such an admirable institution.

SIX THOUSAND MILES

On 2nd October 1943 I found a request on my desk for an officer to attend manoeuvres at Camp Polk, in Louisiana, and received permission to go. John Turnbull, MC, XIth Hussars, fresh from Cairo, was to go to Fort Knox and then to Fort Riley, Kansas. I managed to get permission for John to join me at Camp Polk. His up-to-date experience and distinguished service would be an asset to our British representation, and would add inexpensively to his American experience. I had been told to visit Camp Young, California, 'when the moment came'. Would it not be sensible to go on there and save a whole new coast to coast fare later? We also had to see New Orleans. 'You'd be fools to miss the chance,' they said.' The nearest airport to Camp Polk, though not on the normal route, was in fact New Orleans, from where we could fly to California! The good-hearted Movement Officer agreed to this route though very jealous! But would our colonel sign? The colonel signed. Would the general agree? 'Don't ask him now,' said his lovely secretary Claribel Townsend.

The general and I were pacing Track 14 at Union Station, waiting to greet a Mission from England. The train was late. The general said: 'I am tired of travel, getting in and out of trains and planes and all the rest of it.' 'Yes sir, I see your point. But actually I have a trip in mind with John Turnbull when Humphrey Sykes gets back . . . That is, if you can agree,' 'Yes, yes.' said the General, and he turned away because the train was approaching. I didn't say another word. I worked quietly in the office all day Friday, giving nothing away, but took a long-distance train at midnight with three other officers.

The engine was enormous, unstreamlined, with half the works, a mass of pipes and steam boxes, stuck on the outside. It had a hoarse and penetrating whistle, and a great bell which tolled continuously when the engine moved into yards. There was a long loud hiss as, on the second day, we drew into—great heavens, Chattanooga! We were on the Chattanooga choo-choo! That had been our theme song in hospital and on board ship. We walked round the town where General Grant (of my tank) beat Rosecrans in 1863. Tennessee is charming, well wooded and watered, with friendly-looking hills. In darkness we went through a corner of Georgia and then into Alabama. In Birmingham we took a stroll and had a glimpse and earful of a negro spiritual service in a wooden hut, on our way to the local hostelry for 'Skartch', which we found. Sunday morning saw us through Vicksburg, where General Grant beat the Confederates on 4th July 1863. Then with some excitement we crossed the great Mississippi into Louisiana, flat, mushy and dull. The army met us at Shreveport and drove us 147 miles to Camp Polk and into a luxurious tented Observers' camp.

The four days of manoeuvres were really enjoyable: war from an armchair, almost, with excellent attention paid to our needs. The only drawback was that in camp we were stared at with undisguised curiosity, almost rudeness we felt. But this was part of our job. When John and I went to the PX (Post Exchange) to buy a towel, a seemingly ominous ring of men surrounded us. 'What are you?' 'What do these mean?' Always the same everywhere. I soon had a set answer, which I had to repeat hundreds of times during our three-week trip, and I always carried a card showing badges of rank. Poor John, who was a shy and modest person, attracted even more attention in his XI Hussar uniform with 'cherry-picker' trousers. At a street corner someone pointed at John and said: 'What are those for?' 'To observe the normal rules of decency.' Not a popular reply! But we really enjoyed our strenuous outdoor programme after our Washington life. Back at camp we had our rewards: T-Bone steaks, good beer, warm tents, and piles of blankets to snuggle under with only one's nose exposed.

Thence by car to Lake Charles and a train to New Orleans. We actually achieved our tickets, although British rail warrants had never been seen before. We were told to board 'the Pullman one block up the street': literally so. One solitary sleeping car stood among the shrubbery. A dear old negro porter took our bags and told us we could be away for an hour. There was little local colour and no Scotch. But on our return our Pullman had been attached to a train. We reached New Orleans at 8 a.m.

We wandered about peering into courtyards shops and bars. We drank the recommended Ramos Gin Fizz as aperitifs, sampled sazeracs for our sundowners, and ate oysters à la Rockefeller (because they are such rich dishes) at Antoine's with Liebfraumilch '21. We were about to stagger back to our Hotel Roosevelt when some Americans asked us to join them. It was our duty. We could not refuse! We drank coffee laced with Bourbon, and were then taken on to a Mexican night club, La Lune. We danced around quite happily until our hosts became embarrassingly incapacitated. We extricated ourselves and walked home, not risking being driven back.

There followed a rough flight to Dallas: a solicitous stewardess, poor thing, coped with my misery and malady. Did we hit Dallas? No, Dallas hit us. It was Hallowe'en, and the town was celebrating. The streets were full of exuberant, noisy, squeaker-blowing persons of all ages. The girls were all too busy joining in to spare us a look. Many people thought we were dressed for the occasion and treated us with far too much levity. John, and therefore myself, took refuge in a movie house, soothed by Fred Astaire, whom I had met in Washington, I boasted. Here we were 'Deep in the Heart of Texas'. A great song: but there were no girls for us.

So we spent part of our night dossed down at Love Field because take-off was at 04.45. At dawn we were above the beautiful desert: over New Mexico and heading for Tucson, Arizona. Sweet, unbelievable, change of fortune. Desert and mountains in the early morning sun viewed from the clear blue above, breakfast from a non-spill tray in a luxury chair, air-conditioned and cossetted by a pretty hostess. The Libyan desert had been beautiful too: but there could only be a fleeting pleasure in it. Our day had meant getting up in the cold, moving out of leaguer, peering forward for signs of the enemy, trying to keep exact station with the dimly outlined tanks of the next squadron, wondering if it would be another 'no breakfast' morning. But at least we had had the consolation that if the enemy wanted a fight, we had the sun behind us in the early morning.

Tucson, Arizona! Shades of Wyatt Earp, Tombstone, the OK Corral, etc. But we were tired and became gloomy at the prospect of a twelve-hour delay. No! A kind colonel on our plane telephoned the military air station, a car was sent for us and we were fixed up in a comfortable quarter. That was really decent. Once washed, shaved, rested and revived, we set out to explore 'Toosohn': and it was beautiful. The Pioneer Hotel bar was open, and the manager brought along an elderly Mr Reno who did us a great service by taking us along to the Old Pueblo Club, the social centre of the city. We had a really jolly evening, thanks to members' generosity and the performance of a party of Mexican singers. Two charming girls were about to show us the desert: what a treat! But hell, American Airlines called us back at 11 p.m.

Los Angeles, 2.00 a.m.: our room occupied. John became tough: beds were found quickly. We slept until 11.00 am, then rang the Desert Centre. 'OK, take the train to Indio: we'll meet you' (only sixty-five miles from the station!). It was cold in our tent that night, but deserts are apt to be, and we were well provided for. Next morning, no orders, no set programme. Fine: our plans were all our own. We fitted ourselves out with goggles and other items of field equipment, bunged some tinned rations into a jeep, and off we went with a GI driver to find the battle. Mock battles in a lovely desert are much better sport than we had been used to. We saw four superbly coloured dawns and sunsets. We revelled in this tent life again, getting physically tired, eating 'hard' but well, getting good nights' sleep. We had excellent maps and there were clear landmarks, so we were not so anxious about being lost, as we had been in Libya. We crossed the Colorado River into Arizona, on to Yuma, along the shore of the Salton Sea and the border of Mexico, through the Imperial Valley, rather like the Nile delta. To get home at the end of the manoeuvres—oh yes, we had been properly involved—we had to do seventy-two miles on a desert track. I was a little worried because we had broken one of the desert rules of travel and were without rations, warm clothes and bedding. But our driver was excellent and negotiated several sand-drifts without a falter. It was we who were not setting a good example. . .

Headquarters gave us a lovely surprise by sending us back to Los Angeles via Palm Springs—the desert *par excellence* as dreamed of in Libya. An oasis of pleasure in the centre of the date palm region, at the foot of then snow-capped mountains: cool Mexican-style houses in staring whites and colours. Summer temperatures reach 140°—too hot even for a peacetime season, but in wartime it was season all the year, and we were ready for it. Humphrey Clarke of the British Embassy had given us an introduction to the Farrells and we had the run of the Racquet Club, swimming pool and bar, and a girl to look after us, my goodness;

and she introduced us to Brian Ahearne and his wife Joan Fontaine. We tried to appear nonchalant.

A complete contrast in life followed. The local bus, an elongated Packard holding some fifteen passengers, took us to El Paso station where our train arrived crammed. We just managed to squeeze aboard where the cookie-and-cigarette vendor had set up his shop on eight seats at the end of one car. When we set off, the whole train seemed to want a packet of cigarettes or a cookie. We were squeezed and squeezed again by an unending flow of customers. After an hour or so the vendor took pity on us in our growing discomfiture. He slung two empty boxes out on to the line and told us to sit in the space. Then he decided to take a break and leave us in charge of a few sales to incredulous customers, but only after two train conductors whom we had met on our outward journey vouched for us. They were also ready to fix us up with girls. We gratefully declined.

Los Angeles and the Beverly Hills Hotel: Scotch and sandwiches fixed for us. 'We gasped and giggled' is I suppose how I can describe our reactions on arrival. We were right in the middle of residential Hollywood of the stars. Now what should we do to make the most of it? Humphrey Clarke again, with an introduction. I rang Nigel Bruce, Basil Rathbone's Dr Watson (the best combination ever). He invited us round in the evening for drinks and we goggled at his collection of signed photographs of stars. He was then starring with Maria Montez, and we knew that our Alec Gatehouse had a signed photograph of her which said: 'To the most charming general I have ever met.' How many, I wonder?

'Willie' Bruce sent us off to dinner at the fashionable English-run Cock and Bull restaurant, reserving a table in his name. We stuffed ourselves with steak and kidney pudding, not tasted for years. Afterwards Jennifer Bruce, Willie's daughter, took us off dancing. The next afternoon at their pool we met Jack Bolton, now a US Navy commander, who came up with just what we wanted, a visit to a film studio, 20th-Century Fox, where he worked. We toured the sets, saw Don Ameche filming with Carmen Miranda, and Alfred Hitchcock directing Tallulah Bankhead in *Lifeboat*. Later, Jack Bolton's car and driver were at our disposal for a tour of Los Angeles.

The next diversion was to join Basil Rathbone and Nigel Bruce in NBC Studios for their half-hour Sherlock Holmes serial. They were greater characters than Conan Doyle's. These two even took us to dinner at Lucie's where luckily we were introduced to Cary Grant who was eating on his own. He was at heart still an Englishman, from Bristol. He was most affable and arranged for his wife Barbara (neé Hutton, the Woolworth heiress) to call for us next morning. This she did, and came in a smooth black Cadillac. She took us to luncheon at Romanoffs', *the* place to eat!

The same afternoon we were taken to Columbia Studios to see Cary Grant on the set with Janet Blair. We learned quite a bit about acting in films, but it was the glamour we took most note of, such as Jinx Falkenburg and eight companions on Set No. 7 in a film called *Nine Girls*. This time we did lose our aplomb. John was speechless. I had to tell the story of John's red pants for him. He really was losing his nerve, poor chap. We had dinner again at the Cock and Bull, this time with one Terence D'Abo and 'adequate bits of glamour' whom he brought along. This really finished John. When the news came that we were to go on to a party given by Captain Freddie Brisson (husband of Rosalind Russell, who was unfortunately away), John deserted us at the front door! That was a shame. I needed him.

The party was for Guy Gibson, the dam-buster. The Grants were there and we met Merle Oberon and Ray Milland as a start. The party had been going for some time and was becoming quite boisterous. I got involved in a frightful game called 'Who sir? Me sir?' which goes on: 'Yes you sir! No, Sir, not I sir! Who then sir?' The penalty, I forget how incurred, was a crack over the head with a rolled newspaper which Cary and Co. wielded with delight.

The next day the Baroness de Becker who could view Hollywood with sophisticated continental detachment, and did, drove us round to lunch with Barbara and Cary Grant. We admired their beautiful house and contents. 'Yes, that is a Louis XVth carpet from Versailles. The Louvre wanted it but could not match my bid.' 'Yes, I love India, but Egypt more.' Here John felt at home, having spent six years there. From India, Barbara had bought a mynah bird which in her absence her World War I English chauffeur had taught a foul sentence. When guests didn't understand the bird and asked 'What did it say?', Barbara took pleasure in telling them.

Hollywood provided us with three more memorable firsts: dinner at the Brown Derby, (among dining stars Edward G. Robinson was easy to recognise); the Première at Grauman's Chinese Theatre of the film *Guadalcanal Diary*, with all the attendant razzmatazz—the performance started half an hour late because, until the police cleared a way through the dense pack of autograph hunters and mobbing fans, the stars attending couldn't get in. Finally for us there was a bit of a party at the famous Mocambo night club, where we found ourselves 'dancing on a dime' alongside several of the cast of the film and other stars. The Grants tried very hard to get us to stay on the west coast and go up to friends in San Francisco, but we had been away three weeks and General Gatehouse had been extremely kind.

CHRISTMAS IN NEW ENGLAND

The Baldwins, New England friends who I had met through the McGees at St John's church, made my year by inviting me up to their home at Concord, Massachusetts for Christmas. I arrived on the appointed day and time only because friendly natives had hauled me out of the Boston train for Concord, New Hampshire. Historic Concord, Mass., is delightful. I arrived on a bright sunny day with seventeen degrees of frost. There was an eighteenth century atmosphere, with attractive old houses and former farm buildings of the period. The town centres round the lifelike bronze statue of a Minute Man. The Minute Men were settlers who in the 1770s ploughed with their muskets 'wadded' and ready. Here, in April 1775, an English patrol fearing opposition to their crossing of a stream, fired on the Americans opposite. The Minute Men led by Major John Butterick fired back and a skirmish followed. These shots 'which echoed round the world' were the start of the American War of Independence. By 1943 Concordians appeared to be very pro-English despite having given their blood for their new nation. I met a number of locals and conversation was easy. I just had to battle with a lot of good-natured chaff about England during a Christmas as traditionally English as ever.

'BEAUTIFUL HORSES AND FAST WOMEN'

I was delighted to return to Fort Knox in the spring of 1944, as an observer of armoured force tactics and manoeuvres: valuable for future US/British battle co-operation. My journey to Louisville, the nearest railroad station, on the George Washington train of the Baltimore and Ohio Railroad, was scenic inside and out. An American officer and I gave each other mutual support as we got together with a bevy of delightful young ladies returning to their college, Margaret Hall, Lexington. Our sheep dog flair was put to the test at such close quarters, but we managed to pen two of the comeliest just as the brakeman shunted our coach into a siding for an hour at Charlotteville. When we had been re-attached for the next stage we were at the rear and could enjoy the all-round view from the open rear platform. Coming into Frankfort, Kentucky, the train cuts through a tunnel in the hill on which Daniel Boone, the great frontiersman, is buried, and comes out into the main street. We were able to step straight on to the sidewalk and into a shop for some chocolates. Next morning we were in Blue Grass country—of the beautiful horses and fast women.

I was met by our liaison officer Major Tim Wimbush, R.T.R., the only Englishman among thousands of Americans, and a fine and popular ambassador known as Old Chappie. He became a congenial companion in the hurly-burly of our rugged life. I often heard American shouts of 'I say old fellow', in exaggerated posh, such was Tim's influence. I purposely did not record the military aspects of our partnership. The whole of our time seemed to be spent in a round of leg-pulling and wise-cracking, whether there were Englishmen present or not, but it wasn't. I stayed with Tim in bachelor officers' quarters. The first evening I was physically shaken up by the teenage family of Colonel Barnard, Number Two of the Armored Board, who found that I was a real square but got me jitterbugging, the latest craze. 'I can do the trucking' step!' I boasted. 'Aw, that's out of date! Tut, tut! But still the girls swallowed their pride or something, and took Tim and me to a White Collar Girls' Dance. There we saw some fabulous jitterbugging—almost up to the standard in the great film *Hell's A Poppin'*—in which the negro dancers are the absolute tops.

The duration of this military assignment hadn't been precise, so I was very pleased to devote a day or two to visiting Tim's friends, the Belknaps, out at Land O'Goshen Farm: a 150-year-old brick building. Here I stepped back into *Gone With the Wind*. There was sit-down English tea, watching the training of lovely two-year old horses in the ring, inspecting sheep and cattle on good land 'long time settled'. There was sherry in the well-stocked library by a log fire, followed by a walk at sunset to the old family burial ground among trees, with the slaves buried way beyond. We found the negroes here more friendly and courteous than in the North; especially the dwindling band of domestic servants headed by a fine old-fashioned butler. From the Belknap family we enjoyed listening to a southern view of the North-South subject: and hearing about President Lincoln, who was assassinated before the possible completion of his plan to repatriate the freed slaves to what became Liberia.

Then they got onto the Hill-Billies who in the forties still lived a life of their own. Their music and songs and speech and sentiments were akin to those of the early English and Scottish settlers and testified to their isolation. They were not interested in the benefits of industry. They lived primitive lives, surviving by hunting and small home farming. But the land they had was almost perpendicular, making farming very difficult. Worse still, they grew tobacco, the easiest small acreage cash crop: but it wore out the soil. The government tried to remedy this by paying them subsidies not to grow tobacco. Their shyness and resistance to interference may have given the appearance of being stupid, but they were not. Their whole code of living was unique, I would say enviable. Work was the exception until there was no more to eat or wear. They kept on making their own liquor, 'moonshine', despite the action of the 'Revenuers', the Federal Agents in Kentucky.

The Hill-Billies' law was still the gun. Differences were settled by bullets, and ancient family feuds carried on for generations. Despite an efficient modern police force and local JPs, the solution to private quarrels was killing on the slightest pretext. Here is the *Evening Standard* of Tuesday, 16th July 1944: 'Harlan, Kentucky. Tuesday. Three people lost their lives in a family feud in the wild mountain region of Kentucky in which the men of two families shot it out in the middle of the road after an argument about a poker game, the sheriff announced today. The argument began among the younger members of both families, the older members later joining in the dispute.' Harlan County is the centre of the mountains. Harlan itself, a mining town has a reputation as the shoot'nest town' in Kentucky.'

The last morning was spent with the horses, seeing the Kentucky five-gaited horse; the new gait they called racking, a smooth motion between a trot and a canter. A horse was trained to do this by throwing him off his balance by pulling his head to one side and urging him forward but keeping a firm check on him. A trained racking horse was a beautiful sight with his high-stepping forefeet. This gait was bred into these creatures by the early plantation owners who had to cover long distances in short periods, riding round their estates. The result of riding a racking horse was that the rider was very little fatigued, but the horse was exhausted in a short time.

Next day the Belknaps gave us lunch at the Pendennis Club in Louisville. People gazed at us with curiosity: not an unpleasant sensation here. We were sorry to leave the South. But several other British officers would certainly find a reason to turn up in Kentucky over 6th May period—for the Kentucky Derby on Churchill Downs.

SAN FRANCISCO HERE I COME

When May came round I was up in Detroit again at General Motors, inspecting new internal layouts in tank turrets. I could hardly believe it, but our office there told me I must see AFV amphibious developments (for the Pacific and north-west Europe) at Ford Ord, Monterey, California! John Steinbeck country: Carmel—artists and bohemians —nearby; San Francisco not far. I put my request to the Air Priority Board, and back came tickets.

With a number three priority, not the lowest, I was able to make a direct air connection to San Francisco, and soon there I was over the Sierra Nevada with the early sun behind us turning the snow-peaks to gold. I had an hour to wait for my plane south to Salinas, so I got busy on the telephone to General Motors, the British DAQMG (our senior staff officer on the West Coast) and to the girl friend of a girl friend. I knew I could get back to San Francisco for a day or two before flying home east, and I wanted things laid on.

Fort Ord was a good spot to be stationed: pleasant wooden buildings up a gentle slope behind the sand dunes, with a fine view of the Pacific Ocean. To the east, green wooded hill beyond a vast kitchen-garden valley of lettuces: miles and miles of lettuce fields, dotted with little white farms.

I was up at 04.45 my first morning, and it was cold: but I was on a really novel AFV exercise this time. OK, it was important to get a tank or other AFV to swim ashore, but how soon could one fight in it effectively? As in the mid-west the American personnel at Fort Ord were extremely friendly and kind. When my mission ended the civilian contact I had made in the area was absolute trumps also.

I went no further than the Jeffrey Hotel in Salinas. Here I waited and created quite a stir, like a rare bird blown off course. Oh, I've encountered my twitchers. I was met by Selby McCreery, brother of our great cavalry general Dick McCreery who had commanded the Bays Brigade in France. The McCreery's ranch, Tres Pinos, had a beautiful single-storey house, simply planned with one large high dining/living room with a verandah running the whole length of one side. Cool and easy to run. Luckily I got on famously with Selby and his wife—or they simply had perfect manners. Anyway I felt I had known them all my life. At dinner I made them laugh with stories of John, such as on Cincinatti station when a hearty American came up to him in uniform, slapped him on the back and cried, 'Wha'd'ya know!' John stared and replied: 'I don't know anything at all'. Oh, well that didn't happen often.

Selby gave me a happy day on the ranch, letting me use a ·22 repeater on the ground squirrel pests as we drove to look at various groups of cattle; or when we went to transfer four work horses to a purchaser. I saw a buck on one hilltop such as Colonel Tony Pepys, an earlier guest, had been able to stalk and shoot with Selby's 30−30 although he lost a leg at El Agheila. The Tres Pinos scenery was really lovely: rolling fields of brown, yellow and green; woods and grass-clad hill rising up to 3,000 feet, like a magnified English parkland and with a sugar loaf like the one at Abergavenny. Most of the ranches had been grants of land to Spanish grandees, but the Spanish did not take to the hard work involved and only one ranch now remained in Spanish hands. However the cattle hands were still European. Before I left them, Selby rang up his mother-in-law, Mrs J.D. Grant, in San Francisco, and asked her to put me up and show me round. What a gesture. But he did more, and drove me the forty miles to Gilroy station and got me a good seat on the train.

The countryside became greener and greener, with more and more white houses, till it began to resemble a wine bottle label. The two-hour trip took me past the attractive coffee-coloured buildings of Stanford University at Paolo Alto, among dark cypresses. The train rolled through Burlingame, the social centre of the country set, right into the city. I took a cab to 2200 Broadway. I was amazed at the size and opulence of this house and others nearby, and I admired the taste of the design in pleasant red brick with a stone-pillared portico. A homely Scots maid swung open the huge wrought iron front door—and a fairy tale unfolded. A lift to the third floor took me to a room with a view over San Francisco Bay, and luxury I had never experienced. Tea in the library. *Punch* and *Country Life*. Mrs Grant and friends of her generation in similar circumstances retained many English customs and manners. I met such Americans at dinner, who were using their money and contacts to help the war effort as best they could, in Services welfare for instance. I really felt that Mrs Grant was a good fairy waving a wand over a strange young man dreaming. Mr Monteagle arranged for me to see over the University of California next day. Mrs Grant lent me her car and chauffeur. Dr Gutteridge (History, from Cambridge), took me round: and my visit included a Glee Club Song and Skit Show in the Hearst Greek Theatre. Finally, to make me homesick, in the main library Dr Gutteridge showed me the actual records of the Abbey of Osney, outside Oxford.

I called on Major Barker, the British DAQMG, and he handed me letters of introduction from Barbara Grant, which contained detailed instructions on what to see, where to eat, whom to contact. Here is one of her letters, to Mrs Stanley Page:

Darling Harrie

Again I am imposing upon your kindness to introduce a most delightful friend of ours, Captain Michael Halsted, of the British Eighth Army. He will be in town only a short while, but as he does not know a soul, I am hoping that you and Stanley can manage, somehow, to see him. I know that you will like him as much as we do, for he is, without doubt, one of the nicest Englishmen we know. I hope, darling, that you, Stanley and the children are all well. When are you coming down here? Don't forget you promised to let me know of your arrival in advance, and I am greatly looking forward to your visit.

With very dearest love to you both in which Cary joins me. . .

P.S. Do introduce Captain Halsted to Nini; I would have given him a letter to her, only, alas, I don't remember her address.

I shook my head in gratitude and despair. I needed a week for all that Barbara had planned for me. I only managed to meet one friend. Meanwhile Mr Hall of General Motors gave me a tour of the city, and Mrs Grant swept me off in her grand manner to call on Major-General Galbraith, the Post Commander. Her nephew was his aide. I felt very small, but I did my best to speak up firmly and clearly for Britain. Finally I did manage to meet my girl friend's girl friend, who was pronounced to be OK because Mrs Grant knew her mother. In fact Mrs Grant invited us both to a drink at the top of the Mark Hopkins Hotel—the most spectacular bar in the world. Then she took me to the Burlingame Club for dinner, stopping at her lovely 'South of France' country villa: orange trees, ornamental gardens and statuary at the head of billiard-table lawns. From the terrace we looked across the valley to the mountains where lay Mrs

Grant's ranch in the wine country. I slept on the plane, disbelieving and exhausted.

FAREWELL

I have left my most important memory of BAS service to the last. I had indeed been, as my father had been, under the command of Field Marshal Sir John Dill. As Head of the British Missions he was somewhat remote from us down in AFV. The whole staff never paraded, and we were never directly involved with Sir John, but we felt his presence and personality supporting us and smoothing our way in all that we achieved. Thanks to the Field Marshal knowing Papa, he and Lady Dill once invited me to dinner just by themselves. I was very touched. I hope I behaved well, but the GOC did tell me that I was spoilt! I think that sank in a bit. On another occasion the Field Marshal invited me to tea, just me. I was staggered. He was back from the Tehran Conference; and by the fireside at 2023 Q Street, NW, he told me something of his impressions, and showed me his collection of press photographs of the whole trip.

He was another very great man. He was so kind to both Papa and me. When he died we felt we had lost a real friend.

He laboured well and truly for the cause of Britain and America. The Field Marshal is buried in Arlington Cemetery. He rests among a nation of friends who have honoured him with a place in their burial ground for servicemen and heroes.

The time came for me to leave the USA. In fact I was to return to hospital in the UK. America had been tough but I had some energy left. General Gatehouse had arranged another New York fling, and kindly included me.

Mr Del'Agnesi gave us a 25 per cent reduction at the Waldorf—a fine wartime gesture we thought—so we were not hesitant in dashing up every now and then. On one visit I went on a tour of the FBI and actually met J. Edgar Hoover himself. I think I was most impressed by the Fingerprint department and its gigantic bank—very cumbersome in the pre-computer age.

This time the General's hostess was a Mrs Thomson, who happened to live in the same street as Mayor La Guardia—safer or more dangerous? She was, I recall, 'the essence of American hospitality'. She gave us a wonderful meal, and then produced seats for the new musical *Oklahoma*, the rage of New York. I have only enjoyed *South*

Pacific more. Before *Oklahoma* was released for general enjoyment I was able to buy a set of records at the theatre, which were to come in handy *en route* and at home.

I have never since lived at the level on which Alec Gatehouse and his friends conducted our weekend. We lunched next day at the famous 21 Club, or 'Jack and Charlie's' as it is called—the midday haunt of celebrities. I revelled in the stir caused when Joan Fontaine, who had been absent in Palm Springs, came over to meet the General. That evening, after time for recovery, and no doubt several frozen daiquiris or old-fashioneds, we slid smoothly off in our Cadillacs to El Morocco, another celebrity haunt decorated in African style. That was a good enough ending to my acquaintance with New York City.

Back in Washington, I was given some grand farewells and I have a scroll bearing illustrations and signatures to document it all. Souvenirs which have lasted were three US Navy footlockers which I was able to buy very cheaply at the PX to contain all my loot. These were beautifully lettered with my name and The Queen's Bays' in Gothic script, by Don Hougham. I had also some rather special packing to do for the actual day of departure—by train to New York harbour. Having made armament friends over several visits to Aberdeen Proving Ground, I now found myself the happy possessor of eight different Colt pistols, 3,000 rounds of assorted pistol ammunition, and an early miniature radio receiver. All this had to be crammed into my webbing equipment and worn by me to save anyone asking questions, and against possible pilferage.

A surprise awaited me at the docks on 20th June 1944. I found that I had to board the *Queen Elizabeth*—nothing less for me—together with seventeen thousand US troops! There were so many that they really had to rough it for the five-day voyage; a large number standing up most of the day, some even at night, only able to lie down in relays to try to sleep.

The luckiest or cleverest GI's went into the loos and stayed there 'shooting crap'. It was easiest for the dice to roll on the tiled floors. I found it hard to get in on business. I achieved a certain amount of popularity, when it was known that I was responsible for the evocative music and songs of *Oklahoma* over the ship's loudspeaker system—from my record album.

One morning I found that I had returned to Gourock again. I put on my very heavy fully-filled web-equipment with help, and just had enough strength to stagger off the ship, into a lighter, and then into a railway carriage in a siding, where I collapsed onto the whole length of a seat.

On 4th August I entered an old 'looney bin' which had become Queen Alexandra's Military Hospital, Shenley, Herts. I was walking wounded again, after quite a different campaign. I could get out on a pass occasionally. I had some delightful excursions with a sweet nurse, Dawn, who certainly contributed to my restored health.

Now dear Alec Gatehouse helped me again, for the last time. He had given me this letter to take to General Briggs, now Director of the Royal Armoured Corps. He had been our Desert Brigadier:

My Dear Raymond:

Michael Halsted, who brings this letter to you, has been my GSO III, AFV, for exactly one year.

I am now releasing him to return to UK for further operations to his head wounds at the hospital at Oxford, and I am not filling his post here.

This is to ask you to give him a helping hand when he is again released from hospital into a hard world!

He has done excellently out here, in spite of poor health, headaches, etc., caused from his wounds, and no doubt you can help to place him in some useful capacity. He has mentioned the possibility of an AFV job in Australia, but you will know what the chances are.

Good Luck,

Yours

A.H. Gatehouse,
Major General

Major General Raymond Briggs, CB, DSO,
D.R.A.C.,
War Office,
London, S.W.1.

I wasn't quite up to presenting this, but chance was still on my side. I paid a visit to Bradfield College of which I was and still am tremendously fond. John Hills, the headmaster, could see that I wasn't much use to the war effort as a soldier, and offered me a job as an assistant master. I accepted. John Hills applied for me to be discharged. The War Office agreed and I relinquished my commission on 21st August 1944.

Part Four
War in the Desert

The Desert Itself
Moving about the Desert
No-one to ask the way
Sand, Wind and the Going
Food, Fuel and Water
Desert Climate
Recreation
Battle,Death and the aftermath
Drawbacks and Disappointments
Tactical Shortcomings
Guns and Tanks
A Word about us
Montgomery and Rommel
Bigger and Better Tanks—Just

12

Reflections after my Desert War

War is a terrible waste, and the suffering and damage and death are horrible: impossible to forget, not easy to forgive. Yet despite the loss of many fine friends and the maiming of others, when I look back on those days I know I enjoyed my desert war.

This North African coastal strip, our desert, was far from God-forsaken. Every bit may have looked the same as every other at a cursory glance, but there were, there are, subtle differences of colour and contour and composition which although minute were highlighted and important in the midst of desolation as variety, and even as landmarks.

The chief advantage of fighting in the desert was the nothingness. For four months I did not see a house or a tree. This suited me. I enjoyed the experience. Others, faced with no variations around them at all, and no diversions, became restless, bored and introspective.

Luckily the only inhabitants were seasonal and seldom seen—the Bedouin. They lived in tents which were easily transportable. If a battle was impending we could tell them, so that they could move away with their flocks. They knew they could return for the pickings afterwards, but also that they would have to face the risk of mines and booby-traps. They did well out of us for cash, for which we had little use. We paid them well for the small amount of fresh food they could offer, which we needed rather badly.

No doubt they were rewarded for useful information on German movements and strengths; and vice versa! I don't blame them, after having their ancient grazing areas so rudely overrun.

The desert we were in was not far from the sea, and was sand with a good mixture of soil and rocks. The whole coastal strip was relatively flat and featureless and treeless, and covered in short scrub. A thousand years ago, Libya was an Imperial Roman granary and some of their underground cisterns remain, as do wells dating from the Persian conquest of the sixth century BC. There is water still, and actually rain in the winter months. Not as much as in Roman times, but enough to provide some grazing for flocks of sheep, goats and camels. We enjoyed the green as beauty and the rain as water.

The great and obvious advantage of this terrain was that we had almost complete freedom of movement, except for brief periods during the winter rains, when patches and whole areas become quagmires, such as allowed Rommel to escape after El Alamein. It was wonderful to be able to take our tanks anywhere at any speed. When I first got my troop into the desert to try out our engines, suspension and guns, my sergeant and I were so happy charging about giving our gunners fire orders that we didn't notice that we were imperceptibly approaching one another on a collision course. We struck each other a glancing blow that did no damage. One lesson learned.

We became so confident—or foolhardy—that we found a game to play on the move. We had come across a small stock of Italian aluminium stun grenades with a steel ball inside. They were painted red and easily seen in the raised fist of a troop officer, who would take his tank alongside another, and force another troop officer to close down before he pulled the pin and threw the grenade across. No casualties were reported!

Mobility was vital when contact was made with the enemy. It enabled one to advance rapidly and attack; or withdraw to a safer distance, especially at nightfall when it was necessary to refuel and brew up out of range, and get some sleep. Both sides had to do the same.

My troop and I were very nervous of the desert at first. I soon learned to enjoy it, but I don't think my men ever did. They were always homesick. I know because I had to censor their letters. We were in the midst of nothing; absolutely nothing but sand and scrub. This was sobering. Where were we to go? There was nothing to show us the way and often nothing to tell us we had got there, until we learned to recognise tiny features such as a rise in the ground or an outcrop of rock, or better still a well or cistern. And how were we to get back again? Certainly there were no points of reference such as we were used to at home in order to find our way. No trees, no houses, no hedges, no roads, no villages. It was pretty unsettling. In order to survive and then be efficient we had to learn fast, and what we learned was *navigation*.

MOVING ABOUT THE DESERT

Our journeys, or tactical movements, were described in Orders by compass bearing and distance plotted by protractor and ruler on the maps available. The accuracy of these maps was largely due to remarkable men such as R.A. Bagnold[1] and P.A. Clayton of the Egyptian Survey, in the thirties. They made large-scale explorations at their own expense, amassing knowledge of the desert invaluable to us in the forties, yet their efforts drew little or no attention from official quarters at the time.

One of the early military appraisals under *Considerations for the Operation of a Mechanical Force* (in the Western desert) is No. 2: 'Absence of accurately marked landmarks'. Bagnold and his band did provide a number of accurately surveyed reference points. But one or two were such tiny variations in the drab expanse of sand and scrub, hardly visible to the untrained eye, that they could cause confusion. Montgomery's Chief-of-Staff, General de Guingand, writes in his *Operation Victory*[2] 'During the Battle of Alamein, fierce fighting took place around a feature we named "Kidney Hill". It was a small kidney-shaped contour on the map and we had great difficulty in locating it exactly. Everyone gave it a different map reference'.

During our campaigns it was found necessary also to create our own reference points. Such was the famous sign stuck into two weighted oil drums proclaiming that this spot was Knightsbridge, map reference 37984118. Hence the Knightsbridge Box (defended position) in the Battle of Gazala in May 1942. To have an accurate and easily recognisable map reference was a great help for the whole desert navigation. Another artificial reference point equally useful was Charing Cross, an important track junction where the route to the Oasis of Siwa 200 miles south, branches off the route to Sidi Barrani on the coast. Another was simply Barrel 743, where we were once ordered to rally. It was lucky that there was such an identifiable point on the map—to or from which we could easily work out the bearing and the distance.

[1] He died on May 28th, 1990. There was a fine obituary in *The Times* of May 30th, 1990.
[2] F. de Guingand, *Operation Victory*, Hodder and Stoughton 1947.

In 1500 BC, Siwa was to the ancient Egyptians a centre for the worship of Jupiter Ammon, in the Land of Hereafter. The army of the Persian king Cambyses, son of Cyrus the Great, and conqueror of Egypt in 525 BC, was lost on its way to Siwa. The only trace so far found has been the odd perfectly preserved sandal of the period, turned up in the sand. Anthony and Cleopatra visited Siwa in about 30BC: but I digress.

Our tanks had odometers and some were fitted with aircraft compasses. Although these were fairly well compensated against all the surrounding magnetic fields, they were not robust enough to stand up to all the vibrations and shocks of a moving tank. We preferred to rely on our beautiful army issue oil-filled prismatic compasses. I shall never part with mine. Since these could not be compensated, we first of all had to find out what magnetic error the tank's field induced in our instruments. This meant taking the compass way out in front of the tank, outside any magnetic interference, and lining up the driver on the back-bearing of the actual course given, i.e. 180 degrees directly opposite. Then one got back into the tank, placed the compass on the turret, noticed the error it read from the correct bearing, set the compass on that error, and drove on it very carefully until the tank driver called out the number of miles he had been ordered to go. Then we were there!

A better instrument for desert navigation is the Sun Compass—a rugged instrument for use only in sunlight and we had plenty of that. It was invented by our Light Car patrols of the First World War, who were operating against the Senussi tribe. Oddly enough, a relative of my wife's served with the Light Armoured Cars of the Western Frontier Force in 1916, and some of his quite exciting letters have survived.* The sun compass was later perfected by Brigadier Bagnold, as he became. I think it is worth describing.

A sun compass is quite unaffected by magnetic attraction and very accurate if used correctly. It works like a sundial, but in reverse. A sundial must be carefully set up with its centre-line in a north-south direction. Then the shadow cast by its vertical rod (a gnomon or stil), indicates the time. The sun compass is a bit more complicated in having an outer ring in degrees, a solar plate (for time latitude), a date bar, a central stil, and a horizontal shadow bar. It utilises the azimuth or angle of the sun in relation to one's position to obtain true direction. If the sun time is set on the solar plate and date bar, and local time on the time bar, and the shadow of the sun cast by the gnomon or stil is made to fall on the

*See Appendix I

horizontal shadow bar, by turning the vehicle such as my tank to which the instrument is fixed, then the tank will be pointing north and south. Then the direction required can be laid off. Simple!

The time used is apparent time, i.e. local sun time, in which the length of the hour varies slightly throughout the year; and not the mean time kept by a clock or watch. To maintain direction the shadow bar must be moved regularly to coincide with the sun's moving shadow on the solar plate; and the navigator's watch (which often seemed to be mine) has to be on the same local sun time. On one unfortunate occasion when I was leading troop of the whole Brigade, I had not taken my watch off GMT and put it on local sun time, and as a consequence I led the brigade 30 degrees off course. When this was realised by someone checking at the rear, my ears began to blister from the oaths coming through my earphones, and I was ignominiously relieved by Tony from RHQ in his scout car. Another lesson learned. Indeed I note from 6th January 1942 that when leading the regiment I was congratulated by George, our squadron leader. 'No queries at all from RHQ', it says. Of course it was essential for the commander of large units to know exactly where he was at all times: and I discovered later that there was a staff officer responsible who had a theodolite. He kept it in an ambulance for a smooth ride. It was a vital object that must not suffer damage: unlike the ordinary soldier!

NO-ONE TO ASK THE WAY

So far so good. We had learned how to move about the desert in our tanks—and by day, I must add—but we never fully mastered how to walk at night from one vehicle to another, and be sure of reaching it. I noted in my diary that to be sure of a night's sleep I would take my compass out to dinner with me to the mess tent, and remain sober enough to return to my bivvy on the back-bearing. We lost a sentry one night, and were all very distressed early next morning. Had he been captured? Was he somewhere nearby out of sight? After quite a wide cast around, careful to keep in sight of one another, we came to the conclusion that he had wandered over a hardly noticeable rise and into enemy hands. The adjutant reluctantly reported him missing. But amid general rejoicing he came up with the rations two day later: and we heard his story.

He was trudging conscientiously around his lorries on a dark night, until he suddenly found that there were no more vehicles to be guarded. He had wandered off at a tangent, but of course had no idea in which direction. He sensibly realised that although he couldn't have gone very far, to start rushing off in every direction in turn could probably lead to exhaustion and disaster. So he curled up in a sand hollow in his overcoat and managed a fitful kip. At daybreak he looked eagerly around but saw absolutely nothing but sand and scrub. He was lost. Now he was a bit anxious. In which direction should he start to look for the regiment? Or was he going to die of thirst or starvation? Luckily for him, while he contemplated his fate an empty ration lorry of another regiment was bowling eastwards towards the Delta for fresh supplies, and he was spotted. 'No, we can't stop and look for your effing regiment now. Hop in.' So they rightly took him back to base and handed him over to our B Echelon (supply group) to come up with the next delivery! We didn't laugh at Trooper Kershaw. We took careful note.

If one is lost in the desert one does not move, but concentrates on conserving energy and any food and water, and by day seeks any form of shade. Early on we met a Rhodesian officer whose tank had broken down and he and his crew were on their own for nine days. 'Nine days? Good God!' 'Oh, we were all right; but it was a bit boring' (See p. 73). They had sensibly stayed put and on short commons, but were very annoyed at having so much food and water left when rescued. Later on, right out in the desert, we found a Matilda tank and its crew who had been with it six weeks. 'They are very much desert islanders, but cheerful', I wrote (See p. 78).

There were others, no doubt on both sides, who suffered another form of being lost in the desert, disorientation. One day during the course of a fairly fluid action, a German despatch rider on a powerful BMW motorbike rode into our regimental headquarters, got off and smartly saluted what appeared to be the nearest officer. He was right at this impression, but he was British despite the odd assortment of garments we wore which just passed as uniform, I think, under the Geneva Convention. Now the German's war was over. I was offered a similar BMW once; but I did not accept it. It was not really a practical sand vehicle; and like my personal Colt automatic pistol, it was too nice a piece of precision workmanship to be subjected to grinding sand.

SAND AND WIND AND THE GOING

The mention of sand brings me to a most important consideration regarding operations in the desert, not in fact mentioned under the *Considerations*,and that is the state of the 'going'. The going means the surface over which one needs to drive tactically. The area I was in is very good going: some rock, which wears down tank tracks, but on the whole crusted sand, more like fine earth, held together by scrub bush. Unfortunately our wretched war and the resultant thousands of tracked and wheeled vehicles roaring about broke the stable surface into a choking blinding dust—obscuring the route and vehicles of both sides, especially in a following wind. Aeroplane propellors from the various landing strips such as Buq-Buq added to this incapacitating build up of billowing sand. Not all the time, mind you. But this unnatural activity, which must at least have irritated the Bedouin, contributed to the frequency of sandstorms.

These were most prevalent during the period of the seasonal spring wind of the desert, the khamsin—the five-day-wind (in arabic *khamsa* means five). An Arab saying is that if the khamsin lasts for more than three days, you may kill your wife—so irritated can one become. Another advantage of being a Muslim?

Rather like a cricket report, the BBC mentioned a two-day khamsin, ours, hampering operations. I should think so! It has to be felt to be believed.

Other types of going, as surveyed and recorded by the intrepid adventurers of the thirties onwards, became vital information to the Eighth Army. There were sand dunes—of two types, *seif*, long and thin like a sword, which the word means, and *barcan*, crescent shaped; or there were boulders, or else low sand hillocks, obstacles to us disguised by bushes. There were also whole areas of *wadis*, drainage channels, the dry beds of torrents, or else *nullahs*, which are watercourses not necessarily either wet or dry.

There were really brave and accomplished men whom the high command had to rely upon for routes of possible going in these very broken areas. These men were the personnel of the Long Range Desert Group. They had hair-raising, perilous adventures in the absolute blue beyond the range of help. Before Alamein they assisted in the survey and setting up of a very valuable deception, by preparing a map showing false good going well down in the south in an area through which the Germans might outflank our defences. This map was arranged to fall into enemy hands, which it duly did. We do not know how successful this deception was, but certainly the success of our daring left-hook at the Battle of Mareth on 5th April 1943 was largely due to the correct going information sent back by the LRDG. My regiment took part in this, with the very fine New Zealanders, marvellous men to fight with,

under their famous General Freyburg, VC. Bill Pullyblank wrote to me
in a letter of 8th March 1987: 'Our next big do was at the El-Hamma
left hook, supported by the New Zealanders. What a grand bunch of
chaps they were. You would have thought they were advancing over
Salisbury Plain.'

Major W.B. Kennedy-Shaw, in his book *Long Range Desert Group**
had this to say about their own and—to a lesser extent—our
problems in the desert:

> A good many men in the Eighth Army must owe their lives to LRDG,
> but for every lost man found by us how many are still in the desert,
> now only a skeleton with a few rags of clothing round it, and an empty
> water-bottle besides, and maybe, with its teeth fastened in the dry stem
> of some desert shrub?
>
> For a heedless, unthinking man it was terribly easy to become lost
> in the desert, where whichever way you look the landscape seems the
> same. You drive over a ridge which hides your camp or the last known
> landmark, follow a track which you think will lead to your destination,
> do not bother to remember on which cheek the wind blew or where the
> sun's shadow fell when you started, hurry on, imagining that that cairn
> ahead, that bush, that low rise is a feature which you can recognise, and
> in a few miles are thoroughly lost. Then is the time to force yourself to
> make no move at all for half-an-hour, till you have had time to sit down
> and reason out the situation and not, so strong is the temptation, push
> on because you feel so sure that just beyond that next ridge there is the
> place you seek.

Arab Proverb: 'To the man who knows it, the desert is a fortress.
To him who does not, it is a grave.'

FOOD, FUEL AND WATER

Number Six of the *Considerations for the Operation of a Mechanical
Force* states: 'Lack of water, fuel or any form of food'. Quite true.
In fact, supplies were the key to the whole desert campaign as is
well known. General von Ravenstein commented: 'Tanks in the desert
make a tactician's paradise and a quartermaster's hell.' Just to give one
example: At one point in the Gazala battle, it had been a very near
thing for Rommel. On 31st May 1942 (*Rommel*, by Desmond Young),
Rommel, against the pleading even of his Chief-of-Staff, Bayerlein and
Nehring commanding the Afrika Korps, launched an attack on 150th
Infantry Brigade. This brigade was finally broken down after a very

*W.B. Kennedy-Shaw, *Long Range Desert Group*, Collins 1945, and now Greenhill
Books.

gallant fight. One British officer prisoner protested that if his men could not be provided with food and water they should be allowed to go back to the British lines. Rommel told him sympathetically that they were getting the same ration as the Afrika Korps and himself—half a cup. Then he added: 'But I quite agree that we cannot go on like this. If we do not get a convoy through tonight I shall have to ask General Ritchie for terms.' Alas the chance to finish Rommel in North Africa was perhaps lost that night. Our Army Commander did not know how close Rommel was to giving in after his victory, and we did not attack (Could we have done?) until after Rommel had been re-supplied. But this occasion and what followed is military history and, like Waterloo, the battle which resulted in our retreat to El Alamein was a close-run thing. This was made clear in General Horrocks' admirable TV programmes in the fifties, entitled *Epic Battles*. No more vivid history ever, and no finer man.

We very quickly learned that we couldn't move anywhere in the desert without taking everything with us. You can't pick up anything on the way in the desert—at least not by design, though passing over a former battlefield you may find the very article you need, from—as I recorded—a spade to a tin of graphite grease (invaluable and unprocurable).

Water is the first essential, and under normal circumstances we were rationed to half-a-gallon per man per day for everything. Occasionally we could supplement our meagre RASC supply with rain water, in the winter; or even from an ancient *bir* (well or cistern), though such water could be brackish and undrinkable. Terrible disappointment!

Food was also nearly always in short supply, and the rations and how we divided them up, even down the contents of tins, was always a talking point. The strictest fairness, almost to absurd measures as they would have appeared at home, prevented dissension. Jam, tinned fruit and whisky were our priorities. In certain static situations our tinned biscuits, milk, etc. could be supplemented by purchases in Benghazi by an officer sent off with money in a truck.

Jam was particularly important to us, ideal for the rather horrible biscuits, and full of sugar energy. Once a tin had been opened we learned that below the layer of sand lay perfectly edible jam.

I for one never got tired of bully beef, and still love it. We ate it cold, fried, boiled, mixed with dry potatoes, etc. Only twice did we get fresh meat. This was by barter with the Bedouin.

The other side of the food story, so to speak, I shall never forget. The brigade had had the worst of a running battle in which we found ourselves outgunned, and the three regiments were reduced to one—with serviceable tanks. We were on the run, and no rations could come up to us. I shall never forget our temporary Colonel's reply to my complaint that we hadn't had a prepared meal for four days: 'You don't want food. All you want is ammunition'. Thus was the cavalry spirit instilled into me.

Luckily I didn't smoke in those days. I was later led astray in hospital in South Africa, where I also learned to play whisky poker. If I had been a smoker I would have suffered from cafard with complications very quickly. I could never understand the chaps wandering about looking like Punch cartoon men in a mirage not reaching an oasis, when their smokes didn't come up—even when waiting for a brand described by some as 'camel dung with seccotine'!

But what sometimes did come up—pretty regularly, and often in the oddest circumstances, were mail or comforts from home. The form of mail most used both ways was the airgraph, microphotoed and printed at the receiving terminals. Not quite the same as an original, but still. . .

After feeding us, the Royal Army Service Corps had to fuel our vehicles. I suppose that petrol was really more important than food and water. Humans can go for a day or two without food, but not without water, but if a tank runs out of petrol, that's that. On one occasion a German tank unit did, but unfortunately we were not strong enough to capture the whole force involved and the Germans managed to refuel after dark.

Early in the campaign the British made a costly supply mistake. All our petrol came in thin rectangular four-gallon non-returnable tins, crated in fours in light wood, partly to save weight and materials, I suppose. But as a result these tins just didn't stand up to the transport and handling involved and I think at one time we were losing up to 30 per cent of original quantities. This was too costly and dangerous. We soon learned to copy the admirable German jerrycan, as we called it. This design of container is still in use all over the world, and 'jerrycan' has become part of the English language.

We cooked with petrol pressure stoves but we tank crews, when away from any mess and its cooks and cookers and ovens, found it simpler and more convenient to make our own expendable or throw-away desert cookers very easily, thanks to the versatile four-gallon

British petrol tins. All we had to do to make tea, for instance, was to cut such a tin in half, invert and fill the top half (with the petrol hole in it) with sand, soak the sand in petrol and ignite it. When lit it burned long enough to boil water in the lower half of the tin placed on top. If we were ever blessed with firewood, the whole empty tin could easily be turned into a solid fuel stove by cutting out the top and the lower half of one side, thus forming a chimney. Either model could be abandoned if a hurried move was necessary, preferably after the food or drink had been consumed.

When we were short of food the unexpected *bonnes bouches* from Benghazi or the Delta were all the more appreciated. I don't think we ever over-ate, and no one had a chance to be greedy because tins of pineapple chunks and even peas were carefully counted out into equal portions! But one or two of us, during prolonged static periods, may have over-drunk.

Rum rations were official and much appreciated. Early on, I learned yet another lesson. So keen was I to save some of my mug's worth of rum one night, that I placed the unconsumed portion beside my pillow under the stars. Next morning, when I hoped for a sip, the spirit had evaporated.

KEEPING FIT

Before very long we were all terrifically fit and felt on top of the world physically and on top of the desert mentally. I was never ill and I can only remember one officer being incapacitated by illness. The climate helped. It was hot and dusty, but only when we made it so, or when there was a seasonal wind. Water was short, but we somehow managed to instil the practices of hygiene into ourselves and our men. We owe a lot to our Doc for his stern exhortations. It was his job to keep us fit; and we were very fond of him. Once he diagnosed appendicitis in a man and gave orders: 'Take him back to Div. workshops'. We still trusted him.

When we were halted for more than twenty-four hours or so we had to dig a form of latrine, topped by the versatile empty four-gallon petrol tin. Our own squadron 'throne', as we called it, boasted a wooden loo seat looted in Benghazi. At one long halt I recall a slight tiff with the Doc, who didn't believe that the ground was too hard for us to dig a latrine. He thought we were lazy, but in our position there was an outcrop of rock, as a stick of bombs proved.

I know that later in the campaign there were periods of much greater stress for the officers and men than I had, and that others suffered much more from the elements and the state of play than I did; but this is a personal account and I have more credits to give that desert life.

I think the first is sleep. I had an awful fear of having to fight without sleep, but luckily I didn't. Also I was usually very comfortable because I had a lilo that I could blow up as I lay beside it, and bedding handy on the back of the tank. After I was wounded and lost my tank, I didn't lose my bedding because it was taken off and piled on top of me to protect me from bullets as I was driven off to the Doc on the back of another tank. Marvellous luck.

Both sides, of course, needed sleep, and by the nature of the terrain it was possible to remove one's own force at least some distance out of harm's way for the night, to 'disengage' being the term. We soon learned that the Germans were not all that keen on night fighting. In fact they were pretty nervous at night. We often spotted their whereabouts by their constant firing of their form of Very lights; some no doubt being only guide signals, such as ours, but not all. What really scared the Germans and Italians at any time, but especially at night, were our Gurkhas. I think they are the most formidable fighters of all, with firearms, yes, but more so with their *kukris*.

We had a company of Gurkhas with us on Currie column, and a battery of the RHA, whose power was a mighty source of comfort and joy in daylight. But at night the Gurkhas wrought havoc among sleeping Italians and Germans in their leaguer (or laager—a word we took from the Afrikaans, meaning a defensive ring of ox wagons). They couldn't keep the Gurkhas out. Our Gurkhas looked very pleased with themselves one morning and without enquiring deeply I got the impression that they had managed to cut off some horror-struck sleepy heads during the night.

As I read from our Regimental History, the Gurkhas were constantly coming to our aid as we gradually drove the Germans westward out of Africa. At the Wadi Akarit after the battle of Mareth, there was the following to report:

> Both Germans and Italians put up so fierce and stubborn a resistance to the initial assault that the 51st and 50th Divisions on the right and in the centre were unable to gain their objectives, and the day was only won by the 4th Indian Division on the left. Here the Gurkhas were in their element scrambling over the rocks and getting to close quarters with

their kukris in the dark to win a brilliant success. The Gurkhas sent a Situation Report after this battle which read: 'Enemy losses 10 killed, ours nil. Ammunition expenditure nil'.

DESERT CLIMATE

The next credit I give the desert is its climate, which in the northern strip where we were was cold—well, coldish—from November to April, and hot from May to October. At least we were very seldom wet and miserable; another tremendous bonus for us all. There were occasions when we were pretty cold, but never for long despite my diary references to horrible rain and wind.

We were much more likely to be too hot; but that is not so incapacitating as being too cold, especially as the heat was dry and not humid. Thank God we were not fighting in Burma. Deserts are infinitely preferable to jungle, as I have learned from experience since. The sand and the wind and the khamsin were no pleasure; but the rain did bring pleasure.

The desert, our desert, is extremely fertile. The climate has changed in two thousand years, but the moment any rain falls, up come the tulips and the little crocuses which are a special delight, set off amid the surrounding sand and small, now green shrubs. Wildlife then appears. It was at this period of the year that the Bedouin and their flocks were around, with whom we bartered, another wet weather benefit, I suppose.

What was not so good was the flooding of wadis and the filling up of depressions and the rain turning the sand into a sticky mud. This prevented vital movement after Alamein, and total victory escaped us for the time being.

But what was a pure blessing of the desert was the light and the colours. The desert looks best at dawn and pretty good at dusk. Even on our flat Libyan strip, without the wonderful range of colours that the rocks and jagged hills of the Jebel give at different hours and in different weathers, we were provided with a remarkable variety of aspect on a tiny, intimate scale. Unfortunately there were not many opportunities to record the colours and their changes because the idea of both sides was to attack from out of the sun to have one's opponents' eyes dazzled and gunners confused. We advanced at sunrise; how beautiful, how precious, the scents and bird call, the aromatic fires of breakfast—sometimes. The Germans attacked at sunset: dust and blood-red refraction; the evening cool shatters. . .

RECREATION

As for music, which we felt the need of badly, we had our tank radios. We could tune in to the BBC, at the expense of our batteries, if at rest, but on which our tanks, our lives and our success in battle depended. When we were stationary we hardly dared listen at all. One particular night we could, while the batteries were charging. We had been out-fought, and discretion was thought to be the better part of valour on this occasion. We just couldn't afford to lose any more tanks. We moved east fast for twenty miles, and as we roared along I got the Forces programme on the tank radio—because the batteries were charging. The music was 'March of the Gladiators', and 'Barcarolle' which I have always found moving (See p. 101).

We could have done with more music, but we had no means of obtaining it. In fact we had practically no diversions at all when we were out of the line, and this had its special problem which we had to overcome. If one was luckily provided with books, so far so good; but it was harder for those who were not readers. Nevertheless, most of us, most of the time, were thrown back entirely upon ourselves. Mail from home was a more than welcome diversion and morale-raiser; it enabled one to leave the desert in spirit and to imagine loved ones in their temperate climate surroundings—fields and hedges, and trees and walls and roofs and rivers and ponds and paths, and streets and shops and cars and buses and trains; oh everything in the place of nothing. But as I have said, in this world of nothing, we could do no harm to anybody except the enemy and this was a consolation.

I see now that I was able to use my diary as an occupation and a retreat. I also wrote very many more letters than most of us. I had so many kind friends and girl friends. The others twitted me about all this. Certainly I was luckily never bored. I found great consolation in my fellow officers and men. We were at terribly close quarters at the time. I have since learned that happily married couples feel in need of a little separation now and again, but we didn't get such breaks! We, the officers, managed perhaps because we had originally been brought together by personal selection, so by nature we were likely to get on together and we did; completely, absolutely. I think I was the odd one out in such a marvellous and famous regiment with three hundred years of service. Perhaps I was just lucky in being able to look at us all objectively sometimes. Perhaps we all did so; in between busily looking after our men and machines and ourselves. We spent a good deal of time on such ploys; constructive occupations and diversions.

One valuable lesson I learned from the regiment was not to lie down under poor situations, but to get organised out of them. There was no need to suffer, I found, despite our inescapable overall situation; so the trick was to get as comfortable as possible. That was the mess outlook. No need to rough it: one is no better for that. At rest, good food and drink were skilfully ordered and ferried up from base, admittedly at some financial cost. But other lot-improving efforts were entirely individual and usually fortuitous.

BATTLE, DEATH AND THE AFTERMATH

The desert was dry and the battles ebbed and flowed across it. Consequently there was a mass of abandoned material lying untidily around, which if intact, was still in mint condition so to speak. The desert was an admirable place for picking up, winning, scrounging, making, cannibalising, however you like to put it, just what one needed: from a container and a supply of the vital hard-to-come-by C600 tank engine oil which Pullyblank needed constantly; to the shovel I needed in order to dig 'a better 'ole' for safety; (See p. 111) even 'a walking stick with two notches in it—ideal', I wrote, for 'waving around'. But when? In battle? I wasn't that brave. I wonder who it had belonged to; and how it had been lost. A very sad little human item, so evocative, so personal.

When it did come to action and death around me, I found I could manage. Our desert battles started off all right in January 1942 and the squadron managed to do some damage to enemy transport and take some prisoners. The first fell into my hands, in fact, and George, the squadron leader's voice came over the wireless: 'First blood to you, Michael' (See p. 96). It is difficult physically to take prisoners if one is in a tank, though the soft-skinned trucks and men will surrender soon enough to avoid being machine-gunned.

Unfortunately the German tank forces were too strong for us, and we were out-gunned, although for a time we had marvellous help from our artillery firing over open sights. But of course the gunners were unprotected, and along with their guns were too valuable to risk losing in such circumstances: so, like Laurie Lee, they couldn't stay long. Alas, during a long pause I came across our squadron-major towing a light tank with a big hole in it. It was the tank of one of my admirable corporals, with his body still inside it. My diary reads: 'I soon learned that after the initial shock a dead person is no longer that person at all. The body is the home of the spirit and the soul. When they are gone, the person is no longer present and one just has to dispose of the remains'. In 1942 we, the regiment, lost nine officers and sixty-four other ranks. Sad indeed, but not so shocking nationally as the casualties in that dreadful First World War. In the whole Second World War from France to Italy we lost twenty-four officers and 176 other ranks. Some super chaps were killed. One of our finest generals, Brian Horrocks, later our Corps Commander under Montgomery, wrote in his autobiography *A Full Life*:

> I have always regarded the forward area of the battle field as the most exclusive club in the world, inhabited by the cream of the nation's manhood—the men who actually do the fighting. Comparatively few in number, they have little feeling of hatred for the enemy—rather the reverse!

That is a wonderful tribute; and I do agree with the last sentence. I wrote in my diary: 'I like the Germans as a whole and when fighting feel no more than the normal keenness to fix them'. But I did add that I had never experienced a ruthless attack and I can say also that I did not know about the extermination and concentration camps. In battle one finds oneself simply wanting to get on with the job and remove the opposing forces as quickly and as cheaply in lives as possible. Who lives, who dies, is a very strange question of chance. But the odds are shortened when one becomes a prime target—when the anti-tank gunners are shooting at you. In the attack on Point 333 in the breakthrough at El Alamein, the dice were heavily loaded against our tanks. Stephen Christie-Miller and Freddie Barnado had their tank troops forward on that misty morning with no cover and visibility. They were easy targets for the powerful German 88mm anti-tank guns which did such deadly damage throughout the campaign; and they died instantly. Just before the battle dear Stephen met his elder brother John, who was a staff officer in a nearby division and (as John told me recently) Stephen knew he would be killed. The Doc,* alas, was also killed, but by a very sad chance. He had heard the orders to attack Point 33 and had—without a thought for himself—bravely come up in his scout

216

* Captain Lewis, RAMC, not my Major McGill.

car. But in the poor light, he ran right through our lines and on to a German anti-tank gun.

And yet men such as Captain Liddell of the Coldstream Guards in Europe as General Horrocks recounts, won the VC under heavy fire in full view of the enemy. Leaving his company in safety he managed to climb onto the Ems bridge and cut the demolition wires. He then climbed back, called up his company and the bridge was captured intact, with heavy losses to the enemy. But eighteen days later Captain Liddell was killed by a stray bullet—before he knew he had won the VC.

What can I say? Only echo the words of General Horrocks: 'It was a great tragedy, but it is always the best who die in war'. That is not quite fair, but there is a measure of truth in it. For instance, another splendid officer, Major John Tatham-Warter who had fought famously and had lost one tank under him, was killed later just as he was getting back into another tank in which he was already fighting.

A special loss for us all was Major John Viscount Knebworth. He was killed on 4th July 1942 and his parents, Lord and Lady Lytton, brought out a book in his memory. John deserves to be remembered always by all men. No man has ever set a better example. 'He was,' as I wrote to his parents, 'one of the salt of the earth. His personality made him loved throughout the regiment. His humour was as valuable to us as rations. He would make us laugh all the time, not by telling doubtful stories, but by his sheer personality and power to rise above all the unpleasantness of the desert'. Freddy Barnado, who served under John, wrote: 'His infinite calm and outstanding courage were an inspiration to all those under him'.

From 27th May 1942 until 14th June the Gazala battle raged and the regiment was in continuous action, ending up with only six tanks out of some seventy-five. Unfortunately I was wounded on the first day and the following was—to my surprise—included in the Regimental History:

One final story to complete the day. Michael Halsted who was wounded, had great difficulty in getting back to a Casualty Clearing Station at Tobruk. Eventually, early on the morning of 28th, he found an ambulance carrying wounded officers and men, which had lost its way and had been swanning about the desert all night. As he was being helped in, the following conversation was overheard:

First private soldier: 'Gawd, who's comin' aboard now, Fred?'
Second ditto: 'It's a blinkin' cavalry officer.'
First ditto: 'Thank Gawd, now we shall get somewhere.'

But the officer who saved us was Joe Radice; as you will have read in my diary.

At the end of the main Gazala battle, and as part of a desperate counter-measure to facilitate our withdrawal to Alamein, John Knebworth was put in command of a small force consisting of the remaining six Bays tanks and a squadron of the 4th Hussars. He made of his eighteen tanks a daring mobile column operating behind the enemy lines, actually turning the tables on the Germans, by attacking them from out of the setting sun. They were very successful against German transport, their proper role, until German Mark III tanks attacked them. Finally John's force was reduced to eight tanks in a fighting state and John led his column east again in the night, to cross into our lines. All the way they were taken for fellow Germans moving up, a not unknown phenomenon of the desert war; and they were actually cursed in the dark by sleeping Germans and Italians for driving too close to them! Even at daylight they were still twelve miles out and John decided to be brazen and they drove calmly on. They deceived the Germans completely. They may have been thought to be captured tanks. Anyway, they drove right through several positions without being identified.

Very sadly, John was killed by a single bullet on 4th July, during vital action against a dangerous German infantry and anti-tank force, which had moved up stealthily in the night. I quote from John's sergeant Capel-Barker's own words in the book his parents had published about him:

> The German infantry was bewildered at our lightning attack and my tank had around it sixty to a hundred prisoners with their hands in the air. I started them off towards our heavy tanks. Then in front of me I saw my troop officer's tank burst into flames and the crew abandon. Then Major Knebworth reversed towards it to give them protection. His tank was also knocked out and became a raging furnace as the crew abandoned it. I charged to a small ridge and, keeping a continual fire, silenced the ant-tank gun that had surprised them from the left flank. So now I gave protecting and covering fire to the two dismounted crew who were making their way to the side of my tank. Major Knebworth and Captain Ogier bringing up the rear, the squadron leader marching as though he were on parade.
>
> I had dismounted my wireless operator and myself to assist the men who I found to be badly burnt, when I saw Major Knebworth crumple and fall. Captain Ogier stumbled but remained upright as I ran some twenty yards to assist them. I lifted Major Knebworth, with the assistance of Captain Ogier, on to the side of my tank, where my gunner had rolled out a blanket. I moistened the squadron leader's lips and forehead, but

he remained unconscious and only lived for about ten minutes in this state—he had a clean bullet hole in the left shoulder-blade, rather low down. I also discovered my troop officer had a bullet wound in the leg and was bleeding freely. I got all two crews back to the medical officer, who pronounced Major Knebworth beyond aid. The others went to hospital whilst I, in the last tank, went to bury my squadron leader.

We went a mile from the battlefield and there near a stone cairn we dug his grave; my gunner, wireless-operator, driver and myself. I emptied his pockets. He had everything a soldier should carry and generally doesn't. Then wrapping him up in a blanket, we went to the grave and laid him to rest. There was no clergyman or officer, but just four of his men who respected him. We spoke a few words of the Burial Service as we commended him to God; then gave him his last salute. He was a splendid soldier and a good man. I don't think he would have wished for more.

I had been worried over my reactions to this war of ours, but I was encouraged when I was able to read one or two of John's letters home. For instance:

A few nights I had dinner with C Squadron, about ³/₄-mile away, well within sight of this mess in daylight—almost ten minutes walk. Coming back it was a pitch dark night and in spite of setting a careful course by compass it took me two hours to find my tent . . . One can feel and be absolutely lost a few yards from home on a dark night.

A written comment of mine on John's presence with us you may recall reading, was: 'We've been fighting the weather mainly. A second khamsin and just lately days of horrible wind and sand making us all feel bloody. However, we've had John to keep up our spirits, and he really is enormous value' (See p. 148).

Another letter of John's is particularly interesting:

I have been under fire on several occasions, but I have only had one hit—a track knocked off, which necessitated jumping on another tank. The fire is not as frightening as I thought it might be, especially HE artillery fire which can burst right close to a tank and do no damage, but anti-tank fire is not so pleasant, as one knows that that is aimed directly at one.

A tank crew had a nasty dilemma to face. If an anti-tank shell disabled their tank—with or without casualties, sometimes without—the tank now became a sitting target. But if the crew baled out they became very much more exposed to shell bursts or machine-gun bullets—such as very sadly happened to John Knebworth and in fact to me. I had my driver injured by the anti-tank shell which penetrated our tank and we had to get him out. But we were unlucky. A high-explosive shell got *us*. This was the first day of the Battle of Gazala. I was not to know it but the battle went on for nineteen days, until on 14th June orders were given for the retreat from Gazala to the El Alamein position.

DRAWBACKS AND DISAPPOINTMENTS

We had been retreating since the New Year and it was a sad thing for me and for all of us, to have been through this disheartening period. We were in such good company, from my own tank crew right up to sister regiments and supporting arms; and our generals were congenial and cared for us. Unfortunately all too few of our generals had the right appreciation of the way tanks should be used and we suffered many reverses and casualties in consequence. We had to learn from our adversary, Rommel, who for a long time had superior weapons and tactics.

The campaign started brilliantly in 1941, with the early victories of Generals Wavell and Cunningham of which General de Guingand writes so generously:

> It is the way of life that so little is heard of Eighth Army's successful offensive against Rommel before Montgomery took over command. Admittedly one can't really call an offensive successful unless the victory is consummated. This one ended in a major reverse. But it is only right that full credit should be given to this gallant army who, although equipped with inferior tools, by sheer courage, dogged determination and spirit, defeated some of the finest and most experienced troops in the German Army. It was a wonderful achievement and should not be forgotten. Tobruk was relieved, Benghazi captured and our forces advanced well towards Agheila.

This was us finally; following up these victories eagerly, but alas only to have our hopes dashed. De Guingand continues:

> But once again the significance of the Cyrenaica bulge had not been sufficiently appreciated. Our position was very weak till Benghazi had become a major supply base, and we had gathered strong forces in the area between Tobruk and Tmimi. Rommel once again saw his opportunity and took it. He attacked strongly on a narrow front on 21st January 1942 [This was us for sure] . . . and Eighth Army, stretched and weak in supplies fell back to avoid disaster.

Shots in the Sand

We at the sharp end knew nothing of this. We only felt the ignominy of retreat and the inadequacy of our tanks and their guns. Blaming our tools? Well, yes, and what we felt as reflected in my diary has since been amplified and repeated by a number of authoritative authors, no less than Field Marshal Carver, in his *Dilemmas of the Desert War* (Batsford 1986).

For days we had no idea of the situation. Later we got reorganised. It is all in my diary, blow by blow, recording the fact that the name of our brigade was mud to the Guards' Brigade for this retreat.

Then our brigadier came and made a speech which, for the first time, we were all summoned to hear. That fact was encouraging, even if the speech didn't help much. Our bewilderment was mainly due to an almost complete lack of information at the sharp end. Our wireless communications system and equipment was not nearly efficient enough to give us whatever coded information we could have had from RHQ, for instance. A contributing factor was the poor reception due to desert atmospheric conditions especially at sunset, just when the Germans chose to attack with the low sun behind them and right in our eyes. The wireless sets in those days were cumbersome and fragile and not powerful enough; and also in short supply. Our batteries weren't up to it either—even if never used for listening to the BBC. But the BBC news did give us the overall picture. Nearer at hand, just imagine this: sometimes in order to learn the latest situation and possible future action we in our squadrons had to rely on a visit from the Padre, who was based at regimental headquarters, because he might be able to relay a little tactical gossip. I am sure he knew how vital he was to us with his secular messages. He brought us spiritual comfort too; and he buried Stephen and many other good friends, as he told me.

It was shortly after this that we went out in early February 1942 on the Currie Column for a raid on German advance positions which I mentioned when referring to the Gurkhas (See p. 212). We were not as daring or successful as John Knebworth's column after Gazala, but our activity did quite a lot to raise morale; especially as Colonel Currie did not send us against dug-in German anti-tank guns (of which more below); though he told us afterwards that he was in two minds about it.

Out on Currie Column we were pretty exposed in the open desert ahead of our main forces. We feared enemy air reconnaissance and so only moved at night. We holed up by day disguised as bushes, with ingenious camouflage designed by En-Tout-Cas!

221

Thank God for a Commander in whom we had confidence, who was not taken in by the German trick of encouraging our tanks to attack prepared anti-tank positions. And also for our admirable 'Bing' Crosbie-Dawson, who chaffed the rum-bearing RSM for calling our operation an 'exercise'. Bing is a charming, sympathetic, fully efficient character, the absolute quintessence of a first-class cavalryman of the Queen's Bays. He did much to help us young sprogs to develop into worthy active service officers. I owe him a great deal. He is, I am happy to say, very much alive as I write this.

TACTICAL SHORT-COMINGS

It was in relation to our success in Currie Column with our existing tanks that I wrote in my diary that we were cheerful as long as we were used properly. But overall we had been mishandled, in spite of what the brigadier told us; and that fact didn't help morale. Colonel Rogers writes:

> In 1941 General Cunningham's tactics were based on the theory that armoured warfare was a land version of naval warfare and that tank versus tank battle was an end in itself. That theory was a remarkable misreading of military history. Ground is different from sea and can be used to advantage.

I would have thought this was dead obvious. What were our officers at the Staff College in the thirties being taught about armoured warfare?

> Rommel had grasped the secret of our successes in the great battles in France during the Hundred Years' War. Disciplined calvary striking at the weaker elements of the enemy, and formidable bowmen to deal with ill-used men at arms, were highly successful. Rommel realised that tanks and anti-tank guns were complementary arms. There were periods in the 1941 and '42 battles when we had superiority in tanks, if not in fire power; but on many occasions British armour was blunted against hidden anti-tank guns. The Germans then counter-attacked.

GUNS AND TANKS

The Germans had an excellent anti-tank gun from pretty early on, the long 50mm, which I mentioned in my diary of 10th January and which Field Marshal Carver illustrates in his book. Even our anti-tank guns were 2-pounders to begin with. Like pea-shooters they felt sometimes;

demoralising. They were, as I have quoted, quite effective at short range, but we never seemed able to draw the Germans into any form of trap; nor did we seem capable of setting one.* Furthermore it was quite some time before we had our 6-pounder tank and anti-tank guns. Once these were in service things were much healthier. But again the Germans got ahead by brilliantly converting their 88m anti-aircraft gun into an anti-tank gun. It was a devastating weapon against tanks as I mentioned earlier. Tanks should never have been sent directly against them, but sometimes this was imperative. On other occasions we incurred tank losses when these 88s were very cleverly screened by soft-skinned decoy vehicles.

Rommel's attack from El Agheila in January 1942 was skilfully timed to hit us when our supplies were at their slenderest and unsupported (as happened to him when he drove his furthest east), but we had other problems. We were then equipped with British Crusader tanks which were not bad, but they had serious drawbacks. Time and again my diary refers to breakdowns, e.g. 31st December 1941; 'Peter's Mark VIs have failed him.' These Crusaders were not reliable enough. We even had engineers flown out from the factory in Birmingham; incongruous they looked in their white overalls. But what could they do? They did their best, led by Mr. Hucker. 'Now we had Hucker tanks,' we said. And as for our guns I have actually seen Crusaders' 2-pounder shells bouncing on the ground in front of advancing German tanks while their shells were cracking past our ears. But at short ranges, the pundits write, our 2-pounder armour-piercing capability was as good as the German short 50mm tank gun. Certainly our Crusaders were fast, and manoeuvrable, but they were not nearly so good in these qualities as the American M3 Stuart Light Tanks we also had, known as Honeys. I can't think why they were so called, except that they were fast and reliable; and powered by a radial aero engine. In the right situations and handled correctly they were pretty good for reconnaissance or shooting up enemy ground troops or transport. But they hadn't got very much armour. The crew even looked through open slits as did medieval knights. Poor Cpl Minks was in one. It was a dangerous mistake to use these tanks against German armour head-on. At speed on the flank gave a much better chance; provided one had the reliability to get into range and out of danger! If we had been used properly throughout, I think I would have more confidence in our tanks.

Generally speaking, German tank development was ahead of ours. But as Colonel Rogers says: 'in actual tank versus tank fighting, British

* See Diary Feb 1st 1942 (Top of page 103)

units had shown that they were fully the equal of the Germans. But by the time these tank contests took place the Germans, through Rommel's successful tactic, had a superiority in number.'

A WORD ABOUT US

The cavalry has had a reputation for dash for centuries, and a reputation for gallantry coupled with impulsiveness which, Colonel Rogers remarks, was usually effective though sometimes incurring heavy losses.

General Horrocks went further in his introduction to our updated short Regimental History. 'This extreme gallantry,' he wrote, 'was one of the causes of their many defeats in the Western Desert. Rommel's Afrika Korps, if faced by the cavalry, would halt, withdraw behind their formidable anti-tank guns and wait till the cavalry were mown down. Only then would the Germans advance. Unfortunately their Mark IIIs were more powerful than our tanks, and the Germans also had the deadly 88mm anti-tank guns. So the odds were loaded against us. This was one of the main causes why we were driven back to the Alamein line.'

MONTGOMERY AND ROMMEL

Thank God, General Montgomery arrived when he did. General de Guingand writes of the period between the battles of Gazala and Alamein as a stalemate, thanks to the Navy and the RAF, who alone were capable of destroying Rommel's supplies. He mentions certain short-term offensives which at that time should never have been ordered. Every effort should have been devoted to the accumulation of supplies. Yet a wretched armoured division newly arrived from England, equipped with slow-moving and obsolete infantry tanks, was thrown into battle with little time for preparation and training. They eventually ran into the usual German gun screen of 88mm and lost a large proportion of their machines. But never again! Montgomery would have none of Currie Columns or even of Battle Groups. Tanks under him fought together with sledge-hammer blows.

The name Rommel keeps cropping up in my diary. He was indeed a formidable opponent; and I think we were lucky not to suffer worse reverses at his hands. Apart from the overriding question of supplies, we ourselves might have met with disaster if we had had to fight soon after arrival in the desert or any other warfare. Where can you properly deploy and exercise an armoured regiment, let alone a brigade or division, in Britain? We could hardly have been sent to Canada.

Through Rommel's personality and policy we formed the impression that we were up against gallant and honourable opponents. It was therefore perhaps rather easier to decide to surrender. I even admired the cleverly designed Afrika Korps badge painted on all vehicles. It was a swastika incorporated into the trunk of a palm-tree. Montgomery realised the danger of the widespread soft attitude towards the Germans and he quickly stamped it out. He also insisted on rigorous training, physical and battle. Even more important was his policy of dissemination of information right down to troop level. This had a tonic effect even in the most difficult situations which later occurred.

BIGGER AND BETTER TANKS—JUST

I was in a Grant tank when Rommel began the Battle of Gazala on 27th May. We were ready just in time. The Grants gave Rommel a nasty surprise and us some satisfaction in the fighting of them. It was a reliable tank and its armour and gun, a short 75mm, were a match for the German Mark IVs, so I am told; but the General Grant had serious drawbacks. It was very high off the ground, and thus more vulnerable—very vulnerable. It had a low top turret with all-round traverse, but the same little 38mm gun. Its 75mm gun was low down on the right-hand side in a sponson, rather like a First World War tank, with hardly any traverse. With this odd design one could hardly get into a hull down position and fire the 75. It was not ideal, but it did us pretty well. The Americans as I have since learned, realised that the General Grant was not the answer, but their industrial capacity had not been able to make a large and thick enough casting to take a 75mm gun in a turret with an all-round traverse. However, the 'ideal' tank—of the day—was on its way and the General Sherman, vital to the success of El Alamein, arrived on 10th September 1942. Nevertheless I think that for both sides anti-tank gun development stayed ahead of tank design.

It was early on at the El Alamein position, the line of no further retreat, that General Montgomery's brilliance was really displayed. When he arrived in the desert on 13th August 1942, he remarked to General de Guingand: 'Well Freddie, you chaps seem to have been making a bit of a mess of things.' But very soon the correct tactical handling of tanks was demonstrated at the Battle of Alam Halfa on 31st August 1942, nearly two months before Alamein itself.

General Horrocks commanded 10th Corps. He ordered certain armoured units to dig their tanks in and he had them covered on their flanks by anti-tank guns. We had some 17-pounders by then!

However, before the preparations began the old cavalry inclination tried to re-assert itself—in a distinguished personage, but luckily without success. Winston Churchill, General Horrocks relates, was on a visit to the desert front before Alamein. We had thoroughly learned tank and anti-tank tactics by now; but Churchill was furious to be told that Alam Halfa was to be a defensive battle. 'That is the trouble with your British generals,' said Churchill. 'Attack! Why not attack? That is the way to win battles.' I don't suppose anyone dared tell him that this wasn't Omdurman.

Rommel advanced from the south in a left-hook as anticipated. As his forces got further and further forward, other tank units attacked their soft supply vehicles from both sides. This was the way to handle tanks! I wish I could have been there. This was a classic victory.

After El Alamein came the Battle of Medenine on 6th March 1943. This was another classic encounter in which we lost no tanks, 'and only 130 all ranks killed and wounded'. Only? Ha! I know what that implies. Rommel left fifty-two tanks on the battlefield, though he did recover many damaged ones. However, he left for Germany afterwards, never to return.

The regiment fought on to Tunis; and then up Italy. Here, on Coriano Ridge, near Rimini on 20th September 1944, Four Troop—as Pullyblank and I knew it—ceased to exist.

1st Armoured Division was then commanded by Major-General Richard Hull (17th/21st Lancers). He died on 19th September 1989 and his obituary in *The Times* had this to say: 'Hull's division was committed prematurely at Coriano, and suffered heavy tank losses. The Germans were not as near collapse as General Oliver Leese, the Corps Commander, thought, and the Adriatic foothills of the Appenines proved less suitable for armoured warfare than he had hoped.'

Pullyblank missed the attack. On the advance in the dark his tank's suspension was fouled by fallen electric cable, and despite frantic efforts to clear it he was immobilised for several hours. B Squadron had been mauled the previous day, and now C Squadron with the remainder of B Squadron in support advanced over a low crest down a forward slope to a shallow dip. They were immediately met by a hail of well-prepared fire from 75mm and 88mm armour-piercing shells. Finally, under cover of smoke, three tanks of B Squadron got back, but none from C. At least one C Squadron tank nearly reached the objective. Pully heard on his radio a new young officer reporting excitedly, 'I can see the plain. I can see the plain.' Then silence.

Postscript

Here follows an extract from a moving book by the Reverend James B. Chutter, Senior Chaplain with the South African 2nd Division in North Africa. He was captured at the fall of Tobruk in June 1942.

> On the morning of the attack there were said to be sixty-six 'runners', i.e. tanks ready to fight. By eleven the numbers had dropped to about thirty, by one o'clock to fifteen, by three to seven. When the day was ended, none was left.
>
> The tanks were the same and the men the same courageous souls who had fought so well at Gazala. They were, because of their lightness, no match for the enemy, and I saw many set ablazing by the superior fire power of the German Mark IIIs and IVs—one in particular in a little lone wadi by King's Cross. Out baled some of the crew and then came the black uprush of burning petrol. Those who had not escaped made their last twisted contortions, calcinated within the livid body of that blazing tank.*

Captivity Captive, Jonathan Cape, 1954.

End Piece

When Jill and Margaret, the admirable ladies at Top Flight had completed typing my manuscript I said: 'Any comments or queries?' The single answer which surprised and touched me was: 'Yes, what happened to Leslie?'

Well, Leslie worked for Lord Rothschild for a time, and then had a very responsible career in publishing. We remain good friends.

When I knew that my Diary would be published I wrote to Leslie to ask if she would allow her name and family name to be used just as they occurred, or if she would rather not. Her answer is worth repeating:

> I am so very glad to hear that your book is to be published. I wish you lots of success and happiness with it.
>
> Don't be anxious about references to me—or indeed to the family. Your book is a diary, and that's what happened in your life then. We were all a part of it, and glad that it was so. When I look back at the photographs I marvel how young we all were. But I remember such a lot of affection and laughter amid the frightfulness around us. And I think sometimes that life then was so precious and moved so fast, was so exciting often, and so full of interest, that in a strange way the full realities of the war, and its aftermath, as one sees them now, mercifully didn't register. . .
>
> No, don't be anxious about your 'girlfriend', she can only hope she was not too uncaring, and plead perhaps extreme youth. Dear Miss Oakley-Hill (her headmistress), she did her best. . .

Exactly so.

APPENDIX I

Letters Home

Letters home from wife's cousin who was fighting in the Western Desert in World War I

No. 1 Battery Light Armoured Cars. WFF Egypt. March 20th 1916

My dear Father

We have really had a very exciting time the last ten days or so. I expect you have got my last letter, but I did not tell you about our scrap in it. We caught the Senussi force about 22 miles from here with our 9 armoured cars and one Ford — they had evacuated this place the night before and were in camp when they first got wind of us. Anyhow, they just had time and put about half their stuff on camels, and got under way when we came up with them. We were lucky in having a road to get down and then on. We found them in full retreat to the south of the road, and opened fire with our machine guns. They got one 10-pounder into action against us and 2 machine guns, but all the shells went over our heads, and burst on the road behind us. Both m-guns and the 10-pounder were out of action in about 15 minutes — The Gunners stuck it out till one car was practically on top of them, and were nearly all wounded or killed. We took one or two of them prisoners.

By this time the enemy were very much scattered and it was very difficult to get a decent target. We shot a good many camels carrying shells and ammunition. Some of them blew up. After about 1½ hours the cars had got a bit scattered, so we worked our way back to the road where we found most of the others. Eventually we all got in and the Duke of Westminster started back with some of the prisoners. W.F. and

I were left out with three cars to look after the wounded and prisoners and collect as much of the arms and ammunition as we could. We picked up no less than six more machine guns, making a total of nine, and two more 10-pounders, besides the one that had been in action. We made a dump of all the stuff, and when it got dark we made three sides of a square with the three cars, and pushed the prisoners, who were chiefly Turks, inside. We did not much expect to be attacked, but we were quite ready for them if they came. About 11, B. came up with some of the transport cars and as soon as it was light we piled all the ammunition and arms up, and set fire to them. We worked out there was over ¼ million rounds of rifle ammunition, and a good number of shells and bombs. Altogether it was an awful bit of luck getting into them as we did, and I think it has pretty well finished up this show. Since then we have had another frightfully exciting exploit two days ago when we went miles down into the desert and rescued 90 English sailors who had been prisoners for 5 months, but this must wait till my next letter, as I have no more time now.

My dear Mother

I am afraid I have let some little time elapse since my last letter, but we have now moved back again, and are having a pretty quiet time. I don't think I told you about our second trip in my last letter. The Senussi have had 100 shipwrecked sailors off the aux: Cruiser *Tara* as prisoners since November and through various sources duly discovered the name of the place where these prisoners were supposed to be. They were very anxious that we should have a dash at getting hold of them; as apparently they were having a pretty thin time. By great good luck we picked up a man who said he knew the place, but would not commit himself as to the distance. We started off at 3 a.m. on March 17th with 9 armoured cars and about thirty other cars, all the ambulances and staff cars that could be collected. We halted at the well where we had had the scrap three days before, and filled up with water, and had a bit of breakfast. As soon as it was light we pushed on. The road for about 40 miles was absolutely deserted; we then came upon one man, grazing about 100 camels. We left him alone, but a mile or two further on a party of men and camels crossed our road some way in front of us. Our two cars were doing advanced guard, and we soon came up with them. The men who turned out to be regular Arab soldiers, made off across country but R. in the leading car caught them up and shouted to them to stop, which they did and chucked down their rifles. Two others who had got a bit of a start, however, went on, and we opened brisk fire on them. But they managed to dodge it all right, and got away to the rocky cliffs. The eight men who surrendered said they were two Turkish officers. We were very anxious not to waste more time than we could help, so we collected the rifles and smashed them, and burnt the camels' packs. We had to leave the prisoners as we had no room to carry them.

We got on the move again; and went on and on down the road for about another 30 miles. We then came on a Wolseley motor-wagon, which originally belonged to the R.N.A.S. but had been left behind by them about 5 months before. The S. had evidently been making good use of it, but had obviously had great difficulty in getting tyres. They had run the car on the back rims for a considerable distance, and finally the rim had broken, and there was nothing left of the wheel but a bundle of spokes. They had very ingenious home-made tyres on the front wheels. The outside cover was made of camel's hide, stuffed with india-rubber picked up on the beach and sewn on to the rim with telephone wire. The Turkish flag was flying on the car when we arrived but was soon whipped off by someone as a trophy of the chase. At the 84th mile our guides turned us off the road and we struck across country in a S.W. direction. The going was not very bad.

After 20 miles our guides stopped and had a consultation, by that time we thought we were on an absolute wild goose chase, as even if we found the place (which seemed improbable) the chances were 4 to 1 against the prisoners being there. However the guides said they thought they were getting near the spot, which was a well, slap out in the middle of the desert. After another 7 miles one of the guides stood up on a car, and said he could see the place, a mound on the top of a ridge. We pushed on for the place with the armoured cars as hard as we could and saw a man come to the top of the mound and have a look, when we got within half-a-mile of the place, sure enough there stood a crowd of men, we were uncertain for a moment who they were, but suddenly they shouted, cheering and waving their arms. The scene might have been taken out of a cinema film, or a story book for boys. They were most frightfully pleased to see us and there was terrific hand-shaking. The sailors were chiefly clothed in old bits of sacking and had been given very little food. They had lived chiefly on snails and roots, with a small allowance of goat's meat and rice. The well where they were is called

—— and the S. thought they were perfectly safe there, as it is almost ten days camel march from anywhere and the Arabs themselves very often can't find it. There were 2 or 3 officers among the prisoners amongst them the captain of the *Tara*. He was most awfully nice. The Arabs had taken the gold out of his teeth, which he thought rather a severe measure. Their guard which consisted of about eight men, bolted when they first saw us. They were followed up. The sailors were given food, which had been brought for them, and which they went at like wolves. They were also each given a blue hospital coat. We packed them all on to the cars as quick as we could and started off homewards. It was rather like a Sunday School treat going off. We struck the road just as it got dark and pushed on most of the night, arriving at the well where we had halted in the morning at 2 a.m. The Camel Corps had formed an advanced post for us there, as we got into Camp there and pushed on in at 10 the next morning. The distance out to —— was 110 miles. Our chief trouble was punctures, as the tyres they supply us with now are very bad. However we managed to get all the cars in all right. The ambulances did very well and I think the R.A.M.C. people thoroughly enjoyed their trip.

by Tom Digby to his father Algernon.

Other Accounts sent home by Tom Digby

Armoured Car Chase of Senussi. The enemy are completely smashed up, at a cost of only one slight casualty — it was a magnificent and unique piece of work from start to finish.

It will stand as a classic in motoring annals. It was only by a complete disregard of tremendous difficulties, and a display of high qualities of courage and resources that the expedition was successful. When General Lukin reoccupied Sollum, 10 armoured cars following up the enemy's tracks came upon a remarkable road, which starting in the desert runs to Tobruk, 90 miles away in Tripoli — according to English notions the road surface was execrable but the A.C. enthusiasts declare it to be splendid. Over it the motors had a speed of 55 miles an hour. At Aziza, 19 miles from Bir Waer (the Senussi camp) the cars suddenly came upon the enemy, and dashed into a Turkish mountain gun and 2 machine guns, killing every gunner by maxim fire. Then, without a halt, they charged in line over the boulders, stiff scrub, sandy patches and all the other traps among the widely scattering foe, who were taking to their heels at the approach of the magical instruments of the infidel. The charge continued for 7 miles but the enemy, thrown into the wildest confusion could not be further chased, for fear of a shortage of petrol. Some of the camels, hit by our machine gun fire, blew to pieces as if struck by a high explosive, and then burst into flames. It was found that the Arabs had loaded them up with bombs and petrol.

On returning to Sollum, the Duke of W. was informed that a letter had been picked up in the ruins of Bir Waer from Capt. Gwatkin Williams to Nuri Bey complaining that the *Tara* prisoners were starving and ill, and suggesting that medical comforts should be procured at Sollum. The letter mentioned Bir Hakim as the place of the prisoners' retention. Every prisoner and refugee was interrogated but none knew Bir Hakim, except a man who said he had fed a flock there 30 years ago. Subsequently another man who had been the prisoners' guard, was discovered and the Duke asked permission to attempt a rescue. Every man in the batteries sat up all night and next day tuning up the machines. By midnight on March 16th there were gathered at the Old Turkish fort about Sollum 9 armoured Rolls Royce cars, five touring cars with guns, light cars with supplies and the ambulances — 42 cars in all. No tourist trophy cars were ever more carefully prepared than these. At 3 o'clock on St. Patrick's morning the column moved out of the fort across the few miles of trackless desert, until the Tobruk road was picked up. After 50 miles on the road the column turned on to the desert due south. After 15 miles over desperately rough ground the party began to be uncertain of success. The two Arab guides were arguing as to whether they were on the right track, the man who had not seen Bir Hakim since his boyhood thought they were wrong. The other Arab would not say much. He thought the pace of the cars was greater than it really was and expected to arrive sooner. The desert was now very stony, but the going was fairly hard, 100 miles went by, then 105. That was believed to be the limit of the distance, but still there was not the faintest sign of the *Tara* prisoners' camp. At between 110 and 115 miles nobody spoke, the fear of failure kept everyone silent. A mile further on the Arabs became animated and through the mirage a small height could be seen.

A halt was called at 2 o'clock and the Duke sent forward the armoured cars to the attack. They raced up to within 200 yards of the mound. The first car that of Lt. W. Griggs, the jockey, who regards this as the biggest of the 'Classics' races in which he has taken part. The prisoners were standing silhouetted against the sky-line, absolutely motionless, and as silent as statues, dumb with amazement at the appearance of the rescuers. At least one man threw off a sack covering him and faintly cheered. The crowd staggered forward with the rolling gait of starved men and swarmed round the cars. They could not be persuaded to leave the cars, which were slightly hindered in their advance to tackle the guards, all of whom were subsequently killed. Meanwhile the 22 remainder of the column, seeing the prisoners leave the mound, started a tremendous race to the spot. They ran abreast, caring not for obstacles and punctures, but just tore ahead as fast as the engines would propel them and the air was filled with the cheers of the crews, and the noise of the exhausts.

The *Tara's* dog was rescued and is now one of the 2 mascots of the A.C.Div. (since dead!) the other being the parrot brought from Ypres, which cannot speak, but betrays its former home by making a noise like the flight of a shell.

by W.J. Massey

The prisoners settled down to a life of unending monotony and starvation, their food consisting of about an eggcup full of rice per day and desert snails which they gathered at first in large quantities. The area in which the Bedouin guards (24 in number) would allow their 91 prisoners to wander, was small and soon the snail ration was hardly worth considering. From then onwards it was just a question of who would die first. Several letters were sent to the Turkish Authorities, but there was no answer to these appeals and death seemed certain. The Captain tried to escape to place the case before the Authorities, but owing to weakness he was recaptured and brought back to the —. Here in the presence of his men and the — of the guards who stoned him, he was nearly beaten to death. To take 41 vehicles (some weighing 3 tons) safely through that 250 mile journey without a single serious mishap was a miracle, if nothing was. The sailors said they expected to be moved next day to an unknown destination, further in to the vast desert where rescue would have been impossible.

by Capt. R.P.W. one of the A.C. Officers.

APPENDIX II

Gazala 1942

Farewell address given to the Queen's Bays by the Divisional Commander, Major-General Raymond Briggs, CB, DSO, in June 1943 when leaving to take up a new appointment.

"I asked your Colonel to parade you today because I think it is a good thing sometimes to look back, and, in my opinion, when the history of this war is written, the 14th June, 1942, will probably occupy a place in your Battle Honours along with 'Willems', 'Warburg', 'Lucknow', 'South Africa', and 'The Great War'.

Many of you were present on that day, but there are some of you who were not, so I will go very briefly through the history that led up to the 14th June, 1942.

The battle, which will probably be known as the Battle of Knightsbridge, started for the 2nd Armoured Brigade on the 27th May. Only four days before that date the last Grant tank had been issued. The Regiment in those days was organised; two squadrons of Crusader tanks and only one squadron of Grant tanks. There were no Shermans in the country at that time, and no Priests as artillery.

The Brigade on that day consisted of The Queen's Bays, 9th Lancers, 10th Hussars, 1st Bn. Rifle Brigade, and the 11th (H.A.C.) R.H.A. with ordinary tractor-drawn 25-pounders.

The battle, for the Brigade, started on the 27th May, and that was after the Germans had swung around by Hachiem on the 25th and 26th and overrun a large number of the 4th Armoured Brigade (7th Armoured Division).

On the 27th May the Brigade advanced*, with the Queen's Bays leading, and that day had a considerable amount of initial success. We

---

* Alas, I was wounded early on. M.H.

236

captured 350 prisoners and 18 guns. On the next day—the 28th—the Brigade moved again to help the 22nd Armoured Brigade, and again they had a certain amount of success, knocking out a few tanks, several guns, and taking a few prisoners. The Brigade also had a certain amount of misfortune, losing a whole squadron of the 10th Hussars, who ran into a number of 88mm. guns.

The 29th May was a very memorable day indeed, near a place called Aslagh. On that day, continuously, in a semi-circle, with the 10th Hussars on the right, the Queen's Bays in the centre, and the 9th Lancers on the left, the Brigade—sadly depleted in tanks and only supported by the R.B.'s and the H.A.C.—contained, held, and held off over 150 tanks, of which about 80 only were Italian. German tanks in those days were mostly Mark IIIs with a few Mark IIs and IVs; the Germans had not got the Mark III Specials or Mark IV Specials. The Brigade on that day was helped by the 3rd C.L.Y., who came up very providentially.

At the end of the day—the 29th—the 10th Hussars were reduced to three tanks. I therefore called them out of the line, and those three tanks were handed over to the 9th Lancers.

On the 30th the Brigade were still fighting near the Aslagh area, and on the 21st an attack was made by the 9th Lancers, with the Queen's Bays in support. The 9th Lancers, after the fifth day of battle, were reduced to five tanks, so I sent them out of the line, which left me with The Queen's Bays.

So the battle went on. The so-called 2nd Armoured Brigade, which then only consisted of The Queen's Bays, H.A.C. and the 1st Bn. R.B.'s, sometimes supported by odd squadrons—one day the 4th Hussars, another the 5th Hussars, or the C.L.Y.'s—went on fighting. Sometimes we belonged to the 1st Armoured Division, sometimes to the 7th Armoured Division; sometimes we moved down to the south, sometimes to the west, and frequently to the north.

The Brigade went on fighting each day and every day, and it is this I want you to remember; each day your Regiment fought one, two, three or even four major actions. There was no question of any rest; there was no question of any letting up at all. They were always moving here and there to wherever the fighting was heaviest.

On the night of the 13th—14th June the decision was made to evacuate the Knightsbridge Box. The Knightsbridge Box was a feature, well dug in, wired in, and mined and occupied by the 201st Guards Brigade (the old 2nd Guards Brigade) and the 2nd H.A.C. That was a ticklish business because the Hun was all around this Box. Not very close in because our armour kept him at a distance, but it was feared that, whilst the Box was being evacuated, German tanks might come in and cut them off.

However, that night Knightsbridge Box was successfully evacuated without a single casualty to the occupants. That night, or early the following morning, Brigade H.Q. and The Queen's Bays had orders not to move until all the occupants of the Box had got to Acroma. There were a few alarms that night. The Hun tried to put in some sort of attack, but nothing really happened. Very early the following morning the armour and the R.B.'s moved north through our own minefields, with orders to take up a position in between Acroma and El Tamar and to prevent any penetration being effected. The decision had then been made that the 1st South African Division, holding a line from the sea down to Gazala, were to be evacuated to Tobruk, and they were evacuating along the coast road. Our job was to see that German tanks did not penetrate and so cut off the South African Division from Tobruk.

Quite early in the morning the Brigade took up a defensive position facing South, with the right resting on a little box where there were some anti-tank guns and infantry (South Africans not belonging to the 1st South African Division), and the left resting on another box manned by the 1st Bn. Worcester Regiment and a few guns.

The German attack started about 10 a.m. and increased in intensity all day. In the afternoon the attack was very fierce indeed, and The Queen's Bays were at that moment reduced to two Grants and eight Crusaders. They were getting into pretty serious trouble, but holding their own magnificently, because for some reason which I have not yet been able to find out the occupants of the Worcester box withdrew. That left the left flank of the Armoured Regiment—if you can call two Grants and eight Crusaders a regiment—entirely exposed. However, a certain amount of assistance was given to me as Brigade Commander, and the 8th Royal Tanks appeared with twenty Valentines and a little later the 7th Royal Tanks appeared with four Matildas. While this battle was raging I was given an order—from General Lumsden to take command of everything I could see. Well, the most I could see were German tanks, and I couldn't take command of them!

However, not a single tank penetrated anywhere near that road, and the only ground that was given was not more than two or three miles. Very heavy casualties were inflicted on the enemy. Our casualties were not light, but we had done our job.

When dark fell the remnants of the Brigade were ordered to withdraw to the other side of Tobruk and, surrounded by Germans, with coloured lights going up all around, the Brigade slowly moved in a westerly direction, through Acroma, to the other side of Tobruk.

Now, what can we learn from that? Here is an Armoured Regiment which had fought continuously, every single day, one, two, three or even four actions for nineteen days without stopping for any rest. I think—well, I know—that in my experience of war, the last war and this one, I have never met such an example of dogged endurance and determination to stick it to the end.

Everybody was very tired indeed. I can see now, in the early hours of the morning of the 15th June, your Commanding Officer, Colonel Draffen, and the then second-in-command—your own Colonel now —sitting on a little form on the back of their Crusader. How they didn't fall off I don't know, because they were both fast asleep! Most of the men were in the same condition.

Well, the reason I really got you here today was to remind you of a new page of history which should be, and I am sure has been, added to your Regimental traditions, and to remind you of the Battle of Knightsbridge and in particular of that day's fighting on the 14th June, 1942.

That example should serve to keep up our hearts for what we have to do in the future.''

Glossary

(1)	GOC	General Officer Commanding
(106)	BGS	Brigadier General Staff
(14)	CO	Commanding Officer
(16)	AOC	Air Officer Commanding
(19)	OUTC	Oxford University Training Corps
(33)	RSM	Regimental Sergeant Major
(38)	QMG	Quarter-Master General
(43)	MTB	Motor Torpedo Boat
(45)	MM	Merchant Marine
(46)	RAC	Royal Armoured Corps
(50)	RAMC	Royal Army Medical Corps
(50)	DMS GHQ	Director of Medical Service, General Head-quarters
(63)	BNC	Brasenose College Oxford
(66)	PT	Physical Training
(73)	RAOC	Royal Army Ordnance Corps
(75)	KRRC	King's Royal Rifle Corps
(75)	PZKW	Panzer (Armour) Kreigs (War) Wagen (Vehicle) = Tank!
(76)	RTO	Railway Transport Officer
(76)	Q(M)	Quartermaster General's Branch (Movement)
(78)	LRS	Light Recovery Section (RAOC)
(83)	RHQ	Regimental Headquarters
(83)	RASC	Royal Army Service Corps
(84)	SSM	Squadron Sergeant Major
(86)	2 I/C	Second in Command
(88)	ACV	Armoured Command Vehicle
(93)	SHQ	Squadron Headquarters
(94)	KDG	King's Dragoon Guards

(99)	B. Echelon	Supply column of lorries/trucks
(106)	RV	Rendezvous
(107)	FOO	Forward Observation Officer (Royal Artillery)
(107)	RE	Royal Engineers
(110)	HAC	Honourable Artillery Company
(116)	ADS	Advance Dressing Station
(118)	MG	Machine Gun
(118)	TDR	Tank Delivery Regiment
(119)	REME	Royal Electrical and Mechanical Engineers
(122)	Q Control	See (76) (This time tank and vehicle movements)
(123)	PMC	President of the Mess Committee
(128)	DADOS	Deputy Assistant Director of Ordnance Services
(136)	ESR	Egyptian State Railways
(136)	AA	Anti-Aircraft
(141)	NAAFI	Navy, Army and Air Force Institute
(193)	DAQMG	Deputy Assistant Quarter-Master General
(198)	GSO	General Staff Officer (III = Captain, II = Major, I = Lieut Colonel)
(230)	WFF	Western Frontier Force
(237)	CLY	County of London Yeomanry
(237)	RB	Rifle Brigade

Index

247